D1187428

BANKSTERS, BOSSES, AND SMART MONEY

BANKSTERS, BOSSES, AND SMART MONEY

A Social History of the Great Toledo Bank Crash of 1931

TIMOTHY MESSER-KRUSE

The Ohio State University Press
Columbus

Library of Congress Cataloging-in-Publication Data

Messer-Kruse, Timothy.
Banksters, bosses, and smart money : a social history of the great Toledo
bank crash of 1931 / Timothy Messer-Kruse.
    p. cm.
Includes bibliographical references and index.
ISBN 0–8142–0977–7 (cloth : alk. paper)—ISBN 0–8142–9054-X (cd)
1. Banks and banking—Ohio—Toledo—History. 2. Bank failures—
Ohio—Toledo—History. 3. Toledo (Ohio)—Economic conditions. 4.
Toledo (Ohio)—Social conditions. I. Title.
HG2613.T65M47 2004
332.1'2'097711309043—dc22
                    2004015122

Cover design by Jay Bastian.
Type set in Janson.
Printed by Thomson-Shore, Inc.

Historians will record two outstanding facts—the courage, confidence and character of thousands of our citizens reduced to poverty, and the cowardice, greed and ignorance of Toledo's financial leadership, in whom thousands of depositors had placed their trust.

—Walter Baertschi, in Toledo's *East Side Sun*, June 14, 1934

CONTENTS

LIST OF FIGURES

LIST OF TABLES

Acknowledgments

In any work that is the product of several years of research a large number of debts are incurred. As this one did not begin as a book but as a private interest in the author's own community, the roster of those who offered suggestions, pointed to leads, or assisted in many small but significant ways is probably incomplete. To all who are overlooked, I apologize.

This book was only possible because of the tremendous resources and expert knowledge of the staff of the Toledo–Lucas County Public Library, especially Jim Marshall and his team of dedicated librarians who have made the Local History Department a model of engaged scholarship and preservation. Though I've claimed more than my share of time from everyone who works in the Local History Department, I want to especially thank Greg Miller for not only finding what I asked for, but digging deep into the vault and finding many nuggets that were not cataloged and that I would never have found otherwise.

Over the years I have been assisted by a succession of able graduate students who helped me track down citations, copy articles, enter data into spreadsheets, and perform many other boring but indispensable tasks. Steve Miceli, Doug Wolf, Katy McMillion, Bonnie-Jean Chudzinski, Andrew Wicks, and Holly Hartlerode all took time out from their studies to contribute in these ways. Slavak Lehman amazed me with his rapid ability to translate Polish into English and his patience in spending many long hours in doing so while I transcribed the results.

Many people in Toledo opened their doors to me, and I am grateful to all of them. Sally M. Copeland, Marketing and Promotions Coordinator, and Robert A. Robinson, Executive Vice-President of National City Bank for the Northwest Region, generously made arrangements for me to study some of their older banking records and although these did not provide many facts for this study, this was not for lack of helpfulness. Mr. Robinson also helped arrange an interview with Willard Webb, Jr., and I want to thank them both for extending this courtesy to me. George Jones III shared his family reminiscences with me and helped put me in contact with others whose recollections were important. Though my researches and findings affected him personally, Mr. Jones displayed a mark of character rare in men of his stature, a willingness to pursue the truth wherever it took him. Similarly, Milton F. Knight took time out to share some of his stories with me.

The University of Toledo supported my research directly and indirectly, with a summer research grant, a semester sabbatical, and by supporting the graduate program in the Department of History. I would like to thank Prof. William H. Longton for not only enthusiastically supporting my research as chair of the department, but for listening to all my banking anecdotes.

I must also thank David Simmons and the staff of *Timeline* magazine for finding some terrific photographs that I had missed and for generously sharing their fine photographic reproductions with me. *Timeline*'s editor, Christopher Duckworth, has given me encouragement and support for this endeavor.

Finally, it is my wife, Diana, who keeps me going and puts things in perspective for me, and my boys, my best friends, Griffin, Emmett, and Connor, who make me want to write a book that they might want to read.

BEYOND THE PANICKED CROWD

The image of frantic crowds crushing in upon the ornate doors of a bank is one of the most enduring symbols of the Great Depression. Alongside the forlorn man hawking apples on a street corner, the overloaded Model T's of Okies heading further west and the tin and canvas shacks of innumerable Hoovervilles, the image of the bank run has become an icon of the worst economic disaster ever to befall modern American capitalism. Unlike its kindred symbols that express the human face of the tragedy, the image of the bank run seems to express both the cost and the cause of the disaster. It simultaneously invites the viewer to sympathize with the anxious crowds eager to withdraw their hard-earned savings and posits them as the active agents of their own misfortune.

As is true of most vital American stereotypes, the image of the bank run has been reproduced and retold to ever-new generations through the popular media. Frank Capra, a director whose enduring popularity is in no small measure built upon his talent for filling his silver screen with the characters and backdrops from a modern American mythos, built his 1946 classic, *It's a Wonderful Life*, around a small-town bank imperiled by a panicked crowd of depositors. Just as George Bailey's bank faced no other problems than the skittishness of his quirky neighbors, so too has the popular imagination largely explained the banking crisis of the 1930s as a failure of confidence rather than a failure of management.

Like most popular myths, the idea of the bank panic has its counterpart in academia. Economists have long debated whether the banking failures of the 1930s were "independent" economic events, that is, the result of a sudden loss of depositor confidence, or were a consequence of the erosion of the value of banks' underlying investments and securities. One of the most influential economic analyses of the past generation, Milton Friedman and Anna J. Schwartz's *A Monetary History of the United States, 1867–1960*, claimed that the bank failures of the early 1930s were the turning point that dragged the nation's economy from recession into depression. The direct cause of these pivotal bank failures was what they termed a "contagion of fear" among depositors. Though dressed up in monetarist jargon, this is an academic retelling of Frank Capra's story, though here George Bailey did not get a second chance and the fearful mob with little faith in the goodness of their neighbors succeeded in tearing down their banks.[1]

The most recent and thorough monograph on the subject framed the problem of bank failures in the conventional manner: "Conceivably, banking failures may have been the passive consequence of declining income and prices—an endogenous response. Or, they might have been a purely autonomous response to an unanticipated shock to depositor confidence—an exogenous response."[2] The reader is given but these two options: the Great Depression's banking failures were either a result of panic and mob behavior or an irresistible occurrence not unlike the weather. When a storm comes it is nobody's fault, and though the storm blows down many old and rotten trees, it blows down a few healthy ones as well and one does not blame the tree for falling in a storm. Our contemporary understanding of the banking crisis, by naturalizing it or extending blame over a faceless mob, removes responsibility for the consequence of economic decisions from those who actually made them.

The current popular and academic image of the bank run was not always the most salient symbol of America's worst period of banking failures. Many of those who experienced the bank crashes of the 1930s didn't view the banks as victims and the Great Depression as the ultimate cause of their problems. Popular magazines featured articles analyzing the reasons why banks were toppling across the nation and generally agreed that the banker and not the economy was to blame. "The tendency nearly everywhere," editorialized the liberal *Nation*, "will be to ascribe these bank failures to that anonymous depression which takes the blame for everything on its broad shoulders, but the figures, even on the surface, do not bear out this facile explanation." The more conservative *Saturday Evening Post* shared this viewpoint: ". . . in a word it was unsound banking that caused the bank failures, and not a depression which engulfed well-managed banks." The *North American Review* went so far as to blame bankers for the depression itself, "The banks and the investment houses have thus been fundamentally responsible for the panic of 1929." Even the keynote speaker for the Virginia Bankers' Convention in 1936 admitted, "In the minds of many folks, banks . . . were not the victims of the recent devastating depression, but were the basic cause . . . due principally, if not exclusively, to the inadequacy, the incompetency and the cold, heartless depravity of the bankers."[3]

The plummeting respectability of the banking fraternity was much commented upon and approved of in the press. Noted essayist George Anderson in an article entitled "Are Bankers Intelligent?" observed, "There are certainly many reasons why the average banker has lost his power and his prestige in his community—many reasons and all good."[4] The popular attitude towards the banking fraternity was best summed up by journalist Clifford B. Reeves writing in the *American Mercury* magazine in 1932:

> The title of banker, formerly regarded as a mark of esteem in the United States, has sunk in public estimation to a point at which it is now almost a term of opprobrium. There seems some danger, in fact, that in forthcoming editions of the dictionary it may be necessary to define the word as a peculiar American colloquialism, synonymous with rascal, highbinder, and scalawag, and we may even see the day when to be called a son-of-a-banker will be regarded as justifiable ground for the commission of assault and mayhem.[5]

Moreover, the belief that bankers were personally to blame for causing the Great Depression was not limited to those left destitute by its effects. The Pulitzer Prize winning historian James Truslow Adams observed that "resentment against bankers is rapidly growing" but that "hitherto the anger against banks and bankers has been voiced by the poor and debtor classes, today the strongest feeling I find is among the well-to-do classes."[6]

In the 1930s the public's condemnation of the "banksters" who gambled their savings away took many forms. Cartoons in the most widely circulated magazines portrayed bankers as gamblers and swindlers. In the 1930s pulp magazines added to their repertoire of plots stories built around crooked bankers. Street & Smith's *Best Detective Magazine* began publishing banker mysteries in 1930 with "Thumbway Tham's Bank Account" and other stories themed around crooked bankers such as "Double Liability" (1931), "Simon Trapp Opens a Bank" (1934), and "Buried in a Bank" (1936). A rival pulp, *True Gang Life*, devoted its second issue to "The Bank that Robbed Itself" in 1935. *Ace-High Detective Magazine* carried banker stories such as "Death on the Credit Side." *Complete Detective* offered "Bank Night in Hell."[7]

Even after the public's open furor against bankers began to subside with passage of tough new banking regulations in 1933 and the adoption of federal deposit insurance, bankers remained in disrepute for many years. A survey by *Fortune* magazine in 1936 revealed that 38.3 percent of respondents believed that bankers "abuse[d] their power"—only journalists were more distrusted at 41.8 percent.[8]

How America's popular understanding of the banking collapse has shifted since the 1930s is well illustrated in the changing descriptions of the event in college economics textbooks. College students taking their first macroeconomics course today would find a description of the banking collapse that emphasized the role of depositors. Indeed, many use the term "banking panic" in narrating the event. For example, one textbook in economic history reads: ". . . in October 1930 a wave of bank failures concentrated in the South and Midwest hit the country and produced something new. A general alarm about the banking system spread across the country, and people began converting bank deposits into currency . . . A rumor that a bank was in trouble would literally send people running to the bank to try to get their money out before it closed."[9]

In contrast, a textbook in economic history published during World War II does not even describe a bank run or give any causative role to depositors, but instead describes the collapse of international and domestic markets as the primary cause of the banking turmoil, banker misconduct as a secondary one, and the depositors as victims of both. "Banks failed in droves: 4100 closed their doors between 1930 and 1932 and caused depositors to lose a large part of the $3 billion put with them for safekeeping . . . The public was profoundly shocked by the apparent poor judgment and even downright crookedness of men who had been looked upon as pillars of respectability in their communities."[10] Clearly, the closer observers were to the events of the Great Depression, the more likely they were to blame individuals rather than impersonal forces for the economic disaster that befell the nation.

One place to study this disparity between the modern memory of such events and the discernible facts behind them is Toledo, Ohio. This is because Toledo has much to remember and surprisingly little memory of it. It was arguably the city hardest hit by the Great Depression, both in absolute economic terms and in its relative decline from its equally disproportionate boom years of the 1920s. Most importantly, Toledo experienced the worst banking collapse of any city in America during the Great Depression.

By the mid-1920s, Toledo had enjoyed three decades of booming growth. In the 1890s it was one of the only cities in the Midwest whose economy grew throughout the depression of 1893–1898. Buoyed by a well-timed oil strike in the region, a Gay-Nineties bicycle craze that set its wheel and metal shops humming with activity, and the relocation to the city of large eastern glass works, Toledo outpaced most other midsized cities in industrial and population growth as the nineteenth century drew to a close. In the years leading up to World War I, manufacturing evolved from bicycles to automobiles and from cutting elegant glass punch bowls to blowing most of the nation's bottles and light bulbs, while trade changed from oil speculating to supplying machinery and hardware to the oil-drillers. By the 1920s, Toledo's rate of growth in manufacturing employment led the United States.[11]

Even before the stock market crash of October 1929, Toledo's overheated growth had begun to stall as the city's largest employer, the Willys-Overland Company, laid off thousands in the spring of 1929. But employment stabilized and had begun to rebound by the summer of 1931, when five of Toledo's largest banks failed, an event that locally marked the transition from economic difficulty to economic disaster. All at once, the city that had led the nation in employment growth during the 1920s now led it in job loss in the 1930s.[12]

Toledo was not home to the largest single bank failure during the Great Depression—that dubious crown is worn by the city of brotherly love, whose Bankers Trust Company of Philadelphia held deposits worth over $450 million when it toppled in December of 1930. Nor did Toledo's bank crisis grab national headlines the way that several other large failures did. Six months before Toledo's bank failures, the collapse of New York City's Bank of the United States startled the nation not so much because of its large size (over $200 million in assets) but because of the confusion caused by a name that implied the bank was the official bank of the federal government. Historically, the failure of Michigan's Guardian Union Group in 1933 was the most significant single event, as this banking syndicate's closure set in motion the wave of state banking closure laws, euphemistically called "bank holidays," that culminated in President Roosevelt declaring a national "bank holiday" immediately after his inauguration.[13]

Though they were not the most famous or the most nationally significant of Great Depression bank failures, Toledo's bank failures considered in proportion to the size of the community in which they occurred were unprecedented. From 1930 through 1932, the largest single year's loss of deposits for any of the twelve Federal Reserve districts was that which occurred in 1931 in the Fourth District, the area encompassing all of Ohio, the western half of Pennsylvania, and the eastern half of Kentucky, when over 11.3 percent of the total deposits in the region were lost. The Fourth District's distinction as the worst-affected district in the country that year was due largely to the contribution of Toledo, which alone accounted for three-quarters of the district's losses.[14]

Toledo's banking disaster would have been significant had only one and not five of its banks gone belly up. During the whole of the Great Depression, only nine banks with assets exceeding $50 million failed. One of these was the Ohio Bank located in Toledo. For the year in which the giant Ohio Bank closed, it was the largest bank failure in the United States. Likewise, the 1930s suffered the closure of twenty-three banks with assets between $10 and $50 million. Three of these, or more than one in ten, were headquartered in Toledo, the twenty-seventh largest city in America, with fewer than three hundred

Table 1

Deposit losses per person, FY 1929–1933.

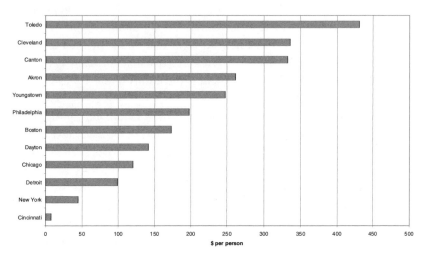

Source: Data gathered from Annual Report of the Comptroller of the Currency, Dec. 1, 1930, pp. 764–68; Dec. 7, 1931, pp. 1034–41; Dec. 5, 1932, pp. 568–74; Jan. 3, 1934, pp. 648–63; Oct. 31, 1934, pp. 776–93; Campbell Gibson, "Population of the 100 Largest Cities and Other Urban Places in the United States, 1790–1990," Population Division Working Paper, No. 27 (U.S. Bureau of the Census, 1998), Table 16; Annual Report of the Division of Banks (Ohio), Dec. 31, 1930, pp. 18–21, 34–39; Dec. 31, 1931, pp. 112–13; Dec. 31, 1932, p. 49; Dec. 31, 1933, p. 32; Dec. 31, 1934, p. 55.

*FY 1933 through March 15 only. All non–Ohio city figures are based on statewide losses.

thousand people. In 1931, one out of every four banks in this category that were lost was located in Toledo, Ohio. If banks were bombs, no piece of the country would have been more devastated than the epicenter of Toledo's financial district, the intersection of Superior and Madison streets.[15]

Because neither the Federal Reserve Banks nor the U.S. Comptroller of the Currency published city-level data for bank failures, it is difficult to precisely measure the relative per capita losses across different regions of the country. Ohio's state Department of Banking did compile such statistics (table 1). From these figures the ratio of the total deposits of suspended banks to the total population of each of the principal cities in the state can be calculated. In 1931, $430 worth of deposits were frozen for every man, woman, and child in Toledo, about a fifth more than the next nearest sufferer, which was Cleveland at $335. Comparable figures are not readily available for most other major cities of the nation, but even overestimating their losses by attributing every dollar frozen in their entire states for the whole of the 1930s to them alone,

Table 2

Percentage decline in annual exchanges of the fifty largest clearinghouses, 1929–1934.

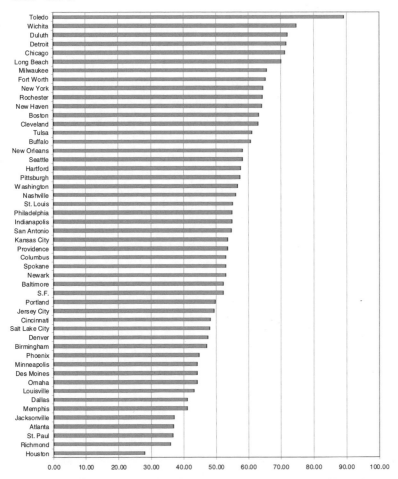

Source: Annual Report of the Comptroller of the Currency, Dec. 1, 1930, pp. 759–63; Dec. 7, 1931, pp. 1029–33; Dec. 5, 1932, pp. 563–67; Jan. 3, 1934, pp. 643–47; Oct. 31, 1934, pp. 772–76.

*Excluding those that did not report totals in this period (Oklahoma City, Oakland, Los Angeles, Little Rock, Davenport).

their per capita deposit losses are minor in comparison. According to this overly conservative method, Philadelphia's ratio stood at $197, Chicago's at $120, and New York's at $44.[16]

Other, probably more accurate, measures of the relative size of bank failures in American cities are the reported annual sums of exchanges handled by each city's clearinghouse. A clearinghouse is a central location where banks can quickly and conveniently swap checks, discount notes, and balance accounts with each other. The volume of money that moves through a clearinghouse is a pretty good indicator of the overall economic health of the city, but it is also a figure that is highly sensitive to banking failures, for when a bank fails its mass of deposits are no longer available to be exchanged or discounted, causing the overall volume of clearinghouse activity to fall in proportion. Comparing the activity of the fifty largest clearinghouses in America in 1929, before the waves of Great Depression bank failures hit, with their totals in 1934, after they had receded, is a useful index to the relative severity of bank failures in different regions of the nation (table 2).

Of the fifty largest clearinghouses in America, none experienced as deep a drop in their annual activity as did Toledo's, which plummeted by 89 percent between those years. In 1929 Toledo possessed the thirty-fourth largest clearinghouse in America. By 1934 the volume of its exchange ranked it sixty-ninth, a rank lower than El Paso, Texas, a city one-third its size. No other city on this list fell as far or as fast as Toledo. Judging by this indicator, no other city suffered as catastrophic a banking decline as did Toledo during the Great Depression.[17]

Though Toledo's banking collapse did not attract as much attention as did the well-publicized failures in New York, Philadelphia, and Chicago, several knowledgeable observers did conclude that Toledo's bank crisis had been the worst. President Franklin D. Roosevelt was probably correct when he called Toledo's bank crisis "the worst banking experience of any city of the nation."[18]

Toledo's banking collapse began on Wednesday, June 17, 1931. That morning the Security-Home Bank, the third largest, did not open its doors. As word of Security's closing rippled across the city, crowds gathered downtown and withdrawals mounted throughout the day at the other leading banks. At 4:00 P.M. the tellers at three of the remaining four largest banks, the Ohio, the Commercial, and Commerce Guardian, pulled down their shutters for the last time. The next morning each of these banks posted notices on their doors explaining that all withdrawals would be suspended for sixty days. When the suspension period ended two months later, all of these banks were closed and turned over to the state for liquidation. With over $125 million worth of deposits frozen in the closed banks, Toledo's economy was devastated.

At the time of Toledo's banking meltdown, official voices joined in a chorus of blame against the common depositors who they said caused the failures by running on the banks. Toledo's *News-Bee* editorialized that "Banks normally safe [were] forced to close by ill-advised and hysterical runs."[19] Ira J. Fulton, Ohio's superintendent of banking, was blunt in his assertion that "Fear, and not mismanagement" was the cause of Ohio's bank crisis and included in his annual report a little homily that he had written entitled "Holy Writ Condemns Hoarding."[20]

Following their lead, contemporary academic, journalistic, and business sources blamed Toledo's bank failures on the bank runs. The first academic study of the causes of Toledo's banking crash concluded that " . . . if the management of these banks had been willing to reduce operating expenses and to sacrifice the higher income of less liquid investments . . . they could have met the depositors' 'run' in the summer of 1931." [21] Subsequent general histories of Toledo place greater emphasis on the role of declining real estate values, but the throngs of "fearful depositors" remain the immediate cause of the crash. [22] The Toledo *Blade* has published a number of retrospective articles over the past few decades on these events, all of which prominently feature the bank run as the precipitating moment of crisis.[23]

In interviews with people connected to the banking industry in Toledo, the same theories were evident. One story that was often recounted was the most popular illustration of the bank run theory. An anomaly in the bank crash was the fact that one large bank, the Toledo Trust Bank, did not fail. The story circulating in financial circles is that the president of the bank, upon seeing the gathering crowds in the street on that mid-June morning, sent workmen down to the basement to stoke up the furnace until the lobby was sweltering hot, successfully discouraging anyone but the most persistent from sweating in line long enough to withdraw their money. This story has gained power to the point where it has begun to spawn secondary mythic narratives. One of the descendents of this bank president told how when he and his siblings went to clear the belongings out of the old family homestead, the furnace would miraculously turn on by itself even after the thermostat had been turned off—whether evidence of a soul forever guilt-ridden or forever proud of an old dirty trick is not clear.

This predominant narrative of a panicked populace and bankers struggling to preserve their deposits to the very end is not surprising or unusual. It follows in the main what college history textbooks today teach freshman.[24] What is remarkable is that Toledoans by 1934 understood a much different version of events. In 1932 a Lucas County grand jury indicted six officers of the defunct banks on charges that they had misapplied the funds of the bank, made false reports to the state, and fraudulently accepted the public's deposits in the waning days of their bank's operation. Those cases were still grinding through the courts in late 1933 when the Ohio Senate Committee on Banking held hearings in Toledo into the failures of 1931. The committee commissioned a special examiner to go over the books, who in just two weeks of auditing documented a trail of misappropriation, fraud, "smart money" insider withdrawals, and sweetheart loans to directors that completely inverted the popular idea of a bank run. From these hearings the public learned that there had indeed been a bank run, only it was a raid on the deposits of the bank conducted primarily by the owners, directors, and officers of the banks themselves. The public also surmised that these facts must have been known by the state Department of Banking, who had control of these banks for over two years and had not made public even one funny entry in any firm's books.[25]

By early 1934 Toledoans saw in print what had long been rumored before, that the first bank to fail, the Security-Home Bank, was brought down by the huge burden of loans and withdrawals made to insiders at the expense of depositors. In the last six weeks of the bank's operations, a little over $3 million in deposits were lost. Nearly half of that amount was withdrawn by the officers of the bank, their relatives, and the other businesses that they had interests in. On the day of the fabled bank run that supposedly shut down Security-Home Bank, the frightened public withdrew $679,971 from their savings accounts. That same day, June 16, 1931, commercial interests and rich investors quietly removed a much larger amount, $1,039,303.[26]

The other banks that voted to suspend withdrawals on the day of the Security-Home Bank's collapse only closed the front door of those banks. While still relatively healthy on the day of suspension, these institutions saw deposits fly out their back doors until they were unable to reopen when the suspension period expired. It was reported by the special examiner that over $12 million was withdrawn from the largest of these banks during the suspension period, much of it to relatives, friends, business partners, and the industrial interests of the principals of the bank. In spite of the proclaimed withdrawal freeze, these banks' daily transactions were quite brisk for those with connections. On the last day of banking, June 17, 1933, savings deposits at the Ohio Bank dropped by $2.07 million. But from the day the freeze began to the day the bank failed to reopen, savings accounts lost another $1.56 million. During the last week of the withdrawal period the bank's commercial accounts lost more deposits than they did on the day of the famed "bank run."[27]

Though all the records of the banks and the men involved in Toledo's economic downfall have been destroyed, enough of the facts remain scattered about the city to reconstruct the essential details of the nation's worst urban bank failure. As it turns out, the essential question to be asked is not what led the banks to ruin but who pushed them over the brink.

CHAPTER ONE

BLOWING UP THE BUBBLE

Toledo's real estate bubble began on a beautiful, clear Sunday in the spring of 1912 when E. H. "Harry" Close, a fastidious man whose flawlessly manicured nails were often commented upon, threw a grand opening celebration for his new rural housing development, "Homewood." This was Toledo's first twentieth century suburb, a subdivision platted not on the city's expanding edge, but leapfrogged out into the northwestern countryside. Many families still in their church clothes rode the free streetcars to the end of the new rail extension to Homewood where, under a large tent, the Overland Automobile Company orchestra played, cool lemonade was served, and salesmen guided customers, few of whom were schooled past the sixth grade, through the fine print of their mortgage contracts.[1] Homewood, cleverly marketed to the growing number of skilled workers at the Overland Company, quickly sold out, and Harry Close, superstitiously fond of the letter "H," ventured to repeat his formula with Home Acres, Homeville, Homewood Park, Hillcrest Acres, Hopeland, and others.[2]

Harry Close's success marked the beginning of a twenty-year boom in Toledo real estate development. During these decades, developers like Harry Close would vastly expand the area of the city and its urban infrastructure. The quick profits that Harry Close and others plucked out of the cabbage fields and oak stands surrounding Toledo seemed to justify an ever-increasing spiral of investment in new projects by local banks. By the 1920s, the subdivision boom claimed the lion's share of the city's bonding authority, bank capital, and political clout. As more and more of the city's economy came to depend on the price of undeveloped lots in a far-flung lattice of empty streets, the stage was set for the tragedy that was about to unfold in 1931.

E. Harry Close's earlier development successes and the favorable conditions at the beginning of Toledo's third twentieth-century decade attracted a flock of real estate speculators. In 1912, when Close built Homewood, there were just a handful of real estate companies in Toledo. By 1924, when he died, Close faced an additional 435 competitors. Some of these new-comers, like the Scott Realty Company and the M. S. Ramseyer Company, opened business with over a million dollars in initial capital.[3]

There were some solid underlying forces supporting Toledo's subdivision boom. Toledo's citizens were making relatively high wages, enough for an unusually large number at this time in history to realize their dream of home ownership. Throughout this period Toledo led Ohio and sometimes the nation in its average wage rates and its wage growth. Largely, this was due to the region's mix of industries that required a high proportion of skilled workers. Toledo's glass industries through the first decade of the century were still the domain of craftsmen, blowing and cutting, fluting and annealing. With nine rail lines converging on the city, the fourth most of any city in the United States, Toledo had more than its share of engineers and telegraphers. Its hardware, machine, and scale manufacturers could not do without their well-paid machinists and tool and die makers. Even the city's auto manufacturers employed as many skilled as unskilled workers up to World War I.[4]

Since the turn of the century home building had kept pace with neither the growth in Toledo's population nor the splendid growth in wages its workers took home. Partly this was due to a shortage of capital in the early twentieth century. Toledo's banks were relatively small before World War I, averaging less than $3 million in deposits compared to the $22 million they averaged in 1930. State banking laws strictly limited the ability of state-chartered banks to make housing loans up to 1908. Most local bank capital was funneled instead into the fast-growing consumer industries of the city. With a number of local industries investing heavily in some promising technologies and products—Edward Libbey and Michael Owens, who were working on their automatic glass blowing machine, the Toledo Scale Company, that was investing heavily in marketing, east side oil refineries always behind the voracious appetite of automobiles, and the Overland Company, that was striving to keep pace with Henry Ford—little was left to build houses with.

Whatever strength there was in the real estate development business was interrupted by the Great War, which strictly rationed raw materials and created the nation's first labor shortage since the last great war of the 1860s. Attracted by the city's high-paying industrial jobs, many migrants, especially from the Upper South, flocked to Toledo. By Armistice Day the city faced a severe housing crunch. In the spring of 1920 many families lived in tents on empty lots while waiting their turn for construction to begin on their homes.[5] The mayor urged residents to share rooms with the homeless, and at least one editor called on those who could to leave the city and return to their farms to make room for others.[6]

The housing shortage proved fleeting, and demand was quickly met by a flood of investment. War contracts brought windfall profits to the area's industries and bulging surpluses to the banks. By 1921 so many commercial borrowers had paid off their notes early that Toledo's banks sat on a million dollars in excess cash. In November the Ohio Bank led the way by slashing its general interest rate from 7 to 6 percent, an announcement that "was especially pleasing to real estate men and builders who see in it a revival of building activity for Toledo."[7]

Within a year of the armistice, Toledo's banks were healthy and eager to service the city's realtors. Many banks began aggressively advertising for mortgage loans, assuring the public that investments in land were sure to grow. One ad for the Toledo Savings Bank promised, "Men and women, having spare sums to invest cannot do better than to put them in well-selected Toledo real estate. . . . land is always safe and, in a city like Toledo, if carefully selected, sure to increase in value."[8]

Profits, as in all businesses, depended on buying low, selling high, and building a market for the product. Buying acres of countryside at low prices was not difficult early in the twentieth century. Still, to get the rock-bottom price, Toledo's realtors often concealed their true development plans. When Harry Close envisioned building an estate village on 600 scenic acres just west of Toledo he contracted with small town brokers to purchase the land, giving the impression to farmers that the land would be plowed, not platted. Luckily for the developers, by the early 1920s the farm economy was in a severe slump and the prices of rural acreage declined.

Even if a developer bought out a farmer for a song, the business of subdividing land was risky. Subdivision development tied up money for long periods and required a strong housing market to absorb the creation of hundreds and sometimes thousands of lots at once. Lots that didn't sell were subject to property taxes, and annual costs could quickly mount if the inventory went unsold too long. The business of subdevelopment was also dependent on the willingness and ability of municipal authorities to extend streets, sewers, and water mains to and through the paper neighborhoods, all of which began as just names and lines on new maps.

But the key to success in real estate in the 1920s was a cooperative bank backing the project. All developers wished to realize their profits as quickly as possible and dispose of their lots in one development so as to free up their resources and draw up another. The common means of doing this was either to sell the lots wholesale to a company that would retail them, or, better yet, if a willing banker could be found, to put up the lots as collateral for new bank loans. In this way the realty company kept control of sales and freed up money for more development. The key to this strategy was finding a willing banker who would exchange good hard currency for land of dubious value.

Harry Close happened to be the son of a banker. His knowledge of the power and the tricks of finance, learned at his father's knee, suited him well for his future career as a developer. Understanding that real estate companies lived and died on the availability of large loans and that this availability often depended on the generosity of bank assessments of lot valuations, Close squeezed himself into the local banking structure. He landed a directorship in the Northern National Bank and amassed the second largest bloc of shares in the Commercial Savings Bank. To the end of his career, which was tragically cut short in 1924 at the age of fifty when he was found cold in his bed by his butler, Close appeared never to lack financing for his projects. By that date, Close had already subdivided over five thousand acres.[9]

Developers became very adept at both marketing their new subdivisions and finding ways of building their value. Realty offices preferred to locate on the ground floor storefronts of downtown office buildings where they could tempt passersby with window displays of both neat workman's cottages and sprawling mansions. It was said by this time that Toledo had more storefront realty offices than any other city in the country. As a group, realtors were among the most aggressive advertisers in the local newspapers. Advertisements and brochures extolled their new neighborhoods' combination of rural bucolic serenity and convenient transportation to the city's center.[10]

Perhaps the greatest selling point of the subdivision, and one that lent the most to its value, was its exclusivity. Each subdivision was organized to attract a specific class of home buyer. There were working class subdivisions, like Close's Homewood with fourteen lots to the acre, and at the other end of the spectrum, there was the estate section of Ottawa Hills where each lot spread over two and a half acres. Those intended for lower- to middle-income buyers usually were arranged on a grid pattern, while those higher up in the income scale were curvilinear with many dead-end streets. To ensure the distinctive neighborhood aesthetic appropriate to each class, restrictions were written into the deeds. The number of restrictions varied also with the wealth of the neighborhood. In lower-income subdivisions, homeowners were not allowed to keep farm animals on their property, to build houses with more than two units, or to sell alcohol. Upscale developments had lists of restrictions that ran for pages, governing everything from house styles to building setbacks, fencing, landscaping, and property uses. All of these restrictions were vigorously policed and enforced by the realty companies, as they bore directly on the value of their inventories of lots.[11]

The most common restriction had the most negative long-term consequences. Section 6 of the list of restrictions for the Westmoreland neighborhood, entitled "NUISANCES," a section that prohibited building "stables, cattle yard, hog pen, fowl yard or house, cesspool, privy vault" and banned "poultry, hogs, cattle or other live stock or any noxious, dangerous or offensive thing . . ." concluded with this paragraph:

> At no time shall any lot in Westmoreland or any building erected thereon be occupied by any negro, or any person of negro extraction, or any Chinese, or any person of the Mongolian race, but this prohibition is not intended to include or prevent occupancy by said persons as domestic servants or while employed in and about the premises by the owner . . . [12]

The language of these racist clauses varied slightly, but the effect was always the same. The line permitting residence of black servants was dropped in lower-income areas. Sometimes the restriction permitted only those of the "Caucasian race" to live in the neighborhood. Occasionally, the term "Ethiopian extraction" was substituted for "Negro." Either way, the city's growing African-American population was systematically excluded from the suburbs. After twenty years of racial restrictions, twenty-one of Toledo's fifty-five census tracts would have no African-Americans. By the 1930s, most of the city's black population would be crowded into just four census tracts, including the two deemed to be the most substandard with the greatest number of houses in need of repair.[13]

Demand for housing was naturally strong due to population, wage growth, and white residents' desire to flee the old city, but it was also sustained by the easy money policies of local banks. The loose credit policies of local banks underwrote the operations of the city's real estate men. The system of financing, though common throughout the local industry, is best documented for the Welles-Bowen Company. William B. Welles, a former hardware salesman, and Badger Bowen, a former door-to-door book salesman, had been partners in the realty business for six years before buying 90 acres from neighboring farmers out at the end of Bancroft Street in the early twenties and drafting an upscale development they called "Westmoreland." With strong bank backing, the Welles-Bowen Company made it possible for their prospects to begin building quickly on their lots. With just 10 percent down, a lot was purchased, with the balance taken over seven and a half years at 6 percent interest. Then, a Welles-Bowen subsidiary would offer the new lot owner a second mortgage, secured by the same property, to help with their home-building costs. Eventually these notes would be given to the bank as collateral for new loans to assist other lot buyers to build homes or for platting whole new subdivisions, and the process would merrily repeat itself.

On paper it all added up very nicely, but the whole system rocked precariously on the ability of the purchaser to keep up the payments. While the first loan was risky enough, based as it was on the expectation that the buyer could pay and the development would fill in and keep up prices, the second mortgage was a real hot potato. If the buyer defaulted, the holder of the second mortgage would have to wait in line for the first mortgage to be completely repaid, with interest, before recovering a penny. But none of this was of immediate concern to the bank as long as the lot-selling market remained strong, thus keeping up the value of the collateral, and the purchasers coughed up their interest the first of every month.[14]

The interdependence of the banks and the real estate developers was soon reflected in the boardrooms of the city's financial corporations. Following the lead of E. H. Close, who directed the Commerce Guardian Bank, real estate men were appointed directors of the city's banks, and bankers became officers of realty companies. Of the twenty-nine heads of realty companies listed in a "Who's Who" book of prominent Toledoans, more than a third were also bank directors.[15] In the other direction, Frank C. Hoehler, a vice-president of the Security Bank, also served as vice-president of the Welles-Bowen Company.[16] Osbert D. Tiffany, president of the People's Bank, was founder and president of at least three different real estate companies, which, given his passion for ornithology, were named the Cardinal, the Bluebird, and the Oriole.[17] Badger Bowen became a director of the Home Savings Bank, while his partner, William Welles, later directed the Security-Home Bank.[18] One of the most powerful of the developers was Walter Stewart, who was a vice-president of the E. H. Close Realty Company, president of his own Walter Stewart Realty Company, and vice-president of the Commercial Bank.[19] C. O. Miniger, director of the Ohio Bank and a leading stockholder in several others, went into partnership with Welles-Bowen to develop a subdivision known as Hampton Park. The Reuben brothers, Al and Zale, who merged their realty company with the E. H. Close company after Harry died, making it one of the largest development firms in the state, got themselves elected as directors of two of the fastest growing banks in town, Al with the Commerce Guardian and Zale with the Commercial. Likewise, Edward Kirby, president of the Commerce Guardian bank, was also a director of the E. H. Close Company and its affiliates.[20]

Naturally, as bank boards became increasingly peppered with real estate interests, a greater proportion of the banks' loan business was shifted into the subdivision business. There was nothing necessarily wrong with this in theory—the development business was booming and its profits were strong in the early twenties—and bankers could reasonably see this field as one ripe for investment. However, it was not simply the field of real estate

Table 3
Largest real estate loans granted by individual banks in given year.

Year	Mortgagee Bank	Loan ($)	Interlocking Board Member and Mortgagor
1921	Ottawa Hills Co.	200,000	Edward Kirby (V.P., Commerce Guardian Bank; Dir., Ottawa Hills Co.)
1921	Devaux Realty Co.	50,000	Badger Bowen (Dir., Home Savings Bank; Treas., Devaux Realty Co.)
1921	B. C. Bowen Co.	100,000	Charles Carrol (Dir., Security Savings Bank; Pres., B. C. Bowen Co.)
1922	Commercial Bldg. Co.	325,000	F. E. Stewart (Dir., Commerce Bank; Dir., Commercial Bldg. Co.)
1922	G. B. Ricaby & Wife	129,000	H. A. Dunn (Dir., Security Bank; Dir., G. B. Ricaby Co.)
1923	Sidney Spitzer et al.	112,500	Sidney Spitzer (Dir., Commercial Guardian Bank)
1923	G. B. Ricaby et al.	120,000	H. A. Dunn (Dir., Security Bank; Dir., G. B. Ricaby Co.)
1924	Stanley Roberts	100,000	Stanley Roberts (Dir., Commercial Bank)
1924	Heather Downs Realty	1,500,000	Ira W. Gotshall (Dir., Ohio Bank; Sec., Heather Downs Realty Co.)
1924	Mount Union. Realty Co	200,000	F. C. Hoehler (V.P., Security Bank; Pres., Mount Union Realty Co.)
1925	Madison-Michigan . Bldg. Co	350,000	C. Miniger (Dir., Commerce Guardian Bank; Pres., Madison-Michigan Co.)
1925	Simplex Realty Co.	110,000	Thomas DeVilbiss (Dir., Toledo Trust Bank; Pres., Simplex Realty Co.)
1926	Baywood Realty Co.	125,000	C. D. Preston (Dir., Ohio Bank; Dir., Baywood Realty Co.)
1927	Lucas County Realty Co.	30,000	E. H. Rhoades (Dir., Dime Bank; Dir., Lucas County Realty Co.)
1927	Heather Downs Realty Co.	575,000	Ira W. Gotshall (Dir., Ohio Bank; Sec., Heather Downs Realty Co.)
1930	Port Toledo. Bldg Co.	260,000	William W. Morrison (Dir., Ohio Bank; Pres., Port Toledo Bldg. Co.)

Source: Data compiled from *Index to Mortgages: Mortgagor, 1921–1930*, Lucas County Recorder's Office, Toledo, Ohio; John M. Killits, *Toledo and Lucas County Ohio, 1623–1923* (Chicago: S. J. Clarke Co., 1923); Business Incorporation Records, Secretary of State of Ohio; Business and Industries of Greater Toledo Collection, MSS Coll. 36, Local History Department, Toledo–Lucas County Public Library; *Annual Report Department of Banks and Banking of Ohio, 1920–1931.*

development that bankers put their money into, but the companies of individual realtors who sat on their own boards. Steadily throughout this era individual banks placed a growing proportion of their loans into land companies controlled by their own directors. According to county mortgage records, at least sixteen times during the 1920s the largest real estate loan given by one of the city's banks in a single year was granted to a company with an interlocking directorate to the bank (table 3).[21]

Interlocking directorates and conflicts of interest between the banks' best interests and the best interests of other companies that bank officers controlled was nothing new in the 1920s. All of the banks in Toledo were heavily invested in companies that were controlled by their own directors. But loaning money to companies with company stock or bonds as collateral was a different beast from loaning money on real estate collateral.

Fundamental to any bank's success was its ability to correctly measure the value of collateral. If a bank incorrectly assesses the value of an asset that it accepts in guarantee of a loan, then it stands to lose an amount of money at least equal to the margin of error in its assessment. If the value of a collateral asset falls, and the bank perceives the drop, it can threaten to call in the loan or demand more collateral to make up the difference. Both stock and bond values, though they could rise or drop rapidly, were readily observable as their value was always pegged to their published closing prices in the stock and bond markets. Real estate loans, on the other hand, were a trickier matter, as each parcel carried a different valuation that varied not only with the market but also with subtle differences in location, amenities, and even intangibles like fashion and aesthetics. Making one initial accurate guess at the value of a house or a stretch of lots in an open field was difficult enough, but reevaluating that guess on a regular basis was a costly practice that ideally required a direct inspection of the property. It was so costly and troublesome that banks usually wouldn't bother except in the case of the most expensive commercial buildings. Just to be sure that the assigned value of collateral was solid, and to cover some measure of erosion that might occur over the life of a loan, good banking practice required that collateral exceed loans by at least 20 percent. In theory, bankers desire to secure as much collateral as they can on each loan, and naturally, borrowers have the opposite interest, seeking to post as little collateral as they can so as to leverage the most money from their property. But theory doesn't hold when banker and borrower are one and the same.

Osbert D. Tiffany was a newcomer to the banking business when he joined the People's Savings Bank in 1908. After he rose to become president, Tiffany ran a rather loose operation. The books were so disorganized that daily overdrafts were not always recorded. Tiffany's carefree management didn't seem to cause him any difficulty as his board, like so many others in this day, simply served as a rubber stamp of his actions. By the 1920s, his People's Bank seemed to be run primarily to support the outside business ventures of its own officers. About $55,000, without security, was loaned to the Eastmoreland

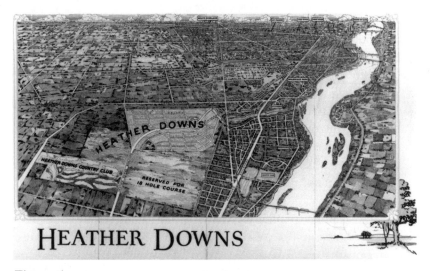

HEATHER DOWNS

Figure 1
The Heather Downs development, on Toledo's south side, was the largest single borrower from the Ohio Savings Bank. (*Source:* Toledo–Lucas County Public Library)

Realty Co., an outfit controlled by bank director William J. Von Ewegen.[22] Tiffany himself borrowed over $100,000 without collateral to support his own real estate ventures, much of it taken without bothering to gain formal authorization of his own board. All told, Tiffany, his family members, and his businesses took over one hundred loans from the bank, often taking new loans to repay old ones in a long compounding process.

The Banker's Trust Company, the youngest bank in town, established in 1927, was also in the habit of throwing money at its directors and asking for no collateral in return. Sidney Spitzer, the president of the new bank, took $25,000. His brother Lyman Spitzer steered seven thousand unsecured dollars to his Spitzer Paper Box Company. Clinton Mauk pocketed about $12,000. M. C. Seeley took about $10,000, and J. D. Hurlbut was relatively restrained, grabbing only about $4,000.[23]

Raleigh Mills had the good sense to marry the daughter of a bank president. Still in his twenties, he was made cashier of Home Bank by step-daddy Marion Miller, and soon moved up, reaching the board room.[24] By the time the decade was out, Mills had managed to accumulate over $200,000 in loans from the Home Bank and its successors, many of them unsecured. Real estate developer and Home Bank director Badger Bowen was given a loan of $79,000 on $4,000 collateral.[25]

Well plied with private and public loans, facing a seemingly endless demand for suburban housing, and reaping the rewards of a decade of tremendous economic growth, it is understandable that Toledo's developers were overly optimistic. By 1926 there were 79 major subdivisions and hundreds of division extensions and additions selling lots and many more being mapped out beneath scopes and stadia rods.[26] It is estimated that by the end of the decade, enough lots were platted to house a population of over one million, four times Toledo's actual population.[27]

The most ambitious developments were begun to the south of the city. In 1924 ground was broken on the Heather Downs subdivision, an 800-acre plat "in the beautiful exclusive up-river section" of the city surrounding an "exclusive golf course" (figure 1). Enough house lots were surveyed to accommodate a population of fifteen thousand people. Though primarily a venture of the Blair Realty Company, it was heavily underwritten by the Ohio Savings Bank, one of whose directors, I. W. Gotshall, was an investor and director in the project.[28]

Given these particular structures dictating real estate expansion, it was almost inevitable that speculative interests would overbuild to the point of crisis. Because of the insider pull of real estate moguls with the banks, capital was loaned with little scrutiny of the prospects for either profit or repayment. Long after the market for houses and lots crashed, loans continued to be supplied for new developments and old loans were renewed on the same terms even though the value of the underlying collateral had deteriorated. City bonds allowed the developers to run their projects with little consideration for the economy of their plans. Not having to tie up their own money in the infrastructure of their developments eliminated the greatest source of the realtors' risk, as it is always easier to gamble with someone else's money.

In addition to the easy loans that the realtors' boardroom clout secured, they also benefited from a huge hidden public subsidy of their business. Most of the heaviest expenses in the development process were actually shouldered by the public, as the city paid for street, sewage, and water extensions with special bond issues and later assessed the lot purchaser a special assessment to defray a portion of their cost. These could be issued upon order of the city's service director or the county assessor, depending on the jurisdiction, and were approved routinely by the 1920s. Even the cost of streetlights was split fifty-fifty between the city and the homeowner.

But the ability to draw on the public tax base to construct the developments themselves proved only one ingredient for the success of a subdivision. Increasingly, as the subdivisions expanded, their value and salability were determined by the willingness of the city to upgrade access to them. Toledo, being a railroad nexus, was crisscrossed with dangerous high-speed crossings. The city, having once been a canal terminus, was also bisected by the abandoned Miami and Erie Canal, which for most of the year was no more than a mosquito-breeding, muddy ditch. The cost of tunneling under or bridging over these obstructions ran into the millions of dollars, a burden the developers demanded that the city shoulder for the public good, though their concern was awakened by their private interest. Occasionally, a developer even put off platting a subdivision until the city bore the cost of tunneling a road under a nearby railroad crossing. The costliest single city undertaking in the 1920s was extending Summit Street across the canal to ease access to the downtown from the south side, one of the largest regions of real estate subdivision growth.[29]

Lobbying alone proved insufficient to shake these expenditures out of city hall. Reformers and city councilmen representing poorer wards often voted against expenditures out of their districts, especially if they smacked of being a special favor to landed interests. Thus in 1928 the city council temporarily withheld its approval for building a new university campus beyond the western fringe of the city, but bordering on a half dozen new subdivisions. Those politicians most closely tied to the city's political machine could be counted to vote for public works as a means of securing patronage and contracts for supporters. However, truly large expenditures required the voters' approval of a bond issue, and voters wisely did not trust the city's politicians to be good stewards of this money. City politics were at a stalemate as far as the private development interests were concerned. These conditions made it necessary for the overlapping banking and real estate interests to claim a greater share of governmental power themselves. The realization of their investments depended on it.

Seizing Municipal Government

It was not an unusual luncheon gathering of the city's movers and shakers that took place at the Exchange Club on a typical Wednesday in September of 1921. Perhaps there were a few extra notables present, being "President's Day," when the heads of the other business clubs were all invited to attend, but not so many that anyone took notice. Of course, no one there eating lunch and chatting up their table could have known that in ten years many of the men in the room would be bankrupt. What they did notice was the unusual entertainment as a fetching young flapper named Hope Eden stood before the head table and was announced as the "miracle girl" who was "the most talented exponent of mind transference." It is not recorded what questions the businessmen asked of young Miss Eden or what her answers were. Earlier in the week someone had asked her about whether to purchase property and she had called upon her "unique psychic gifts" to answer that "real estate values are more or less speculative at present. Remain where you are for at least another year . . ." Perhaps Hope Eden, whose act ran through the week at Keith's vaudeville theater, was the real deal—certainly the advice of the miracle girl was no worse than that freely given by the experts who followed her.

The keynote speaker that day was William H. Yeasting, an up-and-coming young banker, president of the Chamber of Commerce and the Commercial Bank. Yeasting urged his fellow businessmen to prepare for rapid growth. Within a few years, he trumpeted, they would be doing business in a city of 500,000, double its current population.

For Yeasting and the other presidents at the head table, this prediction was not mere idle speculation. These men were about to stake their fortunes and reputations on it. Walter K. Stewart, president of the Advertising Club, was using his influence as a director of the Commercial Bank to secure hundreds of thousands of dollars in loans to pour into his speculative ventures. Al Reuben, president of the Toledo Real Estate Board, was platting subdivisions with his land company and loaning money for construction from his mortgage company. Leroy Eastman, president of the Kiwanis Club and director of the Security Bank, was positioning his bank to underwrite this expected boom. Most everyone else in the room was similarly filled with the booster spirit.

For Yeasting, Stewart, Reuben, Eastman and all the other banking and real estate big shots who regularly attended these elbow-rubbing lunches, this was the dawn of their era. This was their decade—a time in which their ideas, their opinions, and their authority would prevail over all others. It was an era in which the reigns of power and decision-making would come together into their grasp. They would remake the city. They would alter its geography, its neighborhoods, its structures of business and government. These business leaders sincerely believed that their improvement plans for the city and their private interests were complementary. Perhaps they did not realize until it was too late that their twin dreams of windfall riches and of a modern city remade under their progressive leadership conflicted.

So, the story of the banking crisis of 1931 properly begins nearly twenty years earlier, before World War I, with the rise of the real estate moguls and young bankers to civic dominance by the 1920s. Their victory was neither easy nor swift, for to achieve it they had to overcome powerful social currents that had held the balance of power in Toledo since its emergence as a modern city in the 1890s. They had to crush the city's powerful and radical labor unions. They had to break the power of both the progressive Independent political movement and the city's entrenched ethnic political machine. They had to end the hide-bound traditionalism of the city's old-money elites. As each of these obstacles was overcome their influence increased, and those remaining became easier to remove until by the end of the 1920s they had achieved nearly all of their goals.

The first target of Toledo's organized business interests was the city's labor movement, a powerful force not only in the city's factories, but also in city hall. Though the labor movement had never been strong enough to form its own political party or even play kingmaker in city politics, it could muster enough influence to force issues onto the agenda or to block proposals it was strongly opposed to. Toledo's successful independent movement that elected mayors Samuel Jones and Brand Whitlock was most sensitive to the demands of labor, though even the conservative Republican administrations that succeeded them included elements of the labor lobby.

At the dawn of the decade of the 1920s, the influence of labor in local affairs seemed certain to strengthen. Toledo's unions had grown steadily since the outbreak of war in Europe in 1914. In the last year of the war alone, protected by a severe labor shortage, over five thousand men and women joined unions, expanding Toledo's labor movement by 25 percent. By 1919, over twenty thousand Toledoans, or one-fifth of the city's work-force, paid union dues. Unions were growing so quickly that they were having difficulty fitting into their usual halls.[30]

Realtors and developers had a special interest in weakening unions, as the historically strong building trades unions significantly bid up the cost of construction.[31] Throughout 1920, leaders of the local real estate organizations complained frequently of their high building costs, the shortage of labor, and the interference of unions.[32] Additionally, those city council-men beholden to labor votes were stingy, opposing most city building projects on the grounds that they were too expensive and would unfairly burden their constituents with rising taxes.

Most alarming to the industrial chiefs of the city was the rapid recruitment of unskilled workers into the trade unions at Willys-Overland. Organizers from a half-dozen trade unions, spanning the ideological spectrum from conservative skilled trade brotherhoods to the revolutionary Industrial Workers of the World, quietly signed up members in the dark and clamorous rooms of the city's largest factory.[33]

Willys-Overland was the center of the city's fortunes. Already the city's largest employer, it was clearly the engine of the entire region's future growth as well. John North Willys's ambitions were boundless and he had the audacity to challenge the Ford empire on Ford's own turf—low-priced, mass-market cars. In late 1917 Willys unveiled plans to put in production a car that broke the $500 price barrier and sported many more features than Ford's Model T.[34] By this time, Willys was shipping nearly 9,000 cars per month, a pace that was still well behind Ford's 70,000, but gaining hard, enough to earn it second place

among all auto manufacturers in the nation. In the minds of the city's businessmen, the nascent organizing movement in the city's mass production factories was simply a barrier to expansion. The viewpoint from the Toledo Club,
the social center of the business elite, was Manichean: unions were a barrier
to productivity, progress, and their own rightful and enlightened leadership.[35]

The battle for control of Toledo's factories was pitched by 1920. The
city's industrialists were drawn up shoulder to shoulder under the banner
of the Merchants and Manufacturers Association, led by the law firm of Tracy,
Chapman, and Welles. Following the lead of the national Open Shop Association,
the Merchants and Manufacturers Association pressured the city's business
community to revoke their existing labor contracts and to stand united against
the attempts of labor to strike or organize.[36]

No holds were barred in the struggle between business and labor in those
years. Strikers routinely assaulted scab workers and at least once attempted
to bomb a building site. Employers hired detective agencies to spy on union
meetings, recruit informers, and even to assault picketers. Government agents
hired informers and passed along the names of organizers to plant managers who added them to a citywide blacklist. Local police arrested street
speakers and dispersed rallies with their clubs. Local and federal judges issued
injunctions prohibiting union leaders from organizing and union members
from peacefully assembling. It was even rumored that the businessmen's association had helped organize the local chapter of the Ku Klux Klan as a weapon
in its war on labor. These battles went on for the better of two years, from
the great strike at Willys-Overland (that saw two workers shot dead in the
streets by local police) to the Railroad Shopmen's strike of 1922, but eventually the united front of government and business succeeded in breaking
the back of the labor movement in Toledo.[37]

By 1921, Toledo's building trades unions, once labor's bulwark, were in
retreat. The leader of the Central Labor Union confessed that few union
craftsmen were finding work that spring. Unions assessed a special tax on
all their members to continue the fight, but to little effect. Labor's impo-
tence was obvious when the new Toledo Times Building, a highly visible
symbol built for a newspaper susceptible to consumer pressure, was constructed with nonunion labor. In 1921 all three of the city's garment factories, once a bastion of organized labor, survived brief strikes and broke
their unions.[38] That same year the entire wait staff at the swank Toledo Club
were fired en masse when they collectively asked for a raise.[39] So demor-
alized did Toledo's unions become that they cancelled their usual Labor Day
parade.[40] By 1924 an industrial survey of Toledo boasted that "strikes, as
reported by the United States Labor Bureau, do not occur as frequently in
Toledo as in many other cities . . ."[41] With little upward pressure on wages

Figure 2
Walter Folger Brown (holding his hat) at the 1940 Republican National Convention. (*Source:* Toledo–Lucas County Public Library)

from unions from 1925 to 1927, Toledo's average industrial paycheck dropped by 4.5 percent and languished there throughout the decade.[42]

Just as the unions stood as a threat to their control of the local economy, various political factions stood in the way of the businessmen's control of the city government. For the first two decades of the twentieth century, Toledo's business community did not enjoy the access or influence in city or state government that it felt was its due. Toledo's "non-partisan" reform mayors, Samuel "Golden Rule" Jones and his successor, Brand Whitlock, were not antibusiness—Jones himself was a wealthy industrialist—but they did sincerely believe that government should operate free of any special interests. It was bad enough that both Jones, and to a lesser extent, Whitlock, relied on the populist support of Toledo's strong unions and immigrant neighborhoods for political support and both men chose principles above politics in most situations.[43] Far more upsetting to the city's developers was that Toledo's non-partisans pursued a Jeffersonian austerity when it came to spending. As the keenest observer of politics in this era remembered: ". . . they were grim watch dogs of the treasury—progressive enough but resolutely set against fads and experiments with public money."[44]

At this crucial juncture, Toledo's business elite found their savior in the person of an old Roosevelt Progressive whose political star was just on the rise. Walter Folger Brown (figure 2) would accomplish what few other machine bosses could—weld an effective political coalition out of a wary collection of vice-lords, rum-runners, ward bosses, and downtown businessmen.

Brown was a born politician, preferring the corridors of power to its spotlight. When he was a senior at Toledo's Central High School he engineered the election of his friend, Brand Whitlock, as class president, leveraging just enough coed votes by agreeing to support election of a girl to class secretary. After graduation from Harvard University and taking his destined place as a partner in his father's law firm, Brown made the mistake of moving into the inner circle of the city's Republican machine, the youngest of the so-called Ring of Seven Men, just as Samuel Jones' independent movement was rising up from the streets. More errors followed. Brown became the attorney for the city's street railway just as the high cost of fares became the hottest political issue in the city. In 1912, when the party split, Brown went with his hero Teddy Roosevelt into the Bull Moose party and was cast out with the other party splitters when Roosevelt lost to Ohio's favorite son, William Howard Taft.[45]

Brown's connections and ability along with the national spirit of unity among Republicans in 1920 repaired his reputation. When Brown walked out onto the convention floor in the cavernous Chicago Coliseum later that June, he was made kingmaker. Warren G. Harding's choice for his convention floor manager, Harry Daugherty, had been rejected as a delegate by the state Republican party, and Brown was tapped as his replacement. It was Brown who officially nominated Harding for president and helped steer this "dark horse" through the nomination and on to Washington. Harding's coattails were long and the entire state Republican slate was swept into office, including Harry L. Davis into the governor's mansion.[46] In reward, Brown was given all the patronage his state and federal connections could secure. His clout was so large that his closest political associate was appointed collector of internal revenue for the Toledo District over the objections of Republican state senator and former Ohio governor Frank Willis.

Armed with his powerful statewide connections, Boss Brown consolidated his party's control of municipal and county government in Toledo for the first time in the twentieth century. In an election that marked the first appearance of open party competition for local office since before the rise of Samuel "Golden Rule" Jones and the enthusiasm for "non-partisan" elections that had long gripped the city's politics, the Brown machine benefited from the strong candidacy of Solon T. Klotz, a socialist candidate whose 32 percent showing in the election of 1919 scared the conservative Democrats into fusing with the Republicans. Brown's hand-picked candidate, Judge Bernard Brough, an affable and charming bachelor, after winning handily, quickly tossed aside the civil service rules by simply not holding examinations and designating all positions as "temporary" and set about dispensing offices and patronage to the party captains in proportion to their contributions.[47] In an ironic twist of political fate, Brough's administration capitalized on the legacy of the progressive "non-partisans," who had insulated all administrative functions from the city council and placed them entirely in the mayor's hands out of fear of political meddling.[48]

Walter Folger Brown had succeeded in taking control of Toledo's government by forging together an unlikely coalition of mutually antagonistic groups. One pillar of his power was composed of the regular party politicians from working-class and immigrant neighborhoods who served their constituents by distributing city jobs and contracts. Some of these ward-heelers derived powerful support from the city's racketeers, who had long run a flourishing gambling, prostitution, and extortion business. Seizing on the many opportunities presented by the recent passage of the Volstead Act and the beginning of national Prohibition, these well established but petty gangs were beginning to grow into a much more powerful and insidious force than they had ever been. The other important pillar of Boss Brown's coalition was comprised of the politically-active businessmen organized through the city's service clubs. Brown, being a partner in one of the richest law firms in the city and a director of a local bank, was himself one of these men. These men had long viewed themselves as the proper and natural leaders of the community, but had never before enjoyed the political power Brough's election brought to them. Brown and Mayor Brough appointed two leaders of the business lobby to important cabinet posts. The banker and real estate developer and outgoing president of the Chamber of Commerce, Walter Stewart, was made director of finance. William T. Jackson, president of the General Contractors' Association, was picked as city service director, the officer in charge of all public works projects.[49]

The business lobby's agenda was long but simple. They wanted the city to quickly and efficiently improve the city's infrastructure so as to benefit their own businesses and their own development schemes. All of these plans, no matter how self-interested, could be easily dressed up in the clothes of civic progress, boosted as the path to the city's future, and sold to a trusting public.

Toledo's businessmen took pride in being part of a national movement of business leaders who preached that public support for business interests was essential to progress. As president of the National Association of Real Estate Boards (NAREB), Toledoan Irving B. Hiett, a man responsible for sixty of the city's subdivisions, was in a position to advance this idea on a larger stage.[50] Under his leadership, the NAREB lobbied for higher sales taxes to support public improvements and for the formation of city plan commissions "where real estate men are represented" throughout the nation. It was during a conference of NAREB leaders in Toledo, after they had toured Toledo's newest subdivisions and during a working lunch held on board E. H. Close's yacht, *Tillicum*, that they agreed to conduct a national housing survey in cooperation with Herbert Hoover's Commerce Department. Hoover had requested such a survey a few days earlier, expressing his belief that real estate men should take the lead in government housing policy. He wrote to Hiett: "The solution of the problems of sufficient housing and of home ownership lies peculiarly in the field of real estate organizations . . . I hope members of your organization will take a leading part in every town and city . . ."[51] Toledo's real estate men did just that.

In addition to the Toledo Real Estate Board, the city's real estate and financial interests were organized through the Chamber of Commerce. By 1921 the Chamber had a long pedigree stretching back thirty years to the old Board of Trade and the Toledo Manufacturers Association. In between, it had undergone no fewer than five reorganizations and changes of name, reflecting its weakness in the progressive era of Jones and Whitlock. Though it had always combined union-busting with civic promotionalism, few of its proposed projects, including its highest priority, a new downtown railroad station, were built in these years. After Whitlock won his second election the organization seemed to accept defeat and withered into little more than a gentleman's club, with rooms located on the top floor of the Nicholas Building (whose first floor housed the Commerce Bank), where Toledo's elite could dine, play billiards, or lose money at cards.[52]

After 1920 the booming real estate and banking sectors brought new blood into the Chamber of Commerce. In the decade before 1920, the Chamber's leadership consisted of lawyers and bond merchants from old Toledo families. In the new decade, the Chamber was led by a succession of real estate speculators, up-and-coming bankers, and industrial entrepreneurs. The Chamber of Commerce quickly grew in numbers and public influence and by 1922, with a membership of 3,600, claimed to have the largest membership of any Chamber of Commerce chapter in the United States.[53]

The Chamber selected Walter Stewart, a partner in the E. H. Close Realty Company and vice-president of the Commercial Savings Bank, as its leader in 1920. Following Stewart was the banker, W.H. Yeasting, who brought the Chamber to the forefront of the city's politics. The only two-term president in this era was Adam R. Kuhlman, head of a construction company and a director of the Security Bank. Under Stewart's leadership, the Chamber lobbied the city to annex areas to the south of Toledo, some parts of which he later cut up into his own subdivisions.[54] Yeasting and the other Chamber men believed that the city should spend massively on public works, but were steadfastly opposed to a proposed state income tax to raise revenue. Yeasting's Chamber proposed improving St. Clair Street downtown so that it could become the "white way" of a refurbished theatre district. They urged the city to dig subways to separate roads from railroad tracks, expand the city's water system, construct a municipal pier, fill in an abandoned canal bed, and drain urban wetlands. They endorsed the replacement and rebuilding of virtually every school in the city at one fell swoop, a project with a price tag of $11 million.[55]

Under the pressure of the Chamber of Commerce, Mayor Brough and the Republican city council approved development projects until they reached the state legal ceiling on bonded debt. When Brough took office the city's general bonded debt stood at $14,585,598. By the end of Brough's first term, it had grown to $24,424,849.

A majority of this increase was directly attributable to the cost of connecting recently annexed subdivisions to the city.[56] During the long period of the progressive "non-partisan" administrations of Samuel "Golden Rule" Jones and Brand Whitlock, the city had actually shrunk in geographic size. In 1911 Whitlock approved the removal of a one-tenth square mile area from the city limits. In 1916 the nascent real estate boom prompted the city to expand its borders for the first time in a quarter century. When Mayor Brough's business and machine coalition took power, there had been five annexations of subdivisions in the previous four years. Over the remainder of the 1920s, the city would strain under the cost of incorporating two dozen more.[57]

With all the room in the city's bonding authority going to servicing the new subdivisions, the Chamber's wish list of more expensive projects had to be put to the voters. The first of their large projects to move forward under the Brough administration was a proposal to build a civic plaza framed with new public buildings, to be located adjacent to the city's commercial center. Both the Chamber of Commerce and Mayor Brough hailed the planned three-million-dollar civic center as a vital step in Toledo's race with the other fast-growing cities of the Midwest. The necessary bond referendum slated for the languid political off-season of August 1922 would have easily carried except for the loud cries and clever tactics of the city's socialists. Waiting until the day before the election, socialist leaders found a friendly municipal judge and swore out complaints against three leaders of the civic center campaign committee, accusing them of distributing unsigned, anonymous leaflets, a violation of the state's election codes. After warrants were issued for the arrest of the three executives, including Adam R. Kuhlman, owner of one of the largest builders' supply companies and active leader of the Chamber of Commerce, newspapers on election day repeated the socialists' charges that the civic center plan was merely "a plan of real estate dealers to increase property values . . ." Such charges were not outlandish; less than a year before, several parcels adjoining a possible civic center site were purchased by a syndicate led by Edward G. Kirby, one of the city's active real estate developers and a leading director of the Commerce Guardian Bank.[58] Socialists also scored by making an issue of the fact that local business leaders had pressed squads of local Boy Scouts into the service of their publicity campaign, a tactic which struck even jaded city-desk editors as improper.[59] When the vote was tallied, the civic center bond failed by only 625 votes out of 25,319 ballots cast.[60] It was little consolation that the charges against Kuhlman and his colleagues were dropped on a technicality—these men expected such treatment at the hands of local judges. (A few years earlier, speeding charges against boss Walter Brown were dismissed on the grounds that state law prohibited reckless operation of a "motor vehicle," while Brown was clearly driving an "automobile."[61])

These disappointing results caused both the city's professional politicians and its business interests to grow more suspicious of their partnership. The politicos began to wonder if the cost of pushing the Chamber of Commerce's projects might undermine their base of support. As one of the city's editors warned them, "The mayor of Toledo . . . should remember that while the luncheon clubs represent a large, influential and worthy class of citizenship, there is yet a much larger class, all taxpayers, who should be consulted in a project. . ."[62] Leaders of these same "luncheon clubs" believed the negative vote was entirely due to voters' suspicion that any additional revenues or bonds would simply disappear down the Brown machine's partisan maw.

Though their referendum failed, the vote was just close enough to allow Toledo's developers, bankers, and business boosters to believe that they could win at the next election if they just redoubled their efforts. For a time, the Brown machine and the Chamber of Commerce continued to cooperate. Both machine nominees and Chamber men served amicably on city planning boards and commissions, the city council voted overwhelmingly for Chamber-sponsored tax increases and bond issues, and the Chamber's highest-placed city official, Service Director William T. Jackson, did what he could to keep the cost of graft to a minimum.

The Brown-Chamber business boosters tried again in November of 1925, this time audaciously proposing a massive package of bond issues totaling over $32 million, a sum larger than the accumulated debt of the city. Besides bringing back the failed civic center plan, the Chamber heaped onto their wish list tens of millions of dollars of subsidies to facilitate the sale and growth of the newest subdivisions. It included nearly $5 million for new boulevards extending out to the developments and another $5 million for new sewers and waterworks. Two million would go for new parks, nearly all of which would be situated near the largest new developments, rather than in the old parts of the city. Much of the rest would be spent on street widening, bridges, port development, and police and fire substations.[63] On election day, as expected, Brown's Republicans swept all major offices, but all of their spending plans, except for a minor road and rail separation project, were again turned down by Toledo's voters.[64]

The marriage between the activist businessmen and Brown's ward bosses was now strained to the breaking point as each believed the other was the anchor weighting down their grand plans. Mayor Brough's successor, Fred J. Mery, presided over the final rupture between the couple, though he can't be accused of causing it. At first, Mery seemed an acceptable successor to Brough in the eyes of the business lobby, as he himself was a businessman, a proprietor of a neighborhood drug store. But Mery's political instincts were more powerful than his business acumen, and having once been elected to the state legislature, he was more experienced in partisan politics than was his predecessor. From the time of his campaign, Mery was popularly recognized as the ward bosses' man in the Brough administration and several of the Chamber men who had served in Brough's cabinet resigned before Mery took office. After less than a year in office, Mery shocked the city's business interests by firing their last man in city hall, William T. Jackson.

The firing of Jackson forced business leaders to rethink the basis of their power in the city. What was clear to them now was that voters would not endorse massive public spending projects that were to be built by a city administration that had a well-earned reputation for waste, inefficiency, and corruption. No matter that their partnership with the machine and gang elements had driven the foot-dragging non-partisans out of power and delivered city government partially into their hands; it was a coalition that would complicate the task of leveraging increasing tax revenues into subsidies for their enterprises. The business men were now determined to win power alone.

1927 was the year in which the business lobby broke with the Brown Republican machine and established its own administration. In that year's mayoral campaign the business lobby united behind William T. Jackson, the man who best symbolized their newfound opposition to the entangling strings of the Brown machine. Jackson's campaign was headed primarily by the same financial elite that ran the Chamber of Commerce and the city's banks. Jackson campaign manager was John R. Cowell, a recent president of the Chamber of Commerce, yet another banker, and a man who as a past Republican councilman had worked as diplomat to the Brown machine. His campaign treasurer was Sidney Vinnedge, sitting president of the Chamber of Commerce and director of the newly chartered Industrial Bank. Alfred Koch, Toledo's native department store mogul and a director of the Toledo Trust Bank, along with Clement Miniger, perhaps the richest man in the city and a director and majority shareholder in several banks, according to one insider, "became Jackson's (best) workers and gave money and time to his support."[65]

Besides the solid support of the city's business lobby, Jackson gathered support by hammering away at the corrupt administration of "Boss Brown." He denounced the machine's record of inefficiency and waste and its protection of the city's flourishing gambling and prostitution rackets.

The Chamber of Commerce men, while fighting to elect Jackson mayor, hedged their bets by also campaigning for the elimination of the old mayor and his ward-based council and their replacement by a professional city manager and a council elected by proportional citywide vote.[66] This charter "reform" could only be won through a special referendum, as the city's regular politicians saw no profit in revising the city charter so as to separate themselves from their own neighborhoods and their networks of retainers, flunkies, dependents, and friends. Perhaps knowing that an openly Chamber of Commerce–orchestrated campaign would alienate many of the city's working class voters, the Chamber created a front organization, the People's Charter Campaign Committee, to run things. It had a good populist name, though it included two former presidents of the Chamber, A. R. Kuhlman and Sidney Vinnedge, as well as two other bankers, C. C. Whitmore, president of the Security Bank, and Percy Jones, a director of the Commerce Guardian Bank, with a couple of bona fide reformers along for window dressing.[67]

But the machine was not prepared to give up without a fight. The Brown Republicans tapped Dr. William B. Guitteau, a popular former superintendent of schools, as their best hope of clinging to city hall. Brown's experienced ward-heelers resorted to every trick to blunt Jackson's popularity: they entered the former vice-mayor, Grant Northrup, as a third candidate in the race, hoping to divide Jackson's support enough to allow Guitteau to win a plurality; they inflated the voter registration roles and sent repeaters to the polls; they played to the labor vote by trumpeting the fact that Jackson had steadfastly refused to raise the wages of city employees while he was service director. These tactics very nearly worked, as Jackson squeaked into office with a mere 42 percent of the vote, largely based on the solid support of the Old

West End mansion district and middle class voters in the new western developments. Guitteau carried the city's most concentrated working class wards.[68]

With Jackson's election, city hall went decidedly upscale with at least three bankers seated in the cabinet. Jackson tapped his campaign manager, John R. Cowell, to head the Safety Department. Earl Peters, a director of the Security-Home Bank, was made finance director, and the proportion of public funds on deposit at his Security-Home quickly rose during his tenure. Jackson's pick for director of public welfare was the president of the City Savings Bank, John B. Merrell. City committees resembled the rosters of Chamber of Commerce committees. Under their direction, the city embarked on a paving and building program unrivaled in the city's history.

At last the Chamber of Commerce's wish list of building projects could be completed. New boulevards, sewer mains, parks, and police and fire stations and a new waste treatment plant and water works sprung up in the recently annexed sections of the city. A suspension bridge was strung across the Maumee River by the famous Roebling Brothers Company, builders of the Brooklyn Bridge. A convention hall and a public market were constructed. The only stumbling block in the Chamber's development campaign came when a few downtown councilmen demanded that a new three-million-dollar campus for the municipal university not be built in the suburbs. Leading the charge was Joseph Wawrzyniek, whose Polish district bordered on the square mile parcel of farmland that had been bequeathed by Toledo founder Jessup Scott as the future home of the university. They charged that Mayor Jackson and the university board were swayed by two groups of real estate developers—those who wanted to get their hands on the prime land that the city already owned and those who wished to enhance the value of their western subdivisions.

Wawrzyniek and the other nay-sayers were outmaneuvered by Jackson stalwarts who proposed leaving the question of the site to the university's own board. Though this tactic succeeded in bypassing the central city politicians, it also unleashed a frenzy of private lobbying as every developer in town saw the gain in having a university as a neighbor to their subdivision. The university board was barraged with thirty-four proposals and with difficulty approved nestling the university between five major suburban developments, mainly benefiting the Welles-Bowen and Reuben brothers realty groups, even though critics pointed out that the proposed site was a low-lying "muskrat farm" which would cost millions to drain and whose sale price had recently been inflated tenfold.[69]

The city's business leaders, especially its bankers and realtors who were the power behind the Chamber of Commerce, who had pushed for increased spending on road, water, and sewer projects in the interest of city "improvement," had won. They shook off the stalwarts of the Brown machine, seized control of the city government for themselves, and succeeded in creating a vast public subsidy of their land investments. But at the very moment when their triumph seemed complete, the housing market that they had carefully nurtured with public money began to sour.

Until middecade, houses sprung up across the county's fields. With a strong demand for homes and a growing income base in the county, in the five years from 1921 to 1925 Toledo's builders erected nearly twice as many structures as they had in the previous five years.[70] From 1920 to 1923, the number of building permits issued by the city bounded upward at annual rates of 81, 64, and 56 percent respectively. After the middle of the decade, however, the market for homes cooled off suddenly. 1924 still saw positive growth, though of only 4 percent. Dropping precipitously the following year, the number of permits issued fell by 11 percent and would stubbornly decline for eight of the next nine years. Between 1927 and 1929 alone, the number of building permits issued by the city plummeted by 22 percent.[71]

The consequences of the drop-off in home construction were evident in the gap-toothed appearance of most suburban neighborhoods in the late 1920s. New homeowners had few next-door neighbors, and many subdivisions still had the appearance of the farms they overlay. By 1930, of a sample of seventeen subdivisions from all parts of the city, only 11 percent of the lots were built upon. The seven homeowners in Hoover Gardens on the city's east side were surrounded by a hundred open lots. None of the 279 north end lots of Ratterbee's Boulevard Terrace were built upon. In the south the large 445-lot Glenurban addition contained only 63 homes.[72]

There are many reasons why the housing boom of the early 1920s proved unsustainable. Ironically, the policies that Toledo's financial elite believed were the path to the city's prosperity may have actually undermined the housing market and with it the stability of the city's financial institutions. Industry's open-shop campaign successfully destroyed the city's labor movement and kept wages low, but it also reduced the ability of working people to afford their own homes. The Chamber of Commerce realized its civic improvement projects and extended basic services to a patchwork of isolated developments on the fringes of the city. Not wanting to burden business or the developers themselves with the costs of these projects, a large proportion of the curb and pipe costs were shifted to home owners who built in the new developments through special assessments. From 1915 to 1920, special assessments averaged $1.2 million per year (table 4). Over the next five years the yearly average crept up to $1.8 million, an increase of over 50 percent. From 1925 to 1930, it moved up another 55 points, to $2.8 million.[73] Other general costs, such as widening thoroughfares, building bridges and

Table 4
Special assessment bonds and unpaid taxes, Lucas County, 1915–1932.

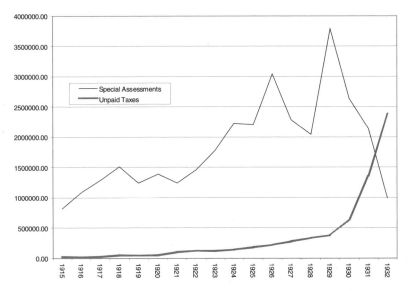

Source: "Toledo Real Property Survey: Final Report," WPA Project #17971 (Toledo Metropolitan Housing Authority, 1939), p. 165.

viaducts under railroad crossings, and large capital projects, ended up as new bond levies and increased property taxes.

The Chamber of Commerce's building spree was paid for out of both current revenue and many years of future taxes through long-term bonds. Over the decade of banker control over municipal finances, Toledo's general bonded debt increased 156 percent, while its population grew by just 19 percent. By 1929, Toledo carried the largest per capita net debt of any city in America of its size. Unsurprisingly, unpaid taxes also grew throughout the 1920s at an annual rate of over 27 percent.[74]

Between the twin prongs of rising taxes and stagnant wages, fewer and fewer working families were able to realize their dream of home ownership. As a result the housing market softened, especially for homes priced modestly. For a few years the increasing incomes of Toledo's businessmen and professionals continued to support the building industry, and the statistics show a considerable rise in the average cost of a home built towards the end of the 1920s.[75] But this trend, too, fell quiet with the great crash of October 1929, which dried up the dividends that had fed it.

It wasn't only the direct costs of subdivision construction but less-obvious effects as well that contributed to rising taxes. As early as 1928, an outside consultant hired to evaluate the condition of the city observed, "If one had known then what is known now and could have controlled the growth of Toledo and the region around it, many things would be different. . . .Unregulated processes of community growth have repeatedly brought uneconomic results. Many of the benefits and advantages which would have come naturally from a deliberate control of the destinies of the city cannot be secured now because of their prohibitive cost."[76] Many of those unnecessary costs accumulated because developers preferred curvilinear streets to the more efficient existing grid system, which multiplied curb, gutter, and sewer costs. Developers also increasingly designed cul-de-sacs and longer blocks into their street plans, forcing a heavier load of traffic onto the city's primary arteries. Ironically, the freedom of real estate speculators to pursue whatever development scheme they could dream up eventually limited their ability to market their lots.

Real estate developers felt the pinch long before the party ended, as their business required rapid turnover of their lots and divisions. As the market price of their assets dropped, their desperation increased, and by the summer of 1927 many were trying to unload their bundles of lot deeds any way they could. Few were willing to auction them and take their losses outright. But there was another way. Local banks had for nearly a decade been accepting lot mortgages, even second mortgages, as collateral for loans. The only tricky part was that a mortgage requires a buyer, and this was a detail that a number of real estate developers found could be finessed. As it turns out, buyers could be bought.

It is a fluke that any details of how this scam worked have been bequeathed to history. The records of this case have been preserved only because one of the principals happened to have been appointed assistant attorney general long after these byzantine business dealings were executed. Being a high public official, Joseph O. Eppstein was subject not only to the usual glare of publicity but also to the heat of partisan politics. Had Eppstein not suffered his career-making promotion, there probably would not be, buried deep in the government archives in Columbus, the traces of how some developers and bankers colluded to save their real estate companies and helped spark the worst bank collapse in state history.

In October of 1927 a group of businessmen chartered a holding company, the Security Bond and Mortgage Company, and distributed shares among themselves. Included in this ring was a troika of real estate men, bankers, lawyers, and one local politician. Henry DeTray and his partner Thomas H. Gardner, who some evenings had to spend time sitting on the city council, had an extensive real estate business run out of one of those storefront offices downtown. Isadore Eppstein was more of an upstairs man, platting subdivisions and arranging financing. Isadore's brother Joseph handled the legal details. On the banking side, the partnership included Frank Hoehler and William Gunckel, president and vice-president respectively of the Security Bank.

The purpose of the Security Bond and Mortgage Company was to liquefy the unsold inventory of a dozen land development companies. These companies, which were essentially bankrupt, would hand over their mortgages to the SBMC, and SBMC would in turn surrender them to the Security Bank as collateral for loans. Armed with fresh cash, SBMC shares would be worth something, thus turning what was junk into gold for its shareholders.

Henry DeTray was primarily responsible for arranging the sales. Of course, in 1928 sales were sluggish, so DeTray paid his employees to pretend to purchase lots from one of the SBMC companies. For example, on September 28, 1928 DeTray's employee Eli K'Burg and his wife Rose mortgaged their little lot in Toledo's far north end to the SBMC for $1,500, a tidy sum for a partial lot located in a marsh. Of course, the K'Burgs did not own the marsh lot (another SBMC company actually did), but the mortgage was filed with the county all the same. SBMC then placed the K'Burgs' mortgage with a bundle of others like it and gave it to the Security Bank as collateral for a ten thousand dollar loan. Of course, it would be too suspicious to have hundreds of mortgages filed under the same name, so the names of friends, relatives, and even perfect strangers were forged as occasion required.

So a SBMC company, such as the Toledo Guaranty Real Estate and Securities Company, which was burdened with unsaleable lots, would deed them to a patsy, even a name out of the phone book. These transactions were nearly legal (though the price of the property was duly inflated and no money changed hands). The dicey part was when a mortgage note had to be forged in the name of the patsy. After all, not only was there a signature to be forged, but the paper had to be witnessed and notarized. Of course, Henry DeTray was a notary, and his employees were seemingly always ready to sign off as witnesses. The mortgage note would then be "sold" to SBMC, and, again, SBMC would surrender the note as collateral and receive real, honest cash in the form of a "loan" from the Security Bank. In just two months in the summer of 1928, at least 160 of these forged mortgages were written. Over the next two years $118,289.61 was borrowed under these auspices from the Security Bank. No payments were ever made on these loans, and when the bank foreclosed on the collateral, it was left holding what a former bank examiner described as "a big bale of nothing."[77]

Not every realtor dared to go as far as outright forgery, but the practice of dumping depreciating real estate on the banks in exchange for good loans became very widespread. By the end of the 1920s, it was observed, virtually every subdivision in town was swapped as loan collateral with one bank or another. Toledo's banks eventually held title to between seventy-five and eighty subdivisions by the time they crashed. In addition to the thousands of mortgages the banks made themselves, somewhere between five hundred and one thousand loans were made on the security of mortgages held by others, totaling in excess of $5 million.[78]

Another variation on a theme was performed by Walter Stewart, a leader of the Commercial Bank. Walter Stewart was a man always alert for the better deal. Not satisfied with being a fast rising young man in his hometown of Quincy, Illinois, he headed to Toledo, where he accepted a job as treasurer of the Willys-Overland Motor Company. Soon he saw the opportunity in Toledo's suburban boom and invested in Harry Close's outfit and got a vice-presidency of the E. H. Close Company in return. Muscled out of Willys-Overland by bigger investors, he bought himself a seat as vice-president of the Commercial Bank and focused on his real estate investments.[79]

Stewart had the appearance of prize fighter, stocky, with a flat nose and hard eyes, and he clearly dominated the board room in which he sat. In 1928, the same year insiders began foisting phony mortgages upon the Security Bank, the Commercial Bank began making large loans to Stewart and his companies. Fifty-six thousand went into Stewart's Federal Pneumatic Service Corporation, a company that was sinking fast, for which Stewart presented to the bank unpaid bills receivable, which, it turns out, he had forged. When Stewart's personal indebtedness topped more than $100,000, he sold to the bank a bundle of land contracts from his real estate company and 400 shares of Commercial bank stock for $210,369.71. The bank stock was worth no more than $90,000, so the bank essentially accepted the land contracts to settle Stewart's account. The same day the deal was completed, Stewart paid off his loan and withdrew his entire account of $110,269.71.[80] Stung once, but willing to be stung twice, two months later Commercial gave Stewart another loan of $30,000 on the security of 195 shares of stock in his Harwood Realty Company.[81]

In theory, bankers protect their banks by carefully assessing the true value of collateral pledged in security of loans and call in loans when this value declines below a certain margin of safety. But given the power of Toledo's realty interests, the interlocking nature of bank and development company board of directors, and the heavy investments of many bankers in development companies of their own, theory didn't hold and banks became awash in junk realty paper.

In the end, the grand schemes of the city's financial captains had failed. Breaking labor unions had dampened consumption. Uncontrolled suburban development had glutted the market for lots and homes, driving even the largest realty companies to the wall. Rather than booming the city into a doubling of its population, the city's capital projects had led to a spiraling of the city's debt. Shifting their personal losses to the city's banks had destabilized them. Thus, all the margins of safety in these various systems had been consumed and compromised by the time the first shock of the Depression would be felt. When the stock market collapsed in October of 1929, its impact reverberated not through a growing, booming urban economy, but a heavily mortgaged and dangerously weakened one.

CHAPTER TWO

BANKSTERS AND BOSSES

While it was important for Toledo's real estate speculators to gain control of the city's government, and thereby push through the building of the necessary infrastructure for their development projects, it was just as critical for the city's bankers to capture the state department that watched and regulated their activities. Though Ohio's banking laws were not rigorous, there were just enough teeth in them that they could, potentially, be rigorously enforced. Both out of fear of the possibility of facing costly regulations and out of desire for the sort of benefits that inevitably flow from having friends in high places, Toledo's bankers were an extraordinarily politically active group and over the course of the 1920s succeeded in extending their reach all they way to Columbus and beyond.

Just as had been the case in Toledo, Ohio's government had gone through a long period of increasing reform and more stringent regulation. If Toledo's business lobbyists could not take sole credit for shifting Ohio's state administration away from populism to a more accommodating view of business—though Toledo certainly played its part—neither were they slow to seize upon the benefits of laissez-faire.

Since the turn of the century, reformism and muckraking had reigned as the political watchwords of the time and politicians understood that their seats depended upon the appearance of independence from powerful business interests. In 1903 Governor George K. Nash required corporations to file annual reports and to pay a capital tax. 1905 brought a reform Democrat, John M. Pattison, to office who pledged to end boss rule and better regulate the railroads. Pattison died after just five months in office, promoting to the executive its last Civil War veteran, Andrew L. Harris, who made most businessmen wish Pattison had been blessed with better health. Harris signed legislation forbidding corporations from making political contributions and inaugurated the state's first regulation of the banking industry.

Ohio elected another progressive Democrat after Harris to the governorship in the same election that sent Taft to the White House. Grover Cleveland's

former attorney general, Judson Harmon, had been the first federal official
to prosecute corporations under the anti-trust statutes. He continued his anti-
monopoly crusade in private law practice and clashed with President
Theodore Roosevelt in 1905 when Roosevelt refused to prosecute the officers of the Santa Fe Railroad for violating federal laws. Harmon was quoted
then as saying: "The evils with which we are now confronted are corporate
in name but individual in fact. Guilt is always personal." Harmon's administration tightened bank depository and public funds reporting laws among
other steps to tighten business regulation. The culmination of this era was
the period from 1913 to 1921 when, for all but two years, Ohio's governor's
mansion was occupied by its most famous Progressive, James M. Cox.

   Toledo's business community was instrumental in shifting both its local
politics and politics of the state away from its embrace of business regulation. In April of 1920 Toledo's Republican faithful, fully backed by the city's
business lobby, elected as its delegate to the Republican National
Convention Walter Folger Brown. Brown led the floor fight that brought
Ohio's dark horse Warren G. Harding into the presidential race. In so doing
Brown gained a stature in the Republican party unrivaled for a man who
held no elected public office since the days of Mark Hanna's behind-the-
scenes power in the McKinley administration. He would soon be recognized, as one reporter described him, as the "czar of Ohio Republicanism,
a political wire-puller whose connections extend almost from coast to coast."[1]

   Brown took a leading role in state politics just at the moment that state
patronage became more meaningful after the election of 1920, when the
newly elected Republican governor, Harry L. Davis, rammed through a bill
centralizing most state offices under single directors beholden only to him.
Governor Davis's "Ripper Bill" solved one immediate problem: it allowed
him to dump out the Democratic holdovers from the previous administration.
But, more importantly, it made department and agency heads more
beholden to the Republican machine by allowing their appointment and
removal without senate confirmation.

   Nowhere is the effect of this change more evident than on the character of Ohio's Department of Banks and Banking. One of the youngest state
departments when the Republicans took over in 1920, it was created as part
of a comprehensive overhaul of the state's banking laws in 1908. Originally
an independent department whose head, the superintendent of banking, was
subject to senate confirmation, as a result of the Davis "Ripper Bill" it was
rolled into a new Department of Commerce whose director no longer needed
to consult the senate about the appointment of his underlings.

   As an independent department, Banks and Banking had been a crusading regulator. It plunged forward with the monumental task given to it by

the legislature—enforcing an untested and complicated law comprised of 120 detailed sections, mandating that it examine every state chartered bank, savings and loan, and trust company twice yearly, and liquidate insolvent institutions. Because none of the state's 460 banks had ever been audited or even required to file a statement of their condition with the state before the passage of the 1908 act, the law gave the banking department a two-year grace period to establish itself. But the Banks Department began closely auditing and requiring sworn statements from the state's banks in its first year of supervision. The department's eight examiners completed 512 unscheduled, surprise audits in one year. Perhaps as a means of putting the state's bankers on notice, the department forcibly closed a bank, the Scioto Valley Bank of Kingston, Ohio, a year before the law was scheduled to take full effect.[2]

By the time the "Thomas Banking Law" of 1908 came into full force in 1910, the Department of Banks and Banking was talking tough and backing it up. In its fifth annual report the superintendent boasted of finding it "necessary to weed out a few of the less deserving banks and trust companies" and expressed his opinion that "the forced retirement of such institutions has clarified the situation and furnished ample assurance to the depositors that the State of Ohio will not tolerate unsafe and unsound banking."[3] Three banks were forcibly closed that year, including one nestled in the state's political bosom, the Columbus Savings and Trust Company, whose $610,000 of capital ranked it as one of the state's ten largest banks. Superintendent F. E. Baxter, a man promoted out the original corps of seven examiners, called upon the legislature to tighten banking laws further, by legally separating savings deposits and commercial banking, saying, "it seems to me that because of the peculiar sacredness of the savings deposits there is every reason why they should be more fully protected . . ."[4] Baxter, going beyond the letter of the law, required a review meeting between his inspectors and the directors of each bank for the purpose of educating them as to better methods of controlling their own institutions and as to their responsibilities under the law.[5]

Overall, the tone of the Department of Banking's first dozen years of reports is populist. Bankers are referred to only as a group that needed to be policed, while the depositors, the public, and the law were the clear protagonists in whose name and for whose protection the department existed. The deeds of crooked bankers who were caught and prosecuted were recounted in great detail and every bank that was closed, even when no individual associated with it was charged with misconduct, was viewed as morally suspect. The superintendent appointed in the Cox administration, Ira R. Pontius, expressed this sentiment well: "A bank officered by honest men, who use every care in loaning and investing the bank's funds, and who manage the bank's affairs within the regulations as set forth in the banking code, will never need to close its doors."[6]

Abruptly with the administrative realignment of the Banking Department under the new director of commerce, the populist tone was wrung out of the annual report. No longer did the banking department use its annual report to lobby for more examiners, stronger bank laws, or the closing of commonly used loopholes. After 1920, though annual reports steadily grew longer, they ceased listing the number of examinations the department had performed, which was, after all, its most basic function. After 1920, there are no mentions of any applications for bank charters being denied (in the last year of Pontius's supervision of the department, one-sixth of such applications had been turned down). Economist J. M. Whitsett observed that during the 1920s Ohio's banking regulators placed few hurdles in the way of investors wishing to become bankers, noting that "almost any group could obtain a bank charter." Instead, the reports of the 1920s sing the praises of the men the department was charged with watching. "Ohio is extremely fortunate in having a large quota of forward-looking men in its banking field . . ." declares the department's lead article in its report of 1926, an article whose title was more than slightly presumptuous for a regulatory body: "Inherent Soundness of Ohio Banks." Other reports cheered the "Growth in Deposits" and "Banking Progress."[7] The idea, as expressed in 1910, that the department's purpose was to "thwart the unscrupulous in nefarious promotions" is nowhere in evidence. Most surprisingly, it appears that the department no longer forcibly closed ailing banks but liquidated only those institutions voluntarily surrendered to it.

State bank examiners, whose neutrality was once highly touted in the first few annual reports of the department, began turning a revolving door between inspecting banks and working for them. Robert T. Sewell was hired as a trust examiner for the department in 1924. Three years later he resigned for a more remunerative position with the Commerce Guardian Bank in Toledo. After three years in Toledo, Sewell rejoined the Banking Department in Columbus, getting out just in time before Toledo's spectacular bank collapse. The possibility of future lucrative employment with the companies a state official inspected was a constant counterweight against tough and thorough audits.[8] As one scholar who was familiar with state banking departments in the 1930s noted, "As a matter of fact, it is customary to look upon a place on the examining staff of most states, not as a life position, but merely as a stepping stone to the vice-presidency of some particular bank."[9]

Investors and bankers, recognizing the advantages of being regulated by the state rather than by the more closely monitored federal laws, increasingly shunned joining the federal banking system. Though both the U.S. Congress and many states engaged in what one contemporary observer coined a "competition in laxity" in an attempt to woo bankers to be federally or state chartered, Ohio seems to have won this competition handily. Over the decade of the 1920s, Ohio quickly rose to be the national leader in the proportion of its banks and financial resources chartered and regulated by state officials rather than federal ones. By 1930 well over half of all the banking resources in Ohio were held by state banks, while the proportion of funds held in national banks actually declined from over a third in 1920 to less than one-fifth in 1930. During the 1920s, Ohio's state-chartered banks grew at a rate over 20 percent faster than that of all commercial banks in America.[10]

After 1920, the state Department of Banking rarely audited banks to verify the accuracy of the mandatory quarterly reports of its member banks, and even when it did these usually occurred on the same days of the year, eliminating the element of surprise that had in the early days of the department been considered the mark of a good inspection.[11] In those rare occasions when the Ohio Banking Department uncovered a problem in a bank's accounts or practices, it rarely imposed any penalties or even threatened to do so. Without an effective threat of punishment, bankers could delay or even ignore the state's orders. After a state audit in the spring of 1930 the Banking Department ordered the Security-Home Bank to stop paying dividends in quarters it actually recorded losses and to restrain its own officers from writing bad checks (vice-president Raleigh Mills had accumulated $686.38 in overdrafts). At the next quarterly audit, the state discovered that the bank had loaned out more of its deposits than was lawful, had not properly charged bad loans to the books, and was $97,000 short in its reserves for loans it had already charged down. No action was taken against the Security-Home Bank to enforce these orders, and when the third quarter's audit was due, the president of the bank, Stacy McNary, wrote to the Ohio superintendent of banking, saying, "We regret that we have not been able to obtain reductions in the loans of officers and directors as we had anticipated . . ."[12] These items were not corrected and the Ohio Banking Department apparently did nothing more about the matter. In fact, after June 30, 1930, the Banking Department never again inspected the Security-Home Bank until the day it failed a year later.[13]

Likewise, in the winter and spring of 1931, the Banking Department head, Ira J. Fulton, sent letters to the directors of the Ohio Bank, pointing out that much of its real estate portfolio was overvalued and nonperforming and instructing the bank to reduce or eliminate dividend payments until the deficits were cleared up. After the Ohio Bank's vice-president, Edward Kirschner, a powerful politician who became the leading dispenser of political patronage when he was appointed Toledo's postmaster, wrote back telling Fulton that he had exaggerated the situation and that the bank would continue with its usual monthly seventy-five cent per share dividend, Fulton did nothing to enforce his orders. To Kirschner that dividend was worth $2,610 every year, a profit that amounted to about a seventh of his annual salary. The other officers and directors divvied up another $39,834 every year and bank president George M. Jones cashed over $25,000 in dividends every year. These men were not prepared to give up these profits without a fight, and there was clearly no fight in the state regulators who watched them. Even after informing Kirschner that the bank's accounting numbers were phony, Fulton's department did not correct them and officially reported them as they were. Kirschner and the other Ohio Bank directors continued to vote and issue monthly dividends even after their bank had announced a moratorium on all withdrawals.[14]

State bank examiners failed to notice that the Commercial Bank illegally inflated the value of its holding of Liberty Bonds, adding $96,920 to its balance sheet that hadn't been earned. (State law required bonds to be carried on the books at cost until cashed.) They allowed other banks to carry other securities that were in default and legally had to be charged off the books. No Columbus officials ever questioned the Spokane, Washington, municipal bonds carried at full value on the books of three of the city's banks as late as 1931 (the Ohio Bank credited itself with $10,000 worth, the Commercial $14,600, and the Security-Home $1,800). Spokane had defaulted on these bonds back in 1920.[15] Perhaps even a trained examiner could overlook one municipal security in a long list of similar bonds, but how did they miss the Imperial Russian bonds credited at full value and carried on the books of the Security-Home Bank until the day it flat-lined? These bonds had been rendered worthless by the Bolshevik Revolution of 1917.

Even when the banking department discovered a problem in security and ordered that a bank's books be corrected, they failed to follow up to verify that their orders had been carried out. The crudest of bookkeeping tricks successfully knocked them off the scent. In 1929, Ohio's Banking Department ordered that the Security-Home Bank write off their books as a loss five hundred shares of Continental Shares, Inc., and five hundred shares of Commonwealth Securities, two worthless stocks that had not paid a single dividend since 1924 but were accounted as a $96,000 credit for the bank. State bank accounting rules required that any stock that had not paid dividends in five years could not be considered an asset, so the banking department ordered the directors of the Security-Home Bank to write it off. Instead, the directors of the bank clumsily jiggered their accounts to continue to

cover up their losses. Their plan left plenty of tracks for regulators to follow if they had bothered. The bankers created a dummy partnership
whose sole asset was the 1,000 shares of the bankrupt Continental and
Commonwealth stocks. Then, acting as the bank's directors, they voted to
give their partnership a loan of $96,000, secured by the same one thousand
shares of stock the banking department had ordered them to dump, and
the $96,000 was never actually paid to the partnership but remained cred-
ited in the general pool of the bank's assets. With the phony $96,000 loan,
the $96,000 stock loss could be taken and the bank's books still balanced,
and as long as all the insiders knew that the note was a phony, that no money
had been exchanged and that no debts were ever to be repaid to the bank,
and with little apparent fear of anything close to a thorough state audit, these
bankers could continue to report bank profits and vote themselves fat dividends. (Two years later, after the Security-Home failed, their scheme suddenly turned around and bit them when some of these directors were suddenly
caught in a fitting predicament—they were suddenly forced to choose between
either admitting that they had committed fraud in their bookkeeping or to
pay back a large loan they had never actually received. Brazenly, these men
chose to keep their money and admit their fraud, not fearing that the county
courts could touch them.)[16]

State bank inspectors also overlooked suspicious manipulations of some
of the largest personal and corporate accounts, activities that may have cost
the state hundreds of thousands of dollars in lost taxes. In 1934 a Lucas County
grand jury discovered that the Commerce Guardian Bank maintained a secret
"bond-purchasing" account that hid profits from the tax man for the convenience of its own directors and biggest patrons. In those days, Ohio's personal property tax assessed about one-half of one percent on the wealth of
the state's richest individuals, although money held in government bonds
was tax-exempt. Federal income taxes took another larger bite each April.
Each year the Commerce Guardian bank transferred the deposits of their
best customers to a special account designated for the purchase of government bonds just before tax day and then quickly returned this money afterwards without ever actually purchasing the bonds. For example, prior to
Christmas, 1928, this account was empty. On the last three days of
December, over $1,500,000 was deposited and then drawn out again after
New Year's Day. When spring tax time rolled around, the account mush-
roomed from zero to $817,107 on the first day of April; then it was com-
pletely emptied two weeks later. When old man 1929 prepared to exit, this
account again went from zero to two million in a couple of days and then
fell back to zip by January 6. April saw the totals bounce again from zero
to half a million and back to zero in the space of a week. Half a dozen of

the bank's own officers and directors squirreled their money away in this way along with a list of local notables that followed very closely the entries in the Social Register. As a courtesy, the accounts of the directors of other banks, including Willard Webb, director of the Ohio Bank, R. D. Mills, vice-president of Security-Home, and Robert Stranahan, the Champion spark plug tycoon and a director of the Toledo Trust Bank, were also sheltered. William T. Jackson, sitting mayor of Toledo, avoided paying taxes on his nestegg of $8,101. But the truly big money hidden from the tax man was that of local corporations: glass giants like the Owens Bottle Co. ($324,883), Owens-Illinois Glass Co. ($502,199), Kent-Owens Machine Co. ($418,407) and Libbey-Owens-Ford ($304,495) topped the list, though real estate holding companies, most of which had interlocking directorates with the banks, accounted for about $2 million of the total. Altogether, in less than three years, at least $7 million in taxable bank balances were hidden in this way, evading over $195,000 in state taxes.[17]

Though a grand jury specifically demanded that Ohio's attorney general prosecute the bond account tax dodgers, neither federal nor state authorities ever actually sued anyone for hiding their assets in this way.[18] Toledo's Republican boss, Walter Folger Brown, had just returned from frolicking among the redwoods with former President Herbert Hoover and seventy other of America's richest and most powerful men at the annual outing of the Bohemian Club—actually he was nursing a bad case of poison oak he brought home with him—when he was contacted by an Internal Revenue Service agent who had some questions about a certain trust account in Brown's name in the Toledo Trust Bank that held a deposit of over ten thousand dollars that had never been declared to the government. Brown, the former deputy secretary of the U.S. Commerce Department, former postmaster general, and former presidential kingmaker, who was then under intense senatorial scrutiny for allegedly taking bribes in exchange for postal contracts when he was postmaster general, was apparently allowed to quietly amend his 1929 income tax return and that was the end of it.[19]

The most significant and dangerous trend of the 1920s, the consolidation of medium-sized banks into financial behemoths, was observed with the utmost optimism by their regulators. In spite of continued start-ups, the number of banks in Ohio dropped steadily through the decade. Such mergers, the department wrote, "are especially desirable" as they "prevent ruinous competition besides curtailing operating expense, increasing loan-power and other banking facilities, and affording greater security."[20]

Freed from the restraining hand of government, Toledo's bankers did what they pleased. Some banks became high-fliers, distributing incredible returns to their shareholders. Merchants' and Clerks' Bank posted a dozen

straight years of 16-percent dividends. Not to be outdone, Home Bank raised
its dividend to 20 percent in 1920 and kept it there through 1923. Union
Savings ratcheted its dividend up steadily through the 1920s from 12 percent to 16 by 1923. Some other banks chose to reward their stockholders
all at once. Dime Bank returned a 28-percent dividend in 1920, while its
neighbor down the street, Security Bank, distributed a staggering 68-per-
cent bonus dividend in 1922. Across the entire roster of Toledo banks, dividends which had averaged slightly more than 9 percent in the five years
before America's entry into the Great War grew to over 14 in the half-decade
afterwards.[21]

Other bankers seized upon the opportunity of lax state oversight to engineer some very advantageous insider deals. The sweetest had to be the takeover
of the little Dime Bank by the coal baron George M. Jones. Dime was owned
primarily by the Bainbridge family, an old pioneer merchant clan whose
scion, Francis W. Bainbridge, died in 1918. Francis's widow, Eleanor, frail
and in her eighties, was probably not hard to convince that it was best to
sell out. Jones and his partners offered $282 a share, $12 above par. After
buying out Bainbridge and other smaller owners, Jones and his junior partners held 1,942 of the 3,000 outstanding Dime Bank shares. Soon after Jones
secured control of Dime Bank, the Ohio Bank tendered an offer of $40 plus
one share of its own stock for each Dime Bank share, a surprising bid given
that Ohio Bank stock was at that moment priced at $350, meaning that the
Ohio Bank was offering $1,170,000 dollars for a bank whose combined cap-
ital, surplus, and undivided profits equaled a little more than three quarters of a million.

Why did the Ohio pay so much for so little? George Jones and his partners were able to walk away from this deal with a fat return of over 72 percent on their investment, or nearly a quarter million dollars, because they
also controlled the Ohio Bank. Jones was the Ohio Bank's president and
largest shareholder, his father-in-law was also a large shareholder and director, and his partners were also members of the board; they were able to tender any offer they felt was fair for their own stock. As a special bonus, a
few weeks before the Ohio purchased its shares from the Jones syndicate,
the Ohio's board voted a two-for-one stock split, thus inflating the value
of the Dime deal even higher.[22]

Jones's profitable acquisition of the Dime Bank had one weakness—when
the deal was concluded the Ohio Bank ended up with 7,000 additional shares
of unsold stock. According to the state's banking law, the directors had two
legal options: they could either tender the unsold shares to the public or
they could write down the bank's capital by $700,000. Writing off capital
would have immediately impaired its ability to make new loans, and

because the directors had already loaned to themselves much of the bank's liquid assets and desperately needed the additional loan cushion, this was not an option they ever seriously considered. Even worse was the idea of selling the shares to the public, for were this bloc of shares to actually be distributed, the men then enjoying the power and insider privileges of sitting on the bank's board might be voted out of their chairs by the new shareholders. How then could these men keep their recent windfall profits from the Dime Bank merger, their loan cushion, and their seats on the board and still act within the confines of Ohio's banking laws? They couldn't, so they broke them.

One month before concluding their takeover of the Dime Bank, George Jones, the Ohio's president, and four of his most trusted directors founded the Vistula Company, named for one of the defunct speculative towns that dotted northwest Ohio during its land boom era of the 1830s. Vistula's initial capital was five hundred dollars—five shares of stock valued at one hundred dollars, with each share representing one vote for the company's board. Each man took one share, though they didn't bother to pay in their one hundred dollars, giving themselves a five hundred dollar loan from the Ohio Bank to cover even that nominal cost.

Vistula's first action was to borrow $725,000 from the Ohio Bank. A quarter million of this loan was actually an illegal transfer from the trust account of a bank director, Thomas Tracy, though neither he nor his son Newton, who was also a director of the Ohio Bank, cared to file a complaint. Newton loaned Vistula an additional quarter million from his own account and another holding company he controlled. The following day, Vistula used all of its cash to purchase the 7,000 surplus shares of Ohio Bank stock. It should be noted that on that day, the Ohio Bank sold the stock to Vistula for $139.29 per share when the open market price was $325. Had Ohio sold its shares through a broker, it would have realized a gross profit of as much as $1,300,000 over what it did. Had the bank had an extra million in cash in the summer of 1931, it might have survived.

Vistula's balance sheet at this point showed a debt of $975,000 against assets of 7,000 bank shares and cash of $500. Over the next three years, Vistula occasionally paid back portions of its interest and its collateral-free loan to the Ohio Bank by borrowing money from Newton Tracy or from the estate of his dead father. When the Tracys needed cash, Vistula simply borrowed money back from the Ohio Bank for them. Back and forth millions went, sloshing from account to account through Vistula, making it appear as though Vistula was solvent when in fact it never owned anything but borrowed bank stock. Every year the Vistula stock was voted as a block comprising nearly a quarter of all votes, and thus every year the same officers and directors were returned to the Ohio Bank boardroom down to the last man.[23]

To cover up the fact that the Vistula was a wholly owned subsidiary of the Ohio Bank, and therefore the bank was loaning money to itself to purchase its own capital stock in direct violation of Section 53 of the banking code ("No commercial bank . . . shall loan money on the security or pledge of the shares of its own capital stock"), a few bank employees were allowed to purchase shares of the Ohio's bank stock for a slightly below-market rate of $300. Only 451 shares were released over the three-year life of Vistula in this way.[24]

Another shaky merger was made by insiders at the Commercial Bank. In 1928 Commercial took over the small and struggling City Savings Bank. City Savings was a young upstart that never got started. After chartering in 1923, it was unable to pay a dividend its first three fiscal years, and remained the smallest of all Toledo banks until the founding of the American Bank in May of 1925, but even American passed it up in size in a year or two. At the time Commercial bought it, City was hemorrhaging money. In spite of its problems, Commercial merged with City, swapping $140,000 of its own shares for the $100,000 book value of City shares. It was a fine deal for the poor City Savings shareholder, who once was a passenger on a sinking boat but had now been rescued and issued a 40 percent increase in the value of his shares. Even better, five months later the Commercial Bank voted to issue two additional shares of bank stock for each outstanding, and as the bank shares had been fully capitalized at the same time that the bank merger happened, this stock split represented a dividend of 200 percent.[25]

Many of these mergers, though profitable to a few insiders, were in some cases enormously destabilizing to the banks that undertook them. Of all Toledo banks, none was more merger happy than the Security Bank. In 1923 it bought out the only independent bank serving the Polish neighborhood known as "Lagrinka," the Opieka Savings Bank (*opieka* is Polish for *care*). In 1926 it purchased the old Merchants' and Clerks' Bank, one of Toledo's oldest banks, whose founder was still president after fifty-four years. "Old Faithful," as Merchants' and Clerks' was known, did reasonably well in the boom of the war years, but had not been able to jump aboard the bandwagon of the early 1920s. In contrast to its 23 percent growth in deposits from 1916 to 1920, from 1921 to 1925 it actually had lost nearly 2 percent of its deposits. Its stock price was down over 10 percent from its prewar highs, even though it had the best record of annual return (twelve straight years of 16-percent dividends) of any bank in the city.[26]

The subsequent acquisitions of the Security Bank made its purchase of the "Old Faithful" look like a good deal. Security's next target was the Banker's

Trust Company, the descendent of the old People's Bank. Banker's Trust was the newest of the city's banks, having just been founded in February of 1927. From its inception, the Banker's Trust company struggled. In its first year of operation it managed to attract just $4 million worth of deposits, ranking it second to last in the city in terms of the ratio of its capital to its deposits. Banker's never earned enough profit to pay even a single dividend in its short life.[27]

In spite of its glaring weaknesses, Security made a handsome bid for the floundering Banker's Trust Bank. In the course of its merger audit, Security's accountants found $1,700,000 worth of assets that were far below their claimed value. When the deal nearly fell through with Security's refusal to accept this large amount of trash, Security compromised, accepting about half of this paper as collateral for a $300,000 loan. At this cost, the deal by which Security expanded its deposit base by less than 20 percent and added four branches was marginal at best. But when, after the merger was finalized, the old directors of the Banker's Trust withdrew their sizable corporate accounts to other banks in which they were more heavily invested, whatever value there was in the deal evaporated and mostly what was left were more bad loans.[28]

But Security was not finished yet; indeed, the weaker it became, the more determined it was to dilute its own red ink into someone else's. A few months after the great October stock market crash of 1929, Security announced it was joining forces with the Home Savings Bank, a former high-flying dividend machine whose climb had recently stalled.

The Home Bank was founded in 1892 and was run conservatively up to the Great War. Soon afterwards, the bank's second largest stockholder, Marion Miller, took over and steered the bank in a new, more aggressive direction. Where prewar dividends averaged below 9 percent, by 1921 they had shot up to 20 percent. In 1924 Miller acquired the tiny Citizen's Safe Deposit and Banking Company and milked the sale for all he could. First, he awarded each Home Bank stockholder a one-for-two split which amounted to a dividend of 75 percent. Additionally, each stockholder was allowed to purchase an additional share for every two he owned at the rate of $150. As a result of the ballooning of the capital base, the dividend was cut to 8 percent, though this represented a 60-percent higher payout in dividends than before. Under the burden of increasing expenses, both operational expenses and the cost of paying a higher dividend, the Home Bank's profits and surpluses began to decline. Net profits peaked soon after the merger and by its last year of operation, 1929, they had declined from that high by 70 percent. Though Home Bank had doubled its deposit base since 1920, its accumulated earned surplus and profits had actually declined over that decade.[29]

As Toledo's banks merged, they did not take advantage of the potential economies inherent in closing surplus branches or laying off redundant staff. At the beginning of Toledo's wave of mergers in 1927, there were ten state-chartered banking companies that maintained 46 offices. After the end of 1930, when all the mergers were complete, there were just five state banking companies maintaining the same number—46—of offices in the city. Rather than making the banks more efficient, mergers actually increased the expenses of banks by adding additional buildings to pay for or maintain, and multiplying staff with each new branch. As banks merged, the size of their boardrooms bulged as well. One local wag noted in 1930 that "a few of the directorates of banks here now, however, are of town-meeting size." Given the customary procedures of Toledo's banking fraternity, additional directors did more than increase the total of executive salaries; they also meant more insider loans draining the bank's resources.[30]

In addition to their costly mergers, Toledo bankers went on a spending spree during the 1920s, spreading new branch offices throughout the city and constructing opulent new headquarters buildings as symbols of their newfound power. Ohio law was unusually permissive when it came to a bank's own capital spending. While two-thirds of states limited branch banking by institutions in their own region, Ohio permitted unlimited branches, even by a bank in its own city. While many states strictly limited banks' expenditures on their own headquarters buildings, Ohio let bankers spend as much as 60 percent of their capital and surplus on bank buildings, an absurdly high amount, but one which Toledo bankers found themselves bumping up against by the end of the 1920s.[31]

In an earlier day, Toledo's banks were far less competitive and their banking houses were conservative to the point of being humble. At the turn of the century, all of Toledo's banks occupied storefronts little larger than the drugstores and flea-bag hotels with which they shared their buildings. In 1912 the Commercial Savings Bank built a free-standing bank building, a sturdy little two-story granite building. Soon afterward the Northern National Bank erected a classically columned temple of finance and the Dime Savings Bank put up its narrow headquarters down the street.

But the gauntlet was thrown to the ground when the Second National Bank completed its new headquarters building, a twenty-one-story tower that ranked as Ohio's second tallest when it was completed in 1913. Besides being the largest commercial building in the city, the bank spent heavily to richly appoint its bank lobby with a gilded ceiling, African mahogany woodwork, and marble wainscotings and floors. All told, the building cost one and a third million dollars, an amount equal to more than one of every eight dollars deposited in the bank.[32]

The building of the Second National Bank tower set a new competitive standard for banks in Toledo. To keep up, the Commercial Bank moved out of its storefront below the Valentine theater and built a six-story headquarters bedecked in marble and bronze.[33] Not to be outdone, the Home Bank ambitiously put up a ten-story limestone headquarters in 1924.[34] The First National Bank, having more stringent regulations as a federally-chartered bank, settled for remodeling.[35] Security Bank purchased the second largest building in town, the Nasby, which when built in 1895 was Toledo's tallest, and poured as much money into Toledo's oldest skyscraper as Second National spent building the newest.[36] This investment, however, only tided them over for a few years. In 1927, Security opened a new more lavish headquarters down the street.[37] Henry S. Thompson, owner of the Toledo Trust, couldn't do much to improve upon the Second National Bank building which he acquired when he purchased both the Northern National and the Second National banks in 1924, so he just turned it into a lighthouse, affixing a powerful beacon to its roof that slowly spun its gloating light for miles in every direction.[38]

In early 1928, George Jones's Ohio Bank scooped them all, announcing the planned construction of a 368-foot-tall skyscraper that would dwarf Thompson's tower across the street. No expense was spared in the construction of what was envisioned as Toledo's signature building. The frame was sheathed in the best quality limestone, corridors and staircases were of Italian marble, office paneling of mahogany, and the outer doors of solid bronze. The massive chandelier weighing four tons and hanging from the 48-foot-high lobby ceiling was specially ordered from Tiffany's of New York. The building epitomized power and stability fitting for the company's motto, "A Giant of Strength."[39]

Even before ground was broken on Toledo's tallest building, the men who controlled the Ohio Bank had already extracted hundreds of thousands of dollars of windfall profits at the expense of the bank from the construction project. The new Ohio Bank skyscraper was built on the site of the old Boody Hotel, once Toledo's grandest, the first building in the city to have had a telephone, site of the 1878 Greenback-Labor Convention, and host to presidents from Grant to McKinley.[40] Just before the Ohio Bank bought out the old hotel, six of the bank's officers (including four of the five who had founded the Vistula company), George Jones, Sr., George Jones, Jr., George S. Mills, Thomas Tracy, Frank Chapin, and Willard Webb, snatched up most of the Boody Hotel Company's stock. It cost them $710,235 to acquire 94 percent of the Boody's preferred stock and 86 percent of its common stock. They then turned around and sold the shares to their own bank for $1,142,392, clearing a neat $72,026 each. The bank then still had to pay yet more to acquire the remaining 550 shares of hotel stock clung to by a few savvy holdouts.[41]

All these new edifices may have added a bit of glamour to the downtown, but they were incredibly costly. While Toledo's state bank assets ballooned in the 1920s by 279 percent, the reported cost of their buildings and fixtures jumped an even larger 420 percent. However, these official figures understated the true costs of the banks' own properties, as many of the building costs were hidden under shell companies and subsidiaries to which the banks "loaned" the money for construction. Banks then paid rent to themselves for the purpose of keeping the true cost of their buildings off the books and evading the legal limits on bank building construction.

For example, the cost of the new Ohio Bank tower pushed the banks' inventory of banking properties over the legal ceiling of 60 percent of its capital and surplus.[42] In order to hide its skyscraper's true bill, and the inflation of it due to their own insider land deal, the directors of the Ohio Bank used the old Boody Hotel Company as a shell from which to borrow two and a half million dollars from the Metropolitan Life Insurance Company to cover the cost of construction. When the building was completed, the Boody Company rented the building to the bank and paid interest to the Metropolitan. The bank then reported the value of the building as well as the value of the Boody Company's shares on the positive side of its ledger, while the mortgage held by the Boody Company was not listed among its liabilities.[43]

In a clumsier manner, the Commercial Bank hid the true cost of its new building by simply excluding its mortgage from the balance of its liabilities, while including its mortgage payments as additions to its assets. By the summer of 1931, the Commercial Bank's mortgage on its headquarters of $340,000 owed to the Penn Mutual Life Insurance Co. was stashed away in a file cabinet and was not discovered and revealed publicly until two and a half years after the bank's failure.[44]

Toledo's banks were top-heavy with their own bank buildings. Besides the new Ohio skyscraper, the Ohio Bank owned ten other bank buildings. Security-Home held title to its headquarters and nine branch buildings. The Commercial paid mortgages on seven buildings.[45] Even judging by their official reports, most banks were clearly burdened by the increasing expenses of these facilities. The Security Bank's buildings and fixtures totaled 3 percent of their total assets in 1926. In early 1930, after the construction of a new headquarters and a network of branches, this proportion rose to over 7 percent of their total assets. Had the Security-Home kept its ratio of fixed costs to assets in line with the other banks in the city it would have had about a million dollars more cash with which to earn income or secure deposits.[46]

Yet for all this, by the time of "Black Thursday," that October day in 1929 when Wall Street's slump turned into a freefall, Toledo's banks, though weak and badly undermined by insider deals and accounting contortions, were still a long way from ruin. There was still a large measure of resiliency to the local economy. The October crash had an immediate impact on Toledo's economy, but its effects were more temporary than is usually assumed. Monthly department store receipts were off by 9.3 percent from the year before in November, though this wasn't a terrible number as growth had exceeded 10 percent in each of the previous two years. Slowing sales continued through the winter and into the spring. February and March figures were off 25 percent, but the ship seemed to right itself in April when department store sales returned to the growth levels of 1929. Likewise, Toledo grocery sales dipped through the winter of 1929 but rebounded to normal levels in the spring of 1930. Industrially, Toledo shipped 50 percent more tonnage into and 65 percent more tonnage out of the city in 1930 than in 1928.[47]

The October crash was a crucial turning point, a moment when bank managers' decisions and strategies could determine whether a bank survived or failed. At that juncture, sound banking principles would have dictated that banks cut back on their dividends and increase their surpluses and reserves. In theory, bankers should have called in slow loans and demanded more collateral from their debtors as equity prices fell. If bankers had acted in the best interest of their institutions, bank balance sheets from 1929 to 1931 would have shown a sharp increase in the level of surplus, a decline in the ratio of dividends to profits, and a reduction in the expenses of the bank itself. As it was, Toledo's bank balance sheets showed just the opposite moves.

For example, from 1928 to 1930, the Ohio Bank's surplus declined from $976,399 to $160,246. But over two-thirds of this drop was caused by a doubling of dividends from $166,500 to $345,000 and an increase in expenses from $2,802,845 to $3,255,443. Gross earnings had actually declined by less than 5 percent. Had the Ohio simply trimmed its own expenses and cut its dividend, its bottom line going into 1931 would have looked remarkably healthy.[48] The Ohio was not alone; between 1929 and 1931, none of the four major banks that would eventually fail cut the amount they paid out in dividends.

As the financial environment slowly worsened, most of Toledo's banks, rather than admit losses or call on their largest debtors to kick up more collateral or repay their loans, began shuffling their assets in a way that would dress up their books and maintain the illusion of their own profitability. To sweep up the mess left to them by real estate developers who had dumped on them millions of dollars worth of vacant lots and deadbeat mortgages, banks exploited their dual character as both banks and trust companies. As trustees, banks could contract to hold and administer property and charge a reasonable fee for the service. These properties were not to be considered assets of the bank, but remained the property of the trust department's customers. Since property placed in trust was not counted in the balance sheet of the bank, bankers discovered that their trust departments could act as a giant dustbin into which they could pour their embarrassing paper.

How this worked is best documented in the case of the Commercial Savings and Trust Bank, though similar schemes were hatched at the other big banks that ultimately failed. In March of 1931, the directors of the Commercial created Trust 694 and placed into it $250,000 worth of dubious mortgages. Trust 694, in turn, issued to the bank $250,000 in "Certificates of Participation" which the bank could then sell to the general public. These bonds represented a share of the income of the trust and promised to the purchaser a 5 percent annual return. From the perspective of the banks' ledgers, there was no net gain or loss as the quarter million of "sold" properties was balanced out by the like sum of participation certificates. It was not even really necessary to successfully sell the certificates to a gullible public, though this was preferred, because the bank carried the certificates it didn't sell as an asset, more importantly, as an asset whose real value need not be assessed.

There was one final flourish to this financial legerdemain. The contract creating Trust 694 allowed the bank at any time to replace properties in the trust with different ones from its own inventory of assets. This allowed Trust 694, and the many others like it, to serve as cover in the unlikely event the state Banking Department would conduct a thorough audit of its books. If an inspector came around, the worst mortgages and properties could be loaded onto a cart and wheeled from the mortgage department's files down the hall to the trust department in exchange for all the notes whose holders were keeping up their payments. As soon as the examiners left, the good and the bad could be switched again in order for the trust to earn money to pay its semiannual interest. Every time Trust 694 managed to pay its scheduled interest, the bank profited twice: once by accounting the interest earned on the certificates it had not sold as a bank profit, and a second time by keeping the margin between the mortgage paid in at 6 percent and the certificates paid out at 5 points.[49]

It was also possible to use these special trusts as a crude pyramid scheme. As trust participation certificates were sold, their principal could be applied to pay a portion of the semiannual 5 percent interest across the whole fund. For a time, if they could be sold at a steady rate, the proceeds derived from their sale, rather than from the actual earnings on the mortgages that underlay them, could keep the whole thing going.

The problem of course was that as the pool of performing properties dwindled, there were fewer "good" mortgages to swap for "bad" ones. After two years, the participation certificates would mature, and they would either have to be redeemed for the face value, or renewed for another two-year cycle, something fewer and fewer people were willing or able to do as the economy slid south. Like all pyramid schemes, this one too was destined for a crash sometime in the future; the bankers who put them together were simply gambling that conditions would improve before the point of crisis was reached.

Trust 694 was only one of several large trusts operated in this manner by the Commercial Bank and one of dozens of others at the Security-Home, the Commerce Guardian, and the Ohio banks. Commerce Guardian Bank maintained Trust 803 for the express purpose of hiding losses and dumping assets that had lost value. Commercial's Trust 694 was not even the largest of the Commercial's funny trusts. It was dwarfed by Trust 636, a million-dollar monster established in 1929.[50]

The Commercial Bank stood out from the pack in the degree to which it broke with established banking norms in how little margin for error it maintained in its accounts. The bank rating service, Moody's, placed great weight on one indicator, the published ratio of "Deposits to $1 of Capital, Surplus, and Undivided Profits." As this rating service explained, this margin "informs the depositor of the margin by which his funds are protected." It also noted that "banking practice has established a ratio of deposits to capital funds of not in excess of ten to one as satisfactory . . ."[51] When the upper limit is nearly reached, it was required that banks solicit more capital to reduce this ratio. In 1927, three of Toledo's large banks, the Commercial, the Dime, and the Ohio, all had ratios over 10. The Commercial's at that time stood at a whopping 18.38. The following year, the Ohio watered its stock by purchasing the Dime Bank and splitting two for one. That left only the Commercial, whose ratio floated slowly down to earth but which by the end of 1930 still stood over 12, which is 20 percent over what was considered safe.

Most Toledo banks stopped paying local taxes on their vast portfolios of properties in 1929. Local officials invoked the maximum fine of 8 percent, but because local ordinances allowed this fine to be imposed only once and didn't allow for interest to accrue on unpaid balances it was far cheaper to pay the fine than to continue to pay taxes. Thus the powerful financial chieftains of the city, who had fought hard and won vast increases in the city's tax levy to finance the building of infrastructure to support their development projects, now refused to pay their share of the burden they created.[52]

As the cracks spread through the foundations of Toledo's giant banks in the winter of 1930 and 1931, the state Banking Department painted a rosy picture of the industry's outlook. Having never closely investigated the practices of Toledo's banks, or even bothered to force them to conform to its own rulings, the department viewed its role simply as encouraging the public to have continued faith and trust in their financial institutions. Picking up the pom-poms in its last report before the Toledo's banking collapse, Ira J. Fulton, Ohio's superintendent of banking, led a hearty cheer for two Toledo banks, the Ohio Savings Bank and the Security-Home Bank, which it placed on the "Honor Roll (of) State Banks."[53] In early April of 1931, the banks reported nothing but smooth sailing to local reporters: "Bankers say the banks have greatly strengthened their positions in the first quarter of this year by the large reduction in loans and the increasing investment in government bonds in proportion to deposits."[54]

Such optimism was based for the most part on highly inflated and even falsified bank reports. Security-Home's first quarter report for 1931 overestimated its assets by more than a million dollars by looking at only the book values of its securities and not their market values. Ohio Bank's wealthiest directors padded their banks assets by depositing over a million dollars the day before the audit and withdrawing the same amount the day afterwards. None of the city banks' official statements are a reliable source of data about their true condition by 1931.

The full extent of misreporting was revealed during the Security-Home Bank's last week of operation. Security-Home's second quarter report was compiled at the beginning of the second week of June. At the same time, under pressure from big-city bankers to provide accurate figures before they would consider merging with it or purchasing it, Security-Home contracted with the independent accounting firm of Ernst and Ernst to perform an independent audit. Coincidentally, both audits assayed the condition of the bank on the same day, June 11, 1931, providing a rare point-by-point comparison of the bankers' own accounting practices to a relatively unbiased standard.

According to the officers of the Security-Home bank, at the end of the day the bank's books were balanced and the bank enjoyed a surplus of $1,500,000 and undivided profits of $545,194.78 (table 5). Ernst and Ernst, however, disagreed, estimating that not only were there no undivided profits at all, but that the entire claimed $1,500,000 surplus had been long wiped out, leaving the bank's balance in deficit by $394,870. Moreover, the dour Ernst and Ernst men in their report noted that their estimate was overly optimistic as "no provision has been made in this statement for possible loss on loans classified by the appraisal committee as of doubtful or undetermined value . . ." This footnote encompassed nearly a quarter of the bank's

Table 5 Official and internal reports of condition, Security-Home Bank, June 11, 1931.

Resources		Reported	Audit
Loans:			
Real Estate		7,100,569.40	6,862,925.07
Demand		3,202,948.97	2,770,145.93
Time-unsecured		3,140,937.31	3,131,450.81
Time collateral		5,471,780.47	5,444,663.97
Past due		1,124,329.39	1,160,932.39
Less allowance for shrinkage		-792,310.15	
	Total Loans	20,040,565.54	18,577,808.02
Securities			
	Total Securities	5,382,303.56	3,131,389.79
Bank buildings		2,087,201.12	1,031,593.24
Furniture and fixtures		140,982.84	130,517.84
Other real estate owned		2,614,964.24	
Leaseholds		140,625.91	
Due from reserve banks		2,399,486.06	2,400,854.57
Cash and clearings		705,586.61	708,815.01
Receivables held by subsidiary		58,538.39	
Remittances		28,849.16	
Overdrafts		981.86	1,125.74
Misc. other claims and receivables		363,245.13	
Customers liability on accep.		36,455.30	6,678.30
	Sub-total	5,399,542.95	7,456,958.37
Total resources		30,822,412.05	29,166,156.18

Liabilities		Reported	Audit
Capital stock		1,500,000.00	1,500,000.00
Surplus		1,500,000.00	0.00
Undivided profits		545,194.78	0.00
Accrual ledger		153,012.65	0.00
	Sub-total	3,698,207.43	1,500,000.00
Demand deposits:			
Commercial		5,065,175.51	5,007,260.19
Public funds		3,506,470.58	3,506,470.58
Certified checks		17,648.13	17,648.13
Officers checks		48,345.40	70,561.81
Deferred items		563.95	
Dividend checks		154.75	154.75
Expense, balance & misc. checks		9,703.38	14,040.82
Bond and coupon		10,199.65	
Demand C.D.'s		58,703.17	58,703.17
Banks and bankers		335,989.20	335,989.20
	Total demand deposits:	9,052,953.72	9,010,828.65
Total time deposits:		14,014,845.26	14,077,413.31
Trust deposits		476,510.46	474,455.50
Bills payable		3,164,839.73	3,164,839.73
Bills rediscountable		375,000.00	375,000.00
Other Liabilities		40,055.45	22,626.89
Mortgages payable			490,669.17
Land Trust Certificates Outstanding			122,000.00
Reserves			323,192.93
	Sub-total	18,071,250.90	19,050,197.53
	Total liabilities	30,822,412.05	29,561,026.18
	Excess Liabilities	0.00	394,870.00

commercial loan portfolio, 5 percent of which was listed as "doubtful" and a whopping 19 percent, or $2,335,372.89, remained "undetermined." As $2,044,330.58 had been loaned to the bank's own officers, and $3,131,450.81 had been given out with no collateral security at all, the chances of much of the "doubtful" or even "undetermined" loans being made good were poor. The green eye-shades also cautioned that "no appraisal of real estate loans or of real estate owned was made prior to the preparation of this report and the amount of deficit as herein stated is accordingly subject to any necessary adjustment." Security-Home not only held $6,862,925.07 worth of real estate loans; it also owned buildings and lots which it claimed to be worth $3,917,701.23 and which were assessed later that year to be worth less than two-thirds that amount.[55]

With their powerful political connections, Toledo's bankers had succeeded in capturing their own regulators and bending the laws of the state to their own ends. They were, as one county judge surveying the local political scene described them, "A mighty power [that] has been builded [sic] up in this city in recent years, so strong, yet so insidious and far-reaching . . . Its influences has been felt in the cabinet and in the policies of national administrations, and is clearly seen in the appointment and selection of our local public officials. In finance its power is unlimited."[56] They had enjoyed a decade in which they had conducted their affairs largely free of state constraints. With the freedom and power they had won for themselves, they maximized their short-term profits, funneled the community's capital into their own private investments, and pushed their losing bets onto the banks they directed. By 1931 their unhindered power had left the banks dry tinder awaiting a stray spark.

CHAPTER THREE

THE SPARK

William H. Gunckel was the sort of amiable sport that everyone liked. Naturally, this short, cherubic Toledo banker was the easy choice of his colleagues to organize the week's entertainments for the Ohio Bankers' convention. His job was not easy. Not only were there a great number of men to be entertained—over a thousand conventioneers overflowed Toledo's hotel rooms—but, being bankers, the association only conducted business before noon, leaving five days of afternoons, evenings, and nights of entertainment to be filled by Will Gunckel. Besides the many details to arrange, he bore the weight of having to boost his city, of having to live up to the honor of Toledo being selected as the host of the convention during that troubled year of 1931. For this one week Toledo would be the object of scrutiny of financiers throughout Ohio.[1]

On the face of things, Toledo's situation appeared bright. Though the city had sagged with the rest of the nation after the Crash of 1929, it appeared to have bounced back since then. The city's employers added workers the very week of the bankers' convention, and the Federal Reserve reported that from February to April Toledo's department stores posted the highest first quarter sales volume of all eight cities surveyed in its district. All of Toledo's banks reported profits and issued dividends the previous week. Even the city's troubled automobile industry seemed to have begun to claw back out of its hole—the largest parts manufacturer, the Electric Auto-Lite Company, was turning profits by producing popular "dollar clocks" that were being distributed by four thousand dime stores nationwide. So, there was some justification for the morning newspaper to welcome the bankers with an editorial that boasted that "the bankers could not have chosen a better city in which to hold their 41st annual convention for in addition to having facilities with which to entertain Toledo can show a good clean banking picture to the visitors."[2]

Gunckel (figure 3) had little difficulty arranging for all of the city's dozen private country clubs to open their doors to the state's bankers. After each

Figure 3
William H. Gunckel, Toledo banker and
director and vice-president of the
Security-Home Bank. Circa 1928–1931.
(Reprinted with permission of the *Blade*)

morning's sessions the bankers could play tennis, hit the links, or ease back
into the deep armchairs of the swank Toledo Club with a sherry and cigar.
For the traditional convention dinner and ball, held at Gunckel's own club,
he focused all his energies. The ballroom and grounds were decorated to
resemble Venice, and hundreds of boats were festooned with lights in the
yacht club's harbor. Then an extravagant dinner was followed by a mock
naval battle and a fireworks show. It was, according to the society colum-
nist, a brilliant and most unusual event.[3]

But William Gunckel had no chance to enjoy the week he so carefully
prepared. He knew better than most of his fellow Toledoans that the condition of his firm, the Security-Home Bank, the third largest in the city,
was desperate. A week earlier, Gunckel was concerned enough about his
ability to secure cash that he arranged for his own bank to advance him a
$10,000 loan on his own home, which it did even though the property was
assessed at only $6,880.[4] Just as the convention opened he heard of the trou-
ble brewing at their branch in the Polish district. A thousand dollars had
gone missing from the vault, and a bank employee had failed to show for

work the next morning. While Will Gunckel and his banker friends were just sitting down to enjoy their convention-opening dinner, Michael Szymanski, a thirty-year-old bank clerk, came home to his wife of six months with a thousand dollars stuffed in his pocket and made her cry by telling her, "I'm going to jail. I'm a crook." He couldn't face her for long and he left in his rented car, a couple of pints of whiskey on the seat beside him. Szymanski parked his car between a rooming house and a used car lot just up the street from the Toledo Club, where his fellow bankers partied. Szymanski guzzled his booze, passed out, and awoke the next morning to find his pockets had been emptied during the night.

Disheveled and hung over, Szymanski drove to a newsstand and bought the morning papers to read about his embezzlement and was surprised when he could find no notice of it. Perhaps he wasn't aware that the president of the city's largest newspaper was also president of the Second National Bank or that other interlocking directorates tied all the city's industries together into one tight web of interest. In such a rocky year as 1931 and with Ohio's bankers in town, what editor in his right mind would risk sparking a bank run by publishing news of embezzlement in a bank in one of the poorest districts of the city? It was bad enough that the papers had to print the reports coming out of Chicago that morning of mass bank runs and the closing of a half-dozen banks. Anyway, Szymanski knew that news, even news that didn't make it into the paper, traveled quickly in his close-knit immigrant neighborhood.[5]

When, later that day, Michael Szymanski turned himself in to the police, Security-Home Bank president Stacey L. McNary found himself staring into the abyss. McNary (figure 4) was the golden boy of Toledo bankers, a young man who began as a bank messenger boy and whose climb since then had been steep. Before he was forty he had become president of the Security Bank, then head of the Toledo clearinghouse, and finally leader of the Toledo Bankers' Club. In the years leading up to Black Tuesday, McNary had helped engineer a succession of mergers that tripled his bank's size. But since those peaks of 1929, Toledo's employment had dropped and the bottom had fallen out of its go-go real estate market. Now with rumors flying across the city about embezzlement at his bank, with news of a wave of bank failures that swept Chicago, and with a deep drop in European bond prices caused by fears of the possibility of a total German default, McNary's edifice teetered on the brink.[6]

In the banking business in those days it was well known that a seemingly trivial incident was often the spark that would burn through a dry and rotten bank. A journalist writing in a national magazine at the time described such a "minor incident of the type that often causes major changes" in which "Mrs. Smith has seen the banker the evening before help a dizzy blonde

Figure 4
Stacy McNary, president of the Security-
Home Bank. Circa 1928–1931. (Reprinted
with permission of the *Blade*)

out of a taxi in front of a night club—and the aforementioned ravishing beauty
was not Mrs. Banker. Secrets like that are usually shared at once with the
general public. Was the banker spending his own money? The question is
asked by a thousand depositors. In the days that follow, funds withdrawn
exceed funds deposited."[7]

McNary's achievement of building Security-Home into the city's third largest
bank had come at a high cost. Each of the smaller banks that were taken over
brought with them a heavy load of rotten loans that had not been properly
depreciated in the bank's books. Each merger expanded the size of the board
of directors, increasing the number of men in a position to favor themselves
and their companies with sweetheart loans. In 1926, the Security bank had
nineteen directors. Five years later the boardroom was nearly twice as
crowded, with thirty-four directors.[8] When McNary acquired Banker's Trust
in 1929, he also took over $355,144 in loans held by Banker's Trust's direc-
tors, about the same amount Security-Home had lent to its own officers. After
purchasing the Home Bank in 1930, Security-Home swallowed an additional
million dollars in insider loans that had been made to the Home Bank's directors. By the fall of 1931, over $2 million, or one out of every ten dollars loaned
by the bank, had been lent to the men who approved all loans.[9]

In making loans to themselves, the Security-Home board tended to be more trusting and forgiving than they were to the person who walked in off the street. Nearly one in five of the dollars lent to directors were loaned without any security whatsoever (18.9 percent). Another 20 percent were loans given solely on the security of shares in real estate companies and real estate trusts whose major asset were thousands of unsold lots. The collateral pledged to secure the remainder of loans consisted of a mixture of equities and real estate shares that even during the peak markets of the 1920s fell short of securing one hundred percent of the loans.[10] Had these loans been given to anyone but those who ran the bank, they would have been called in long before the bank began to tip into the red. At the very least, the bank would have demanded more collateral as the value of pledged securities dropped. Instead, when it was clear the bank was headed for the rocks, the directors voted to renew their own loans without any change in their terms. In the six months prior to April of 1931, bank directors renewed $75,983.52 worth of their own loans. In the ten weeks before the bank closed, they extended the terms on their own personal loans amounting to $959,767.30.[11]

Each time McNary absorbed a smaller bank, he acquired its financial skeletons as well. By 1931 McNary's closet had become quite full. There was the phony $96,000 loan that McNary and his fellow directors had put on the books to cover a huge stock loss. There were the mortgage loans issued to a company controlled by a former director that were based on forged mortgage papers. There were the loans given to companies controlled by directors without collateral and then forgiven. There were the bundles of worthless South American bonds that were still carried at their face value on the bank's accounts.[12]

Now the skeletons were coming to life. While rumors of the embezzlement at the Opieka Branch prompted a few working class Toledoans to remove the tens or hundreds of dollars in their savings accounts to some hiding place in their homes, these didn't amount to much. The real trouble came when a few major corporations, tipped off by bank insiders, decided to pull the plug. The Electric Auto-Lite Company withdrew $56,000 on June 11. American National Co., which had as much as a hundred grand on account, began drawing it down until only thirty-four hundred remained at the end of the week. Libbey-Owens-Ford, the world's largest maker of auto glass and one of the largest corporate depositors, began making substantial withdrawals.

Fearing collapse, McNary met with his bank's largest shareholder, the industrialist Clement O. Miniger, and told him that a merger was the only way to save the bank. There were only two other banks in the city with assets large enough to submerge whatever rotten liabilities Security-Home carried. One possibility was Toledo Trust, the second largest bank, which was

owned collectively by the old-moneyed families of Toledo and conservatively steered by Henry L. Thompson, a somewhat stodgy holdover of a
bygone era in finance. The other was the largest bank in town, the Ohio
Savings Bank, run by Miniger's own brash son-in-law, George Jones, a self-
made man who amassed his first fortune in the rough-and-tumble of running southern Ohio coal mines. Being a hard-headed businessman,
Miniger knew that whatever shaky foundation Security-Home rested on
probably underlay his son-in-law's bank as well, as it too was the product
of a recent flurry of mergers and takeovers, so, instead, he passed over kin
and turned to Thompson for help.

Henry Thompson might have been willing to extend a helpful hand to
a fellow banker whose house was on fire, but only as long as he was amply
and richly rewarded for his effort and there was no risk of being singed himself. Before he would even negotiate he ordered an independent audit of
Security-Home's books, a reasonable but time-consuming demand.
Anyone connected with Security-Home worried that an independent
audit would kill the deal, as it might reveal the truth behind the bank's cooked
books—that the bank had nothing but debts to merge, over 16 percent of
its loans were unsecured, a large proportion of its mortgage loans were backed
with worthless lots, and another 10 percent of its loans were in the hands
of the bank's own directors.[13] A valiant attempt was made by some
unknown insiders to spruce up the books when a flurry of commercial checks
were deposited totaling a million dollars on June 11, the day that the logs
and ledgers were to be examined by Thompson's accountants.[14]

While they waited for the results of the audit, the Security-Home's board
of directors voted to issue a stock dividend of sixty-two and one half cents
per share, or a total of $37,500.99, on Tuesday, June 9, just as they had before
at the end of March. Dividends are a return of profits to the investors in
the corporation, but in this case the bank had not turned a profit since the
close of business on January 28. When the March dividend was declared,
the bank's official ledger claimed it to be profitable, but the insiders knew
this to be untrue and that it in fact had lost over eighty thousand dollars in
just the first quarter of the year. To keep the books balanced, someone had
shoved three and a half million dollars in real estate loans, seven hundred
thousand in securities, and over eight hundred thousand in commercial loans
that were not being paid into a "non-accrual" list that were not declared
as losses. When the directors, fresh from their banking convention revel-
ries the night before, voted to reward themselves, their corporation was another
twenty thousand dollars in deficit. Such a vote, at the moment when the
failure of a bank is a real possibility, took money directly from the depositors, for when the bank was liquidated, every dollar short was one less to

repay those who were owed their savings. Moreover, it was one of the few things bank directors could do that was expressly prohibited by state law.[15]

A week after the Security-Home board meeting in which the directors personally walked away a little over fourteen thousand dollars richer (that being their share of the stockholder dividends), a meeting was called for 8:30 A.M. to hear the report of the independent audit of the bank. Besides the usual group of directors, the superintendent of banks for Ohio, Ira J. Fulton, was present with his staff attorney and head examiner in tow. The news could not have been worse. The audit revealed that Security-Home's claimed surplus of $1.5 million had long been wiped out, leaving it with a deficit of $394,870. Superintendent Fulton, the son of a bank president himself, seemed unfazed by the numbers and urged the directors to redouble their efforts at obtaining a merger and suggested that a committee of three be picked to meet privately with Thompson, Miniger, and himself to iron out the details.[16]

Apparently, nobody but Fulton had any hope left at the conclusion of the meeting. As soon as the meeting broke up, the Security-Home Bank directors headed downstairs and quietly began emptying their accounts. Being on the teller side of the cages allowed them to avoid the lines that were just forming up outside the doors. President McNary put $483.23 in his pocket, leaving less than $30 in his savings account. Director L.G. Pierce withdrew just a little less, $450. Vice-president Raleigh D. Mills managed to walk out with $1,000 in his own cash though he had only $180.86 in his account (he later made good on the overdraft). Director Sidney Spitzer withdrew $654.09, the last of an account that weeks earlier had held $3,687.14. Director Julian Tyler snatched five grand from his account.

Will Gunckel was a very busy man that day. As secretary of the board of directors it was his job to keep the official minutes of that morning's meeting. When it was done, he too went downstairs and began salvaging what he could of his and his friends' money. Of course he took out the last of his own money, $1,822. Then he closed the accounts of friends—over two thousand for Jennie Kibble; over ten thousand for Marcel Metz, about a grand for Mary E. Haskins, and an even two grand for Florence Morris.

The bank's employees were lining up to take out money from behind the counter as fast as the public was lining up in front of it. S. R. Dority, the manager of the safe deposit department, emptied his wife's account of $1,300. Treasurer Karl Naugle cleaned out his account. Of course, the secretaries and assistant secretaries were best positioned to quietly pocket their own money. Carl D. Rideout closed out his and his wife's account, then swept clean the accounts of family members Oliver and D. P. Rideout, the last one holding over fourteen thousand dollars. Theodore Klinksick closed his own account, his wife's, and that of his brother. And James R. Newell made off with all of his wife's account and his son's little nest egg of $122.63, although through some small mathematical error he left a total of seventy-eight cents in two other accounts of his own. Newell also did a big favor for Jeremiah Bingham, a retired industrialist, and withdrew his savings account of $114,000.[17] Assistant Trust Officer and Assistant Secretary F. J. Klauser took a bit more than he had on account and owed the bank about a buck and a half when it closed. His colleague J. W. Wilson also erred and left an over-draft of $2.81.

Other directors had no need to wade into the panicked chaos on the banking floor—they had drained their accounts a day or two earlier. Badger Bowen took his last two grand the previous Saturday. Amos Lint withdrew about ninety percent of his account the day before, netting over fifteen thousand. The same day George Moore cleaned out ten thousand. Earlier, director J. D. Hurlbut managed to draw down his accounts from over seventeen thousand to a balance of about twenty-five hundred and those of Phillip A. Hurlbut from nearly twenty-five hundred to just seventy-eight dollars.[18]

J. E. Rundell, being a former director of the Security Bank and not currently sitting on the bank's board, was late in arriving on the bank's last day of operation and when he tried to cash in his two certificates of deposit for a whopping $179,666.67, the tellers could not scrape up enough cash. The barrel now being empty, Rundell settled for a bank check for that amount to a bank in Cleveland. Unfortunately for Rundell, the next day when he presented his checks in Cleveland, the banks refused to honor them. He was too late.[19]

But it wasn't the hundreds of thousands withdrawn by the bank's directors and officers that delivered the coup de grace to Security-Home. The death shot to the balance sheets came when the bank's officers scrambled to defend the assets of other companies they were connected to. The City Auto Stamping Company, a large auto parts manufacturer, shared four of its six directors with the Security-Home Bank, and while the bank was sinking they helped liberate about four hundred thousand dollars of its cash. Another large Toledo company, the Woolson Spice Company, luckily had both its own president and vice-president on the board of the Security-Home Bank. Woolson usually maintained a balance of between eighty and eighty-five thousand but was left with only eleven dollars and twenty-nine cents before the day's accounts were finally tallied. The Toledo Grain and Milling Company shared its treasurer with the board of Security-Home and on the last day it managed to free $26,000 from its corporate account.[20] Rufus H. Baker, vice-chairman of the board, and director Leroy E. Eastman were also partners in Smith, Baker, Effler, Allen & Eastman, a leading corporate

Figure 5
The ironic final advertisement of the Security-Home Bank in
the summer of 1931. (Reprinted with permission of the *Blade*)

law firm. They set about draining their firm's own deposits and those of
their most important corporate clients.

Superintendent Fulton's hopes for a merger that would clean up the mess
at Security-Home before it became an embarrassment to his department
could not have lasted for long that day, if ever they truly existed.[21] C. O.
Miniger, the bank's largest stockholder and the man Fulton felt was key

Table 6

Cumulative deposit losses, Security-Home Bank, May 15–June 16, 1931.

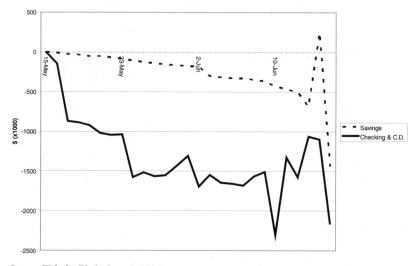

Source: Toledo *Blade*, Jan. 5, 1934.

to working out a deal with Thompson, apparently had no illusions that the bank was salvageable. While Fulton attempted to work out a deal, Miniger withdrew the last of his personal account, $141,504.55. Later that evening, Fulton assembled the Security-Home directors one last time so they could vote to officially close the bank and turn its assets over to the state for liquidation. Perhaps when he called the question, Security-Home's president, Stacey McNary, recalled the speech he had given two years earlier before the Epworth Men's Club, when he had proclaimed that bank panics like that which had occurred in 1907 were now "practically impossible" because of the advent of the Federal Reserve system. At that moment the irony of one of the bank's last newspaper advertisements became palpable. Four days before, a quarter-page Security-Home advertisement (figure 5) that made a pitch for the traveler's business was headlined "Au Revoir."[22]

In the last six weeks of the bank's operations, a little over $3 million in deposits were lost (table 6). Nearly half of that amount was withdrawn by the officers of the bank, their relatives, and the other businesses in which they had interests. On the day of the fabled bank run that shut down Security-Home Bank, the frightened public withdrew $679,971 from their savings accounts. That same day, June 16, bankers with commercial interests and other insiders quietly removed a much larger sum, $1,039,303.[23]

On Wednesday, when the Security-Home Bank failed to open, a more general panic began. Each of the banks in the financial district was beset by crowds of people, clutching their passbooks. On the busy corner of Summit and Cherry streets, crowds lining the sidewalk in front of the Commerce Guardian bank stood beneath a massive fourteen foot high lighted sign whose message "Save To-Day" became an instant mockery.[24]

Some members of the crowd who succeeded in emptying their accounts suffered a pang of guilt afterwards. A few more civic-minded men obeyed their consciences. One man took out $1,400 and walked around the block. Drawn back to the doors of the bank, he hesitated, then walked around the block again, until finally, he gave up, stood back in line, and redeposited his money. Another made it home with his life savings of $4,000 but couldn't sleep that night and returned his cash to the bank the next day. Another man briskly walked out with over a thousand dollars cash in his pocket and was robbed once he rounded the corner.[25]

Inside the city's newest skyscraper, the Ohio Bank tower, two dozen directors of the city's largest bank weighed their options. Long before the panic caused by the collapse of the Security-Home bank, the Ohio, too, had been in trouble. Six months before, the state Banking Department had grown alarmed at the bank's mountain of loans to shaky real estate companies and its accumulating pile of second mortgages on undeveloped lots, a pile that amounted to about 60 percent of the bank's assets. Bank superintendent Fulton insisted that the Ohio Bank suspend issuing dividends and instead build up its reserves so it could write down the inevitable losses from those sour investments. In response the Ohio Bank sent a letter to Fulton signed by its most politically well-connected officer, vice-president Edward Kirschner, who explained that the bank had ample reserves and capital to weather any storm. Though Fulton wrote again with the same demands on March 21, the Ohio's directors simply ignored them and continued to drain the bank of $22,500 each month in dividends, knowing the Banking Department was a paper tiger and Fulton was a servant of political forces over which they had substantial influence.[26]

However, with the situation in the street beginning to spin out of control, the Ohio Bank's directors were faced with a stark choice. They could liquefy as many assets as they could and borrow heavily from banks outside the district to meet the demands of those clambering for withdrawals, or they could invoke a rarely used legal provision that would allow them to suspend withdrawals for up to sixty days. Being the largest bank in town, the Ohio Bank stood the best chance of weathering the storm of withdrawals, especially if the bank began calling in its least secured loans and selling off some of its vast holdings of real estate. Moreover, if the bank adopted this course of action and met depositors' demands, it would probably stand to gain business in the long run as smaller institutions failed.

Though by all objective measures converting assets to cash and calming the panic by making lots of cash available was the best choice from a purely business perspective, it was made impossible by the personal interests of the men who controlled the bank. As the Ohio Bank's own officers themselves owed the bank $139,000 in unsecured loans and $2,519,660 in mostly under-collateralized loans, and as firms that the bank's officers were invested in or controlled owed the bank another $6,650,000, calling in loans was a very unpopular idea. The directors were also handcuffed by their own past deceitfulness. Had the bank begun selling off its mortgages or its lots, the true value of these holdings would be revealed and this would force the bank to account truthfully for its long-term losses. If the balance sheet was corrected in this way, the bank would be forced to suspend dividends and it might even be compelled to admit its previous false reports, leaving the bank's officers open to prosecution or civil suits. Even worse, from the perspective of those who ran the bank, if the bank attempted to calm the public's fears by piling up cash to meet the demands of common depositors, there might be less cash left for themselves in the event their house of cards toppled.[27]

Instead, the men in charge of the Ohio Bank chose a course that doomed their bank, but best preserved their own fortunes. A vote was called and a motion was passed that read: "Due to unreasonable demands to withdrawals of savings deposits, the (executive) committee unanimously resolved to put the 60-day notice rule into effect on all time deposits beginning Thursday morning, June 18, and continuing until further notice, but subject to certain exceptions at the discretion of the officers and tellers of the bank." This meant, in effect, that any of the board members, at their own discretion, could withdraw funds from the bank, though the bank was closed to the public. After the Ohio Bank board adjourned, a copy of the resolution was sent to the newsrooms for publication in the morning papers. Apparently, the bankers thought it best to edit their resolution for public consumption and dropped from the copy they gave reporters the clause explaining how bank insiders could approve withdrawals. This fact would remain secret until revealed by a state senate investigation three years later. This vote probably made vice-president Claude Campbell feel a bit foolish, as he had earlier that day arranged to ensure recovery of his own savings account by having the bank grant a $5,700 loan for his wife secured by a flimsy second mortgage. Had he waited, he could have just withdrawn the money.[28]

Down the street filling with lines of depositors, the officers of the Commercial Savings Bank sat around a long oak table and discussed the growing crisis.

The Paramount Theatre marquee visible through the window advertised its newest feature, "The Vice Squad," and a bit further up the block the Valentine offered "The Laughing Sinner" with Joan Crawford. Like all the bank boards in the city, this was an august group of notables. This assemblage of directors, for example, included the ambitious lawyer and Democratic politician, Frazier Reams, who within a year would be elected the county prosecutor and would eventually represent the region in Congress. A year later, Reams would find himself in the uncomfortable position of having to prosecute bankers for their actions during this crisis. Seated across the table from Reams was Harold Fraser, a leading trial lawyer and the man who would eventually defend his fellow bankers against Reams all the way to the Ohio Supreme Court.[29]

According to their public statements of assets and liabilities, these men had little cause to worry. But many of the men seated around this table knew the public books weren't to be trusted. Some knew about the forged notes used as collateral for loans to a company that one bank director himself controlled; others knew how depositors' funds had been used to buy New York stocks on hot tips with brokers' commissions going to the director who arranged them and losses shunted off to dummy subsidiaries; there were the Florida bond losses illegally held off the books; there was the 200 percent dividend declared in 1928 at the conclusion of a year in which the bank showed a loss. At one end of the table President W. H. Yeasting was aware of allegations that the manager of the Ashland Avenue branch was passing loans through fictitious names to speculate in stocks and splitting the profits with a brokerage firm run by his brother.[30]

But it would have been business suicide and, perhaps, jeopardizing of their own liberty to make these things known, so the directors agreed to endorse a reassuring advertisement to be placed in the papers: "The general banking situation in Toledo is such as to warrant confidence. Calm reflection will convince everyone there is no reason for concern . . ."[31] Of course, some of the directors had just beaten the rush in the street by quietly making "loans" to themselves (which they knew would later be swapped for their deposits), or, in the more creative case of director L. H. Hartman, by just that morning arranging for the bank to purchase bonds with money from his savings account on his behalf. Like the other bankers meeting that day, the Commercial's directors made two momentous and contradictory decisions. First, they voted to join with the Ohio Bank and impose a sixty-day moratorium on all withdrawals. Then, they authorized the executive committee to issue a quarterly dividend of one and a half percent, or $10,500, nearly one-third of which would flow directly into the pockets of the thirteen men gathered in the board room.[32]

When the Commerce Guardian bank followed suit and joined the others in suspending withdrawals, its president, Edward G. Kirby, told reporters, "There is not a particle of sense to all these rumors and this hysteria. All I have to say is that our bank is sound—a member of the federal reserve system—and it will remain sound. We will treat all patrons alike." Like the other big banks that were frozen, Kirby's bank had some thawed spots that those in the know could reach through. Over the next sixty days, nearly four million dollars, or 17 percent of all deposits, would drain through holes in the ice.[33]

From the beginning of the crisis, all of the city's newspapers backpedaled the story. The *Blade*'s first report of the closing of the Security-Home Bank reported that the bank's directors closed the bank due to the "unwarranted fears" that led depositors to run on the bank. The suspension of withdrawals by three of the four largest remaining banks in the city did not make the *News-Bee*'s headlines, but was buried in paragraph six of a story entitled, "Patrons Return Funds" and after the soothing subheadings, "Situation Safe, Sound" and "Toledo Banks in Good Shape, Presidents Say." Likewise the *Blade* didn't mention that banks had frozen accounts until the fourth paragraph of its story, whose headline read like a hypnotist's chanted suggestions: "Banks Are Sound, Presidents Aver; Confidence Urged—Institutions Capable of Meeting Normal Demands, Heads Say; Sane Thinking Asked." Before getting around to the actual story that most of the large banks in the city had closed their withdrawal windows, the *Blade* attempted to ease readers' minds by reporting that "powerful offers of support [had come] from nearby financial centers—Detroit, Cleveland, Pittsburgh and even New York. But Toledo banks and bankers have the situation so well in hand that it was not necessary to take advantage of these offers." The *Blade*'s report appears to have been wholly fabricated, as all evidence indicates that only Toledo Trust received any outside assistance during that time and the other banks were forced to sell assets at a loss to raise funds. With one last article on the day after the bank suspension whose headline, "Bank Situation Back to Normal" summed up the sunny gist of the story, the daily newspapers drew a curtain of silence around the banking situation.[34]

While the daily newspapers reassured the public that the panic was unwarranted and the banks were sound (figure 6), newspaper insiders rushed to close out their own accounts. The same day the *Blade* printed stories extolling the city's citizens to do their patriotic duty and keep their money in the bank, it withdrew over twenty thousand dollars from the Security-Home bank, depleting an account that a month earlier had held over fifty thousand to just under five thousand. The *Blade*'s editor, Grove Patterson, low-

Figure 6
Bank placement of advertising in Toledo newspapers remained on its regular schedule up to the day of failure of many banks in 1931. (Reprinted with permission of the *Blade*)

ered his own Security-Home account from a high of $855.47 to $183.26, while his fellow editor at the Toledo *Times*, R. C. Patterson, rescued nearly half of his ten thousand dollar account before the bank collapsed. Officers of the paper were able to skip to the front of the panicked crowd because of its close connections to the bank. The *Blade*'s president, Barton Smith, was the senior law partner of two members of the Security-Home board of directors. The president of the Toledo Blade Printing Co., its printing plant subsidiary, was W. C. Carr, who was also a director of the Security-Home bank.

All the molders of opinion in the city swung into action when the enormity of the bank crisis became apparent. The editor of the suburban *Sylvania Sentinel* in a rare front page editorial entitled "No Time for Hysteria!" declared, "Our banks our sound, they are safe, they are well governed, so let us all be loyal to our community and to its institutions . . . by keeping calm." Mayor William T. Jackson issued a statement saying, "I feel that financial conditions do not warrant the scare of yesterday." But the most authoritative voice in the heavily Catholic city was newly installed bishop, Karl J. Alter, whose first official action was to instruct all parish priests to counsel their parishioners to remain calm and to act in the public interest by keeping their money in the bank. "If the people withdraw their confidences in all their financial institutions," wrote Alter to his priests, "they will precipitate a condition which means business failures, closed factories, loss of employment and a host of evils such as despair, injustice, hatred and ill-will." Therefore, Alter explained to his priests, they should instruct their parishioners, "It is a duty at present dictated by justice and charity to be calm and reasonable," or, in other words, to keep their money in the banks.[35]

The Better Business Bureau purchased a full-page ad in the *News-Bee* addressed "To the People of Toledo" urging them to "stand fast . . . We advise that you pay no attention to the many unfounded rumors which have been afloat and which without a doubt have caused the unwarranted withdrawal of funds from substantial institutions by a hysterical minority." In the same issue readers would have seen other advertisements telling them their patriotic and moral duty was to stay home and keep their money in the bank. The Irving B. Hiett company, one of the leading real estate companies that had overbuilt the subdivisions and had burdened the city's banks with many unpaid loans, paid for an ad that said "Keep Your Money in the Banks . . . It is the safe thing to do. We know that every such going institution is perfectly solvent." The Toledo Real Estate Board sent open letters to the presidents of each of three banks that suspended withdrawals thanking them for protecting the deposits of the citizens of Toledo. Wilk, Clarke & Co., brokers, paid for an ad that was most to the point, saying simply, "Stop Worrying and Trust Your Bank."[36]

For some that week's crisis was all they could take. Martin Burneth, a 51-year-old unemployed carpenter, waited until his wife left for work and then closed all the windows, put a towel under the kitchen door and unscrewed a cap from an unused gas line on the floor. Mrs. Burneth found his body when she came home that evening. According to Toledo's mortality statis-

tics, Burneth was not the only person to have been driven to despair around
this time. In 1931 there were 43 percent more suicides than the previous
year and 35 percent more than the average for the previous five years.[37]

In an ideal world, the sort of place imagined in business textbooks, when
a bank ran short of cash its financial Solomons judiciously sold some assets
and used the generated cash to reestablish normal banking. The purpose
of a moratorium was to give the bankers breathing room to gain the best
prices they could for their notes and equities, rather than having to throw
them into a fire sale and suffer a huge loss. Reality, however, is just not so
neat, and bankers are men, not philosopher-kings, and the sixty-day withdrawal period was wasted as bankers sold off whatever they could and then
withdrew the cash themselves as fast as it came in. Even though there was
no immediate pressure to discount their assets and sell them overnight, because
the bankers themselves were eager to liquefy bank property so as to rescue
their own accounts, deals were made with little regard to the health or profit
of the bank as whole.[38]

The panicked directors of the Ohio Bank heeded neither their fiduciary
responsibility nor even the law in their haste to raise ready cash. With nearly
two-thirds of the bank's assets in the form of real estate, mostly lots and
mortgages, many of which were second liens and many others near
default, the bank could not easily cash out its investments. As it would have
been impossible to sell the notes and parcels individually in a short time,
the bank's leaders looked to sell a huge portfolio of notes in one bundle.
Large insurance companies were ready buyers for mountains of mortgages,
for they had the capital and the long-term investment horizon to wait for
these properties to perform.

Ohio Bank found just such a prospect interested in a bundle of their notes,
the Metropolitan Life Company of New York, but in order to make the deal
they had to rifle through several trust accounts, swapping good mortgages
out of these supposedly sealed trusts in exchange for dogs from the bank's
holdings. Apparently this was not enough to seal the deal. Metropolitan Life
took full advantage of the fact that the Toledo bankers were laid out on the
rack and secured a guarantee that the bank would pay the arrears of interest,
principal, and taxes on many of the notes both in the past and for an undis-
closed time into the future. Such payments were clearly contrary to state securities laws, as was made clear to the Ohio's directors by a representative of
the Department of Banks. But, as was customary, state officials made no attempt
to back up their orders, and Ohio Bank directors made over $300,000 in ille-
gal mortgage payment advances to Metropolitan Life. The cash generated
by the sale made possible the millions of dollars of withdrawals made by insiders through the rest of the moratorium period.[39]

"Smart money" withdrawals hurt the banks in two ways, in the obvious way by drawing down its remaining cash at a time when it was supposed to be building it up, but also by setting the stage for an even bigger bank run at the end. For smart money withdrawals could not be kept secret. Whispers of big smart money deals spread throughout the city as the sixty-day deadline neared. As the public increasingly suspected that the smart money was cashing out, so did the numbers of those determined not to be the sap left holding the bag. As the public's anxiety level increased, so did the smart money's judgment that there was little hope for the banks, and so they took more of their own cash out. Insider withdrawals fed public rumors which in turn pushed insiders to withdraw more in a deteriorating spiral that doomed the banks long before the sixty-day holiday ended on Monday, August 17.

When the leaders of the three large banks announced they were suspending withdrawals, they left large loopholes in their policies. None of the banks applied their suspensions to their commercial accounts, allowing most of their corporate and business customers to empty their accounts by check. Nor did they suspend payment on certificates of deposit, which were used by the wealthiest customers to park huge uninvested sums of capital. Trust accounts, stuffed not only with retirees' pensions but also with real estate companies' mortgages and remaining cash, were also exempt and open to drain. Every bank also overlooked its own rules and granted numerous exceptions to insiders. Only the Ohio Bank didn't break its own withdrawal policies, but this was true only because it specifically authorized any director or officer to allow withdrawals in a clause in its minutes withheld from the public.

Smart money withdrawals at the Commerce Guardian bank were so heavy that they exceeded the potential withdrawals scheduled to occur when the bank reopened by several multiples (table 7). During the period of suspension, smart money withdrawals amounted to $5,123,000. At the same time, general depositors filled out withdrawal slips due after August 17 totaling only $1,131,373. Of the forty-two trust accounts held by the bank, all but six were zeroed out before August 17. To pay for these withdrawals, the bank was forced to sell two-thirds of a million dollars in securities and borrow over three million dollars from the Federal Reserve.[40]

Similarly, the Commercial Bank was a sieve of smart money during the summer suspension. Over two million dollars in commercial accounts fled first; $120,350 in certificates of deposit were cashed. Then another $1,197,208 was withdrawn from regular accounts while the bank was closed to the public. Given that the Commercial had about fifteen million dollars on deposit before the summer began, smart money amounted to over 20 percent of all its deposits.[41]

Table 7

Cumulative deposit losses, Commerce Guardian Bank,
June 12–August 15, 1931.

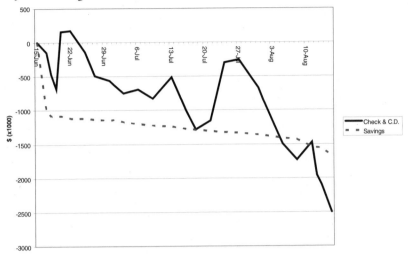

Source: Toledo *Blade*, Nov. 25, 1933.

In order to pay out such a large proportion of its deposits, the Commercial Bank resorted to selling off a huge portion of its real estate portfolio at a steep discount to the Prudential Life Insurance Company. Beginning on June 26, the Commercial transferred twenty-six properties to the Prudential and continued to sell an average of half a dozen properties every business day through the summer. By the time it closed it had sold to the Prudential mortgages worth $974,249, or one-fifth of its entire real estate loan portfolio.[42]

The smartest money was in the Ohio Bank, whose insider withdrawals exceeded those of all the other banks put together. A staggering $10,334,512 secretly flowed out of the Ohio Bank during the suspension period, roughly half from commercial accounts and CDs and half from regular deposits (table 8). Being the largest commercial bank in northwest Ohio, the Ohio Bank enjoyed the lion's share of the region's large corporate accounts. When the banks teetered, large corporations were quick to pull the plug. Electric Auto-Lite, the company founded and owned by the father-in-law of the Ohio Bank's president, withdrew $865,990. The Willys-Overland Company, whose president was a director of the bank, pulled out $720,122 in July. Owens-Illinois Glass cashed out $230,604. Kroger Foods withdrew $573,881. Ford Motor claimed $99,966, a drop in the ocean compared to its capitalization. The law firm of Tracy, Chapman, and Welles, whose senior partner, Newton Tracy, was a director of the Ohio Bank, closed out its account

Table 8

Cumulative deposit losses, Ohio Bank, June 12–August 15, 1931.

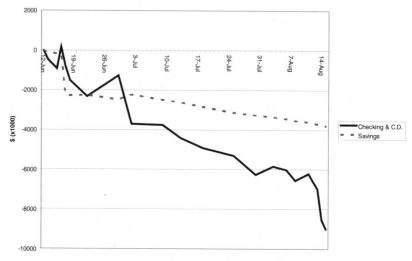

Source: Toledo *Blade*, Nov. 24, 1933.

of $44,036. Newton Tracy's father, Pratt Tracy, was president of the Air-Way Appliance Company, which walked away with $181,432. In all, local businesses took over three million dollars out of the frozen bank.[43]

Though no complete listing of all individual withdrawals was ever made public, a few select and incomplete inventories did surface that reveal a glimpse of the connections that made smart money intelligent. There are the expected family connections—Margaret, the wife of John Cummings, an Ohio director emeritus, ten years retired from the bank, had access to her savings of $705.25. Alice and Eleanor Walbridge, wife and daughter of the Ohio Bank director Sinclair Walbridge, salvaged their savings.

There were also courtesies extended to fellow bankers. J. D. Hurlbut and Clifford Whitmore, whose Security-Home bank he helped guide into the dirt two weeks earlier, were allowed to cash out $26,000 and $958.49 from the Ohio, respectively. The Ohio Bank allowed Florence Tiedtke, the wife of Ernest Tiedtke, who was a director of the Toledo Trust bank, to withdraw $4,135.75 on the first day of the suspension. It also gave back $500 to Carrie Pierce, whose husband Lawrence was a director of the Security-Home bank. F. C. Fuller, relative of Rathbun Fuller, who directed Toledo Trust, was loaned $11,275 against his Ohio Bank savings account of $12,452.

It also appears that pulling political wires could yank money out of the bank. On the Friday before the Ohio Bank closed for good, Margaret O'Dwyer, wife of the head of the county Democrats, Kevin O'Dwyer, was given a loan of $1,500 against her savings account. Robert C. Dunn, past president of the Lucas County Republican Club and later remembered as "one hell of an after-dinner speaker," put $300 cash in pocket. Most spectacularly, Toledo's powerful Republican federal judge, John M. Killits, the judge who had crushed the Willys-Overland strike of 1919 with a flurry of restrictive injunctions, was allowed to borrow over $100,000 from the Ohio Bank on one of its suspended days.[44]

From the fragmentary records that exist it also appears that bankers made allowances for clubs, charities, and service organizations they were affiliated with to rescue their funds. F. A. Fleischman, the assistant treasurer of the Commerce Guardian Bank, signed off on the withdrawal of the Toledo Woman's Club of $2,145. Commerce Guardian also handed back the $2,000 banked by the Women's Relief Corp. The bank's vice-president, G. L. Mills, helped his Rotary Club get its $5,000 back. The Commercial Bank gave back $1,000 to the Toledo Post of the American Legion, $5,500 to the Y.M.C.A., $1,750 to the Jewish Federation, $4,000 to the Toledo Public Health Association, and $1,034 to the Brotherhood of Railroad Trainmen Local 397. The Ohio Bank allowed withdrawals on behalf of the Toledo Catholic Charities ($2,000), the Toledo Firemen's Pension Fund ($700), and the Toledo Museum of Art ($10,000).[45]

In those banks where the board resolution suspending withdrawals did not allow exceptions as the Ohio Bank's did, the preferred method used by insiders to empty their accounts was to make loans to themselves.[46] All knew that it was far better to owe a closed bank money than vice versa. Even better, in the event that a bank held both a customer's loan and a customer's deposit, the two would likely cancel each other out, making the loan the same thing as a withdrawal. This strategy worked regardless of what collateral was offered to back the loan.

The directors at the Commercial Bank used the suspension period to grant themselves loans of this kind. Director E. H. France would wait a month and then arrange for himself a $30,000 loan backed by 367 shares of his own bankrupt real estate company. Future county prosecutor Reams would also take out a sizable loan, but to his future relief as a politician it was reported that he backed it up with solid A.T. & T. stock. Stanley Roberts, the third largest stockholder in the boardroom, waited a couple days before turning title to a downtown warehouse and a $5,000 certificate of deposit into a $73,000 loan. In late July B. L. Boyer, a mortician, accepted an unsecured loan from his bank of nearly $10,000 for himself and another worth nearly $5,000 for his mortuary. A couple days into the suspension period, U. Denman, whose measly five shares in the bank made him the smallest investor among the directors, took two unsecured loans for himself worth about a grand and another in partnership with Frank Miller, the manager who cooked the books of the bank's Ashland-Bancroft branch, for over $3,000.[47]

Four weeks into the withdrawal suspension period, Commercial Bank director Harold Fraser, one of the leading trial attorneys in the city, arranged loans for himself from his own bank totaling $35,500. As collateral for this cash, Fraser threw a pile of securities at the bank, much of which were worthless. There were hundreds of shares in near-bankrupt real estate companies such as the Second Mortgage Security Company and the City Hall Realty Company.[48] Fraser even had the audacity to include fifty shares of Commerce Guardian Bank stock, though that bank had seized up too. Moreover, by accepting bank stock in a frozen bank as collateral on its loan, the Commercial risked being saddled with the cost of double-liability payments if Fraser defaulted and the Commerce Guardian was liquidated. The only things of value in Fraser's stack of certificates were five hundred shares of Electric-Auto Lite, amounting to about four-sevenths of the value of the loan.[49] A year later Fraser would lead the defense team representing bankers accused of misappropriation, false reporting, and other crimes.

Two weeks after the Commercial Bank suspended withdrawals to the public, its president, W. H. Yeasting, enclosed a letter to "our family of stockholders" along with their dividend checks. In his letter Yeasting praised the hard work of the bank's staff and the fortitude and dedication of its officers in that frenzied bank run. So devoted to the institution were they that Yeasting wrote that he did not know "of a single officer or director, or stockholder either, that drew out of his savings account . . ." A month later Yeasting would execute a complicated series of maneuvers whereby the bank purchased government bonds and then swapped them with Yeasting for his cash deposits and trust interests, rescuing over $25,000 of his family's deposits.[50]

Loans were the preferred method of grabbing cash at the Commerce Guardian bank. That bank accumulated an additional $3,000,000 in "loans" during the sixty-day suspension period. According to one journalist, "The loans which were made to intimate friends of members of the banks were not registered in this bank as assets but were merely offset, in other words the loans were considered lost and covered up because the bank was holding their collateral in the form of nothing more than pass books and certificates of deposit . . ."[51]

However, when the end of the sixty-day period neared, insiders abandoned the more cumbersome method of taking loans in favor of a direct raid on the vault. Toledo Mortgage Company, one of the shell companies owned by Director Zale Reuben's family, successfully withdrew over

$5,000 from the Commerce Guardian bank on August 3. With less than a week to go until the bank opened withdrawals to the public, $200,000 was being taken out of the Commerce Guardian bank every day, the climax coming on the day before the bank was scheduled to reopen, when $275,929 was withdrawn.[52]

As the sixty-day suspension deadline approached, state officials searched for a way to avert another panic. By Saturday, August 15, the Commodore Perry Hotel was bursting at the seams with nervous bankers and scrambling accountants. The Ohio Department of Banks booked several floors of rooms to house the sixty examiners and assistants, virtually the entire department staff, brought to Toledo to clean up the mess. Upstairs suites were filled with bankers from New York, Chicago, Detroit, and Cleveland who had come to hear merger offers from the drowning Toledo banks. Other rooms were occupied by country bankers who had rushed to Toledo to salvage what they could of their reserve deposits held by the big banks.[53]

Again, the best hope of saving the banks lay in a massive merger of all the banks that had imposed withdrawal suspensions. Though pooling their assets would not straighten their balance sheets, a combined bank would give the appearance of strength and perhaps leverage more outside cash. To make the plan work, an infusion of fresh capital was needed to tide the new bank over long enough for confidence to be restored so that the money that smart insiders had squirreled away (by one estimate over fifteen million in cash had been stuffed into bank safe deposit boxes) would be redeposited by them. Over time, with new deposits and a rising proportion of performing loans, the bank's bad loans could be gradually charged off the books. The sum of twenty million was what the accountants and consultants concluded was needed to effect the plan, and a syndicate of out-of-state investors were ready to buy in to the merger provided they could be reassured that there was sufficient local support and leadership to see the merger through to success.

No transcripts or records remain of the Commodore Perry conference. No reporters were admitted into the conference rooms where men, some desperate, some angling for a bargain, some needing to be convinced, argued across a paper-strewn table. What was widely known was that the deal hinged on two men whose mutual enmity had grown over more than a decade of personal rivalry. No deal could go through without the cooperation of George Jones, the primary stockholder and president of the Ohio Bank, and Henry Thompson, the president of the Toledo Trust, the largest bank still operating in the city.

According to one report in *The Nation*, the bad blood between Jones and Thompson originated in Jones's success at locking Thompson out of the subdivision realty market in the 1920s and deepened when the two men fought for control of the Willys-Overland Company after John N. Willys decided to sell out and retire in 1929. In their struggle for ownership of the largest company in northwest Ohio, the two resorted to both legitimate and underhanded tactics. According to one account, "deals were made and unmade, reputations were blackened . . . [and] the wounds of that battle were never allowed to heal." Though Jones offered to purchase four and one-half million dollars of stock in the new combined bank and Thompson pledged one and one-half million, they could not easily agree on the details of the merger. *Business Week* reported that the big city bankers were dismayed to find "a feeling verging upon bitterness" between these two captains of Toledo industry and quietly pulled out of the deal because of this "lack of cooperative spirit."[54]

By eight o'clock in the evening, after the big city bankers pulled out, Superintendent of Banks Ira Fulton met with the heads of Toledo's largest banks and had no more hope to share.[55] With no merger prospects, no outside infusion of cash, and little cash on hand, all three of the four largest banks in the city, the Ohio Savings Bank, the Commerce Guardian Bank, and the Commercial Bank, were closed and turned over to Fulton's department for liquidation. After the meeting broke up, the city's authorities were alerted to expect trouble.

As soon as he was told that the big banks were not going to open the next morning, Mayor Jackson ordered a full mobilization of the city's forces. Police chief Louis Haas quickly recalled all the men on vacation and ordered every detective, cop, and desk jockey on the force, night and day shift, to be on duty in the morning. Mayor Jackson called Colonel Gilson Light, commander of the 148th Infantry Brigade of the Ohio National Guard, and discussed contingency plans for a military mobilization to protect the downtown banks from looters.[56]

Early on the morning of the sixtieth day, Monday, August 17, crowds began to form in the financial district. The police roped off streets in several directions, turning the once busiest corner of the downtown over to the jostling crowd. At the usual banking hour of nine o'clock those closest to the bank doors saw the notices hung on the lobby doors—the banks were not going to open. According to the Polish-language newspaper, "the news hit people like a lightning bolt from a clear sky."[57]

The police presence was heavy enough to keep the leaderless mass from rioting. Downtown there were three officers posted to every intersection. Every closed bank had more police stationed inside the building. The only protest recorded that day was one angry depositor who picked up a bottle and threw it through the glass door of a branch of the Ohio Bank located

in the heart of Polonia, at Central and Lagrange. Even the few "communist agitators" spotted in the crowd by an alert reporter were unusually quiet,
and simply talked among themselves and watched the throngs pass by.[58]

At the end of the block, Toledo Trust, the only large bank that hadn't
suspended withdrawals for the previous two months, opened unusually early.
Henry Thompson had heard the night before that his rivals had decided
not to open, and he recognized opportunity in the midst of disaster.
Thompson, long frustrated by his competitors who had locked him out of
the booming mortgage business, now saw his chance to build Toledo Trust
into the preeminent Toledo bank. All he needed to do was to hold out against
another day's storm of withdrawals and he would cement the confidence
of his depositors. Even more importantly, he knew that as the failed banks
were liquidated or consolidated by the state Banking Department, their remaining cash would be transferred to any remaining banks in the city and, in
spite of their overall insolvency, there were still millions of dollars at stake.[59]

Besides opening his bank early in a bold expression of confidence, Thompson
relied on the feds for backup. As the largest member bank of the Federal
Reserve in Toledo, run by a banker politically well connected to the
Hoover administration, Toledo Trust's plea for help rang the fire bells at
the Federal Reserve in Cleveland. That morning two armored cars roared
out from Cleveland loaded with $11 million in cash and sped down state
Highway 20. About a mile out of Fremont, in its haste the lead truck smashed
into a sedan driven by Mrs. H. Banaszak of Milwaukee, breaking her foot
and giving her passenger, Irene Czechorska, some nasty bruises on her head.
As a crowd of onlookers and rubberneckers gathered, some of the guards
brandished tommy guns while others began transferring heavy sacks of currency from the wrecked van to another.[60]

An hour later the line of people stretching out from the bank on
Summit Street parted to let the armored car through. The exhausted guards
began carrying the locked sacks to the vault but were stopped by a bank
manager who had come up with a novel idea. He directed the guards to
unload the stacks of bills in the tellers' cages, where all the people in line
could see the great hoard of dollars. The trick seemed to work, and as the
day progressed the line dwindled, some deciding at the last minute not to
withdraw their savings, and by four in the afternoon, an hour before closing, business was about back to normal. Toledo Trust would emerge from
this crisis as Toledo's largest and fastest growing bank.[61]

Though it seemed impossible to find any optimism in the week's events,
the Chamber of Commerce issued a public letter urging businessmen to
"keep a level-headed attitude" towards the city's banks. The letter tried to
strike a positive note, saying, "The basic factors that have built up Toledo

industries in the past are, of course, still here . . ." Perhaps more than a few wags noted that this letter was signed by the chairman of the Chamber's industrial committee, Adam R. Kuhlman, a man who was also a director of the failed Security-Home Bank.[62]

Others panicked, however. J. M. Wilson, the director of the Ohio Bank branch at Dorr and Collingwood, was nowhere to be found on August 15 when the Ohio Bank closed for good. Along with Wilson, a sum of ten grand or more was missing and it was rumored that he had fled to Canada with the loot.[63]

Toledo's bank crisis attracted the attention of the nation's largest press outlets. *Time* magazine called it "as grave a financial crisis as could possibly overtake a large U.S. industrial community." *Business Week* compared Toledo's situation to that summer's collapse of German banks, "Toledo, O., has been furnishing a clinic on how Americans behave under conditions they had been reading about in Germany."[64]

Toledo's banking collapse shook the financial markets of the entire nation. According to *Barron's* financial magazine, it was news of Toledo's closings that "disturb[ed] the delicate balance of a highly professional market." While the market had suffered from some "speculative uneasiness" after the Chicago banking problems earlier in the summer, such feelings "immediately became general" after Toledo's spectacular failures. Word of Toledo's bank collapse sparked a broad sell-off on Wall Street after a rare week of steady gains. That August one economist observed a "large upswing" in the amount of money in circulation as unnerved depositors chose the mattress over the vault, a circumstance he attributed to "banking difficulties in Toledo."[65]

With over $100 million frozen behind the locked doors, the city of Toledo was suddenly plunged backward in time, back to a barter economy. Thousands of businesses without any liquid assets and tens of thousands of citizens were left without the savings which they needed to get them through stretches of unemployment, sickness, and old age. Local industries, whose cash was tied up in the shuttered banks, were often unable to pay their suppliers or honor their contracts. The financial disruption was passed down the business food chain until businesses far away from Toledo felt the pinch.

Banks are legally required to deposit a large proportion of their cash reserves in other banks, and for convenience and by custom most maintain those reserves in neighboring banks. As a consequence, when the giant banks of Toledo plunged over the precipice, they dragged down with them all the eleven building and loan companies in Lucas County and over a dozen small town banks that held the savings of hard-pressed farmers for a hundred miles in every direction. The more than $100 million in frozen assets in the city's banks were now joined by nearly $50 million held by the city's building and loans. Though the impact of Toledo's bank disaster extended for hundreds of miles, people in Toledo were not always aware of these ripple effects. News of the death of an official of the recently closed National Bank of Defiance did not go far beyond the small town newspapers, especially as police ruled that his death, alone in his garage with his automobile running, was an accident.[66]

Among the smaller banks crushed by the weight of the toppled giants was the American Bank, an unusual bank founded by Toledo's labor unions in the early 1920s. Led by the Toledo's glass workers union, the American Bank gave Toledo's unions control over their own assets, and the dues of most of Toledo's working men and women were pooled there.

In the spring of 1931 at the same time that the larger banks in Toledo were voting large dividends, salaries, and loans to their officers, the union members, who viewed the American Bank not as a business proposition but as a tool of their labor movement, rushed to shore up its condition. To make up for the securities in the bank's portfolio that had sunk in value, the American Flint Glass Workers Union purchased them at their full book value of $157,830. The bank's president, William P. Clarke, reduced his salary to zero. When the large banks imposed sixty-day withdrawal restrictions in June, American followed suit, though few of its depositors clamored to withdraw their money. On August 15, the American needed to pay out only $1,667.36 to meet that day's requests.[67]

State banking law required the American Bank to deposit the bulk of its cash reserve in the larger banks in the city. American Bank possessed $143,944.70 in cash, more than 10 percent above the legal minimum, but could only keep $14,558.88 in its own vault. A larger sum, $18,227.64, sat in the basement of the Commercial Bank, and an even larger chunk, $77,864.59, was locked up in the Ohio Bank, only three blocks away but far beyond their reach. Another $21,990.62 was held by a correspondent bank in New York City. When the day of reckoning came for Toledo, the American Bank, one of the few banks in the city that had more cash on its balance sheet than necessary, closed simply because it couldn't get its own money out of the larger banks.

When the American Bank failed, nearly all of the unions in the city, who had loyally deposited all of their funds in the labor bank, were suddenly bankrupt. The president of the Stationary Firemen's Local wrote, "Our funds are all tied up in the American Bank but one consolation is that there are thousands in worse shape than we are." Among those worse off than the firemen were the glass workers, whose union had chartered the American bank. Toledo's glass workers had their wages garnished to pay the American Bank's double liability as, technically, they were the shareholders.[68]

With their treasuries frozen in a failed bank, Toledo's unions struggled to continue their routine activities but found themselves confronted by the extraordinary situation of employers who responded to the city's economic crisis by declaring huge wage cuts. The Bentley Construction Company led the way by announcing a cut in the wages of bricklayers working on a new wing of the Toledo Art Museum from $1.50 per hour to just $1 per hour. This was doubly galling as James Bentley, in addition to being a partner in Bentley Construction, was a director of the Commerce Guardian Bank. The editor of Toledo's labor weekly fumed that "The eminently respectable people who, through control of industry or business employ workers, take advantage of the misery of their workers at such a time as this to lower wages are a hundred fold more dangerous to society than all of the bootlegging and hi-jacking racketeers that can possibly evade the law . . ." But with unemployment spiraling upwards 25 percent between May and October, workers could do little except talk tough but toothlessly about waging "warfare" against wage-cutters that "will be started at once and carried on to the bitter end . . ." From 1930 to 1932 the average annual wage among building trades workers fell from $1,616 to $955.[69]

The bank failures struck a coup de grace to the city's budget. Beyond the $1,350,000 of city funds that were directly frozen, the city also suffered as tax collections plunged in the wake of the bank crash by 15 percent, or another $1,100,000. By badly tainting anything having to do with Toledo, the bank failures made it nearly impossible for the city to market its usual volume of municipal bonds, leaving some $1,846,062 of them unsold.[70]

While all departments of the city government felt the hit, the worst affected was the one most needed. The city's relief committee had just issued $289,000 in bonds to pay for the burgeoning food program that provided groceries to thousands of unemployed workers each week. Just as the schools opened in September the board announced that the school year would be cut by four weeks and the salaries of teachers were slashed by 10 percent and most of the city's school nurses were dismissed.[71]

While there are no complete and reliable unemployment statistics for the city in these years, there are many indicators of how deeply the job axe fell after the bank crash. Between May and October of 1931, between the days when the city's banks were still all open and after the long collapse of the summer was complete, the fifty-one leading industries in Toledo laid off 5,243 workers, or 26 percent of their total workforce. As it was estimated at the time that these fifty-one companies represented 40 percent of all workers, the total number of people who lost their jobs during the bank crisis is probably closer to twelve or thirteen thousand out of a total workforce of approximately sixty-four thousand. This estimate is close to the Ohio

Industrial Commission's figures that calculated overall employment dropping by 10,884 from 1930 to the end of 1931, the largest single decrease for any year of the 1930s. This is also near to the total of 14,800 men and women who were eventually employed by the Works Progress Administration in Toledo at the peak of that program in 1936, when it was the city's largest employer.[72]

As the grim city prepared for winter, the private desperation of many Toledo families broke into view. Families too proud to ask for help scavenged in the parks and open lots and gleaned the fields at the edge of the city. One man brought home a bag of mushrooms to feed his hungry family, and before morning four of them were dead and two others lay critically poisoned in the charity ward of the hospital. The squatter's camp expanded along the banks of the Maumee River, less than a quarter mile from shiny new downtown banks. Just as the snows began to fall, the police descended on the camp and forcibly drove off its residents, then set fire to the shanties that had just been strengthened against the cold. In October the annual charity fund drive for the relief of unemployment was cancelled because, as the city's welfare director admitted, it would be futile because likely donors "have been struck so hard by the bank failures we could expect no help from them." With but a few weeks to go before Christmas, the Salvation Army reported that its bell-ringers had brought in only eighty-six dollars, the lowest total ever in the Army's thirty-nine year history.[73]

Five weeks had passed since the banks' final collapse when President Herbert Hoover stepped from a train at Toledo's Union Depot and gave a short speech to a sparse crowd in front of the station. As he finished and walked back towards the platform, Hoover turned to one of the local politicians flanking him and asked, "How are banking conditions in Toledo now?" He walked back to his train silently after receiving his grim answer. Within a fortnight Hoover announced his first major initiative, the National Credit Corporation, a voluntary program whereby stronger banks would make more funds available to help weaker ones. Undoubtedly, Toledo's dire example played some part in spurring the administration to take the banking situation more seriously.[74]

CHAPTER FOUR

THE POLITICS OF LIQUIDATION

Almost a year to the day after the Security-Home Bank closed for good, the auctioneer began gaveling away a large collection of antique furniture, grandfather's clocks, safes, and paintings. From the look of things, it appeared that the lavish "palaces of finance" that were the most visible symbol of the excesses that had brought the city of Toledo to ruin were being dismantled. Though much of the "lavish surroundings" of the "richly furnished" bank lobbies and executive offices were being inventoried and placed on the block, the truly important equipment was kept intact. Those attending the auction could not bid on adding machines, file cabinets, postal meters, and such sundry accounting equipment because they were still needed and would remain in use for over a decade to come.[1]

It is commonly believed that when a bank closes, its activity ceases. In fact, a closed bank is a beehive of activity, and its closing merely marks a new phase in its business. Though a closed bank no longer accepts deposits, it still collects interest, deals in bonds, stocks, and real estate, and acts as a landlord, broker, and agent. In fact, the payroll of the banks under liquidation in Toledo actually increased when they closed, as there was much more "business" to be done than when they were open. Suddenly every outstanding loan had to be called in. Every last scrap of pledged collateral, which previously simply sat on the books, had to be revalued and much of it sold. Every skyscraper, warehouse, factory, bungalow, and lot mortgaged to the bank had to have its value assessed at the current market rate. Every stock, bond, and note had to be cashed in or sold. Within forty-eight hours of Toledo's banks closing their doors, the state Banking Department had assigned sixty examiners and accountants on a three-shift rotation to augment the existing staffs of the banks in beginning these tasks.[2]

A closed bank is not like any other business that, once closed, merely needs to sell off its inventory, machinery, and properties and repay its creditors with the proceeds. A bank is different from an ordinary business. A bank is merely a collection of promises, not a physical thing. Its value consists of promises to hold and return deposits and promises to repay loans. Its property is merely tokens and records of those promises.

Before a bank has anything to actually "liquidate," it must turn promises into things. But what happens when promises are broken? What happens to debtors who claim they haven't the ability to make good on their promises? Someone needs to be in charge of negotiating and compromising all the thousands of claims for and against the bank. Here is the great complication and political nature of bank closings. He who controls the process of negotiating these promises controls how the money pie is cut up. If he is honest and neutral, he can act to maximize the pressure on debtors and recover the greatest sums possible to distribute back to the common depositor. But if he is self-interested, corrupt, or pursuing some other hidden agenda, he can use his power for his own ends and favor friends, punish enemies, cover up old misdeeds, and even rob the bank a second time. For those well-placed and alert to their opportunities, the closing of a bank was a tremendous windfall.

The first legal skirmish fought in the wake of the banks' collapse was over just this question of who should be in charge of the process of liquidation. One enraged depositor filed suit in local court to place the Security-Home bank in the hands of a court-appointed receiver so as to safeguard its assets in the interest of all general depositors. Though the suit named the directors of the bank as defendants, it was the superintendent of banks and Ohio's attorney general's office who fought the action. Joining the State of Ohio alongside the names of the directors of the bank in their rejoinder, the assistant attorney general on the scene in Toledo proclaimed that he would "resist to the last ditch any effort at private receivership." Backing up his promise, the attorney general's office brought out its big guns, enlisting Brown and Sanger, the law firm of Republican bigwig Walter Folger Brown, to assist it in the case.[3]

In heading off the movement to appoint a private receiver, the attorney general's office was interested primarily in keeping control of the bank liquidation process within the confines of the Department of Banks. Were the process to take the route of a normal bankruptcy, all the essential investigations and decisions would be in the hands of a local judge and all the receiver's actions would be placed in the public record. Both the attorney general's office and the superintendent of banks wanted to be sure that they would have control over not only the disposition of the bank's assets, but also the auditing and gathering of information about the circumstances of the collapse itself. Since, as their subsequent actions would reveal, the state used its control of the process to prevent the release of embarrassing details to the public, preventing the appointment of an independent receiver was essentially the first step of what would become a long cover-up.[4]

In very short order the court ruled in the state's favor and allowed the Department of Banks to run the liquidation. Toledo's civil court, though ostensibly the watchdog of the liquidation process, seldom second-guessed the actions of local bank liquidators and rarely questioned the decisions of state bank officials. According to state law, it was the court's responsibility to approve each sale of securities or properties and to give the public at least ten days' notice before passing on the issue so as to guarantee that the interests of all the depositors were being protected. But soon after dismissing the motion demanding a private receiver, a county judge granted blanket permission to the deputy superintendents in charge of liquidation to sell securities and properties when and how they deemed most advantageous to the bank.[5]

From that point most of the liquidators' decisions were not recorded or reported as the law required. The selling of tens of millions of dollars of assets, the compromising of millions of dollars of loans, and the disposition of tens of thousands of depositors' savings took place in secrecy. Though this policy may have given the liquidators the flexibility to sell properties when the market was advantageous, it also introduced the possibility of sweetheart deals for insiders made well out of the public's view.

Ohio's Banking Department assigned its own employees to head the liquidation of Toledo's banks, a move which lent the appearance of neutral government supervision to the process, but actually employed the banks' existing officers and staff to run things. Though these official "deputy superintendents" in charge of liquidation were outside professionals with no vested interests in the banks they were appointed to supervise, they had no hand in the day-to-day operations of their banks. Deputy Superintendent in charge of the Security-Home Bank, J. C. Van Pelt, later recounted that when he was called in to oversee the bank he relied entirely on the existing Security-Home staff because "there was considerable confusion in the Department by reason of that closing and due to the lack of experienced persons." The scale of the bank, the height of the mountain of paper to be turned into cash, the seemingly endless extent of files to be opened and reassessed made it "physically impossible," Van Pelt explained, for him to actually examine or review any of the assets himself. So rather than actually get dirty in the paper himself, Van Pelt issued guidelines and policies and allowed the bank's own officers to assess and negotiate its properties. "I merely prescribed the form," Van Pelt confessed, "and directed others in the preparation." As a result, some of the most egregious frauds evident in the bank's accounts were easily buried by the very bank officers who had profited by them. It was seven years later before the first of hundreds of forged mortgages surfaced out of the muck.[6]

Even higher officials of the failed banks kept their posts and now drew their checks from Columbus as assistant liquidators. James W. Eckenrode, the long-time assistant treasurer at the Ohio Bank, was kept on as an assistant liquidator. Karl Rumpf, the assistant secretary of the Security-Home bank and former vice-president of the Dime Bank, kept his position running the mortgage loan department. This was a key position, as Rumpf had the power to negotiate compromises and offsets with those owing the bank money. One former bank official later testified under oath that Rumpf was quite accommodating to this fellow insider, forgiving much of his indebtedness.[7]

The most sensitive areas of the banks, their trust departments, remained in the hands of the same bank officers who had run them for years. According to another deputy superintendent, William M. Konzen, "in my experience in every instance [the] men [put] in charge have had previous trust experience and were in the various trust departments prior to the closing of the bank."[8] These were the most significant departments to have such a continuity of management because it was in the trust departments where evidence of the most clear-cut fraud and malfeasance was to be found.[9] These departments moved money-losing subdivisions off their books and shifted them into real estate trusts. These trusts would either "purchase" the bad paper from the bank, or, more commonly, they would pool the trash properties into one shell corporation that would issue shares back to the bank. The shares could then be carried at full value on the bank's ledger while the trust hid the true losses the bank had incurred. Konzen later noted that "Toledo banks I think are particularly noted for carrying real estate and various assets in trust securing commercial obligations," and estimated that between 500 and 1000 such agreements existed in all the failed banks whose total face value ran up to eight million dollars.[10] Trusts were also the place where fictional government bond accounts were set up for the convenience of insiders and high rollers to hide their money from the tax man. When the state allowed bankers to keep active managerial control over their trust departments, it effectively granted them the ability to conceal their most dangerous secrets.

Control of the banks' trust departments was also prized because trust funds were deemed privileged deposits by Ohio's courts. While general deposits would be paid back a small fraction at a time as loans and properties were sold, trust accounts were liquidated and returned individually. For those wealthy folks fortunate enough to have exclusively cash in their trust accounts, their deposits would be returned in full. Other individuals whose trust accounts held mainly securities would receive their notes and certificates back. Only in cases where the trust was owned in shares by investors would the trust's assets be sold or compromised for cash.

The privileged status of trust accounts provided yet another backdoor means for the well-connected to recover a higher proportion of their deposits than the average person. As soon as the banks closed, several trust department managers began shifting cash that was held in commercial accounts to their trust accounts. In less than three weeks after it closed, insiders at the Commerce Guardian Bank had transferred $317,595.75 from the general pool of deposits to trust accounts, to cite just one example from one bank that came to light.[11] Every dollar moved in this way cut into the sum that regular depositors would someday recover.

Next to bank managers themselves, the other critical area of staffing for the liquidation department was in the field of assessments. Before the banks could begin to negotiate the repayment of loans or the selling of batches of mortgages, the true value of these properties had to be determined. The banks' own estimates of their value were useless, as banks had routinely inflated values so as to balance their books or to maximize the leverage of the collateral of favored debtors. No one could ignore the fact that vacant lots which could not fetch $40 in 1929 were listed on the books of the Security-Home Bank for $1,500. Worthless bonds were carried at their face and the worth of shares in real estate trusts were anybody's guess.

Here again, the need for independent and unbiased appraisals was paramount, and the danger of self-interested distortions of actual values was high. Many businessmen owing loans to the bank hoped for a high assessment on their collateral so as to walk away clear or even earn a profit when the loan was cancelled. In the most direct way, overvalued assessments ate away at the body of cash to someday be returned to the thousands of ordinary depositors. Though the task of selecting neutral assessors may have been one of the most important tasks in the hands of the county courts, a party functionary like Judge Charles M. Milroy probably viewed the opportunity to hand-select seventy-five men for decently paying jobs in the midst of mass unemployment as a partisan bonus. Besides the usual political flunkies who now owed the party a favor come election time, Milroy selected a surprising number of Toledo bankers to assess Toledo bank assets. The first group of seventy-five assessors were charged with assessing the mortgage portfolio of the Ohio Bank. Eight of those selected were present or past bank directors, including Carl Mehring, a director of the Commercial Bank, Charles L. Medaris, director of the Commerce Guardian Bank, and John Huebner, who not only sat on the board of directors of the Security-Home Bank, but owed it $11,475 when it closed.[12] Judge Milroy then picked Claude Campbell to lead the seventy-five men in their work. Campbell was then a vice-president of the Ohio Bank.[13]

For the more potentially scandalous task of assessing the value of commercial and personal loans in the Ohio Bank, a committee of five assessors was selected by Judge Milroy. Three members of this committee were each directors of the other large busted banks, and a fourth was the assistant secretary of the Security-Home Bank. Likewise, eight of the nine appraisers appointed to do the same job for the Security-Home Bank were bank directors, including one, W. C. Carr, who was its sitting director! Just in case one of these nine men could not complete the work, the judge appointed Albert V. Foster, a vice-president of the Security-Home Bank, as an alternate. Whereas the lowly mortgage assessors earned a piece rate of $3.00 per assessment, those serving on these special committees were reported to have been given a flat salary of $1,000, paid for out of bank assets.[14]

Almost immediately after the assessors began, complaints were made of the slipshod way they did their work. The *Blade* reported the manner in which some of the appraisers went about their work:

"What is the size of this lot, about 30 by 40?" [asked an appraiser]
"No, it is about 50 feet by 60 feet," the appraisers would be told.
"What do you think the place is worth, about $3,000?" the appraisers would ask.
"Yes, I would think it would be worth about $3,000," the tenant would say.[15]

More than a few of the appraisers seem to have followed this sort of routine. Those who were paid by the assessment had an interest in finishing them as quickly as possible. Others had obvious potential conflicts of interest. No complete published figures of these assessments exist, though an indication of how they ended up can be glimpsed in one fragmentary document that was later publicly released. Two years after the assessors completed their work, their estimation of the value of the properties that the banks owned outright was published. This estimation did not include any of the properties or securities held as collateral, only properties held free and clear. Before they closed, the banks appraised their own real estate as being worth $13,438,363.94, a sum acknowledged to have been wildly inflated, while the court-appointed appraisers, after months of work, estimated their worth at $13,177,632.94. In the end, the court's assessments of bank-owned real estate varied from the bank's own stated values by less than 2 percent, a ludicrously small margin.[16]

The greatest power that bank liquidators wielded was the authority to grant offsets. An offset is a bargain whereby a person who owed a sum of money to the bank while also holding a deposit in the bank exchanges the one for the other. The deposit is offset by the loan and both deposit account and loan are cleared off the books. In theory this is a very rapid and low-cost means of liquidating bank assets, as there are no brokerage or lawyers fees or other costs associated in collecting on the loan. But in practice, offsets provide a means whereby some privileged depositors are able to reclaim their frozen deposits at the expense of all other depositors. This occurs because those depositors not owing loans to the bank will ultimately reclaim only a fraction of their money, and that only over many years of small dividends, while those with substantial loans are able to reclaim a larger percentage of their deposits immediately.

While the banks were in the process of collapsing, and while they were still under private control, anticipated offsets were employed by bank insiders, the so-called "smart money," as a devious means of closing out their deposit accounts. After they failed, even though their titular control passed to the state, because the state Banking Department retained the banks' old staff and officers to serve as their liquidators, offsets continued to be a means whereby the "smart money" could rescue their cash, and, in some cases, even take advantage of the bank's failure and turn a tidy profit.

Of all the aspects of the bank failures in Toledo, the least well documented is the scope and nature of the offsets that were granted to some depositors. The local courts did not require liquidators to file a complete report of these compromises that would have entered the public record, as required by state law. After the Toledo liquidations were declared to be complete, all the detailed records of these transactions were sent to the incinerator. All that the historical record contains are the total figures for each bank. But even in the aggregate, it is clear that the power of granting offsets was abused.

Immediately after the banks were closed and handed over to the state for liquidation, the market value of deposits lost over two-thirds of their value. The savvy and impartial liquidator would therefore never think of granting offsets on an equal dollar-for-dollar basis between loans and deposits. Instead, he should take a larger share of loans to deposits proportionate to the shrunken worth of the average depositor's bank book. Debtors who don't like the deal are free to repay their loans as previously contracted, but most, in the Depression environment of tight money, would likely take the deal rather than incur more debt or sell other assets at a loss to make good on the loan. Therefore, the leveraged power of offsets should show up in the bank's liquidation reports as each dollar of offsets retires a greater percentage of outstanding loans than do dollars taken in payment. For the Toledo banks, where frozen deposits were generally accepted as being worth about 30–35 cents on the dollar, when the total cash income of the liquidated bank is subtracted from the total of cancelled loans, the remainder should exceed offsets by a significant factor.[17] By the time of the first accounting of the progress of the liquidation of Toledo's four largest banks, offsetting deposits leveraged an average of just 6 percent additional loans. More puzzling, the bank whose deposits had arguably fallen to the lowest value, Security-Home Bank, managed the lowest leverage percentage of offsets in the city—just 4 percent additional value.[18]

A very few instances of the practice of offsetting made it into the press. In November of 1931, the Stollberg Hardware and Paint Company swapped a deposit of $10,633.11 for $10,232.48 that it owed to the bank, a margin in the bank's favor of just 3.8 percent.[19] More suspiciously, the liquidators of the Commerce Guardian Bank cancelled a $200,000 loan to the Detroit and Toledo Shore Line Railroad in exchange for a $500 savings account. This may have had something to do with the fact that Walter Lint Ross served as both vice-president of the Commerce Guardian bank and a director of the Detroit and Toledo Shore Line Railroad.[20]

In the case of only one bank are even aggregate numbers of offsets available. During an Ohio Senate investigation in November of 1934, the state's investigator reported that the Ohio Bank had made $1,332,272.09 by offsetting deposits. By the end of 1934, the Ohio Bank had offset a total of $10,886,034 worth of its deposits. Comparing these numbers indicates that on average, the bank allowed 89.1 percent of the worth of deposits in offsets.[21]

The scale of Toledo's offsets dwarfed anything seen in the state before. In just six months, $9,815,425 worth of deposits were offset in exchange for an unknown sum of credits. This amounted to 61 percent of all the offsets allowed among the twenty-seven largest bank failures in the state in that year. The volume of offsets granted by both the Ohio Bank and the Security-Home Bank were double the total of any other institution in Ohio.[22]

As the bank liquidations dragged on into the winter months of 1931–1932, the mechanism of offsets became a great potential source of profit for the banks' wealthiest debtors. One of the first public actions taken by the Department of Banks was to issue a certificate of claim to every depositor who brought his or her bank book into a bank to be verified. Though they were probably not meant to be so, these certificates were fungible, allowing for the sudden creation of a new and lucrative market in the buying and selling of bank deposits. Offering dimes on dollars, brokers would purchase the certificates of destitute depositors who were desperate to get whatever cash they could immediately. They would then turn around and sell them to those owing large loans to the banks. Those purchasing the certificates would then present them as offsets for their debts to the bank and free themselves from their obligations for a fraction of the face value of the loan. In this way the very bankers who had given themselves large last-minute loans and thereby hastened the bankruptcy of Toledo's banks found yet another way to profit from the financial destruction they had helped create.[23]

A burgeoning market for depositors' claim certificates provided a ready means for those with both money and debts to actually turn a profit from the bank failures. For example, one unnamed county official owed one of the banks $27,000 on a real estate investment. He purchased $45,000 in other depositors' claims for thirty cents on the dollar, costing him a total of $14,000. After he swapped these certificates with the bank wiping out his debt, he cleared $13,000, or a 48-percent profit.[24]

Banks accepted claim certificates in lieu of cash when selling off their assets as well. This allowed investors to gain twice by the liquidation—once by purchasing property at fire-sale prices and a second time by paying for them with discounted deposit certificates. Again, no records of these deals were kept by the banks or the local courts, but one newspaper did detail one such bargain that occurred in January of 1933. The Ohio Bank sold $20,000 in Allen County, Ohio, bonds to an unnamed investor for $23,188 in deposit certificates. At the time, the bonds sold for cash for about $9,600 and the certificates for about $7,000, netting either an immediate $2,600 profit or the potential for the bonds' ultimate redemption at face value sometime in the future.[25] David A. Yoder, the president of a large dairy company, arranged an offset that "caused much comment about town." Yoder happily exchanged $266,000 worth of claims that he had purchased from brokers at the going rate of around 35 cents on the dollar, swapping them at full face value to cancel out a loan of $266,000 he owed the Ohio Bank. The Ohio Bank was known to grant up to 100 percent credit to corporations it was itself heavily invested in, yet credited the city of Toledo only 38 percent in offsetting its loans and deposits.[26]

Sixteen loan companies and brokers competed to purchase depositors' claim certificates by the end of 1931. The field was fertile enough to encourage a half-dozen additional companies to enter the business over the next year. Among the claims brokers who engaged in this business were a number of Toledo's prominent bankers. Kenton D. Keilholtz, a director of the Security-Home Bank up to the day it went bust, was also first vice-president of the Financial Securities Corporation, a no-collateral personal loan operation. Pratt Tracy, who directed the Ohio Bank to ruin, was vice-president of the Toledo Citizens System Company, which offered "character loans to wage earners." Tracy's partners in this venture were Robert J. West, a director of the Security-Home Bank, and Harry W. Wachter, director of the Commercial Bank. Interestingly, Toledo Citizens System Company's president was none other than Mayor William T. Jackson, the political figurehead of Toledo's financial titans.[27]

The most prominent and aggressive of the newcomers to the claim certificate business was organized near the one-year anniversary of Toledo's
bank crisis by a number of former bank executives. Named the Toledo Guaranty
Corporation, it was run out of the old east side branch of the Ohio Bank
by O. D. Tiffany, former president of Peoples' Savings Bank, U. G.
Denman, former director of the Commercial Bank and former attorney general of Ohio, and W. R. Parmele. Unlike the other bank deposit brokers
who swapped claims for cash, Toledo Guaranty looked for greater profits
by offering depositors shares of the company's own stock or their own bonds
that sported an irresistibly high interest rate on their face.

Most of the money Guaranty received from its first sale of deposits went
into an extensive advertising campaign aimed at convincing those still holding onto their claims to deed them over the company: "WE CAN PUT
YOUR CLOSED BANK ACCOUNT TO WORK!," screamed one full
page ad, ". . . [we] have a unique, financially sound plan for putting closed
bank accounts to work."[28]

Though he was president of the firm, O. D. Tiffany began to smell a rat
when his manager, Parmele, refused to let him examine the books. Tiffany
quickly resigned, suspecting correctly that the company was little more than
a pyramid scheme.[29]

The large scale of the market in bank deposit certificates was not made
clear until years later. The state Department of Banks did not report figures for the amount of savings bought and sold in this way until 1935. By
then $13,672,087 worth of deposits had been sold to the four principal banks
being liquidated. This sum was equal to roughly 25 percent of the total amount
of deposits written off their books by that time. Statewide, only about 5
percent of deposits were retired in this way.[30]

By March of 1933 the proliferation of storefront brokers specializing in
deposit certificates reached the point where the attorney's general office felt
compelled to step in and warn all dealers that only those firms holding a license
to trade in securities were legal. Toledo's Better Business Association formed
a special committee to investigate the industry. Both the actions on the part
of the state and those of local businessmen were aimed not at restricting the
market in deposits but merely at eliminating the smaller fly-by-night brokers. The Better Business Association's committee included real estate
developer Zale Reuben, whose Reuben Securities Company was a prominent
dealer in deposits, and W. C. Carr, a banker who went directly from pilot-
ing the Security Home Bank onto the rocks to profiting from the trade in
bank deposits with the B. K. Blanchet Co.[31]

Unfortunately, the Better Business Association proved a poor watchdog.
During its tenure an apparently reputable firm, the Louis B. Storer Co.,

enticed Ada E. Wilson, a retired elementary school teacher, to swap her $2,200 in Security-Home Bank claims for some other stocks. Soon after taking her claims, Storer closed up his shop, and Mrs. Wilson never heard from him again until he stood before a county jury and was declared guilty of fraud.[32]

Judge James S. Martin, who was at that time one of the jurists supervising the liquidation of the banks, condemned the entire deposit certificate business, criticizing "those who prey upon depositors forced to sell accounts for the necessities of life," but he also understood that little could be done legally to curtail it. Instead, Martin suggested that the state Banking Department provide the public with a frank estimate of the likely pay-out of each bank and a calculation of the fair cash value of deposits at the current time. Such a step would help ensure that those selling their claims would not be exploited by businessmen willing to exploit their desperation. But, Martin concluded that the state Banking Department would never provide the public with the real figures because it would be just too embarrassing.[33]

Apparently Judge Martin's suspicions about the Department of Banking were correct. Throughout the process of liquidation the Banking Department jiggered the numbers released publicly so as to make it appear that the banks were repaying a greater proportion of their deposits than they actually were. It was not until 1935 that the department revealed the sum of deposit certificates that had been sold to the banks, though the practice had gone on since the early days of the liquidation in 1931. Before 1935, the department did not report the total shrinkage or loss of resources as a result of liquidation, an important indicator of the likely returns to depositors. Most significantly, the Department of Banking reported a total figure for the percentage of deposits returned to depositors that did not reflect the fact that different classes of depositors received different rates of return.

For example, in 1935 the department boasted that it had returned over 70 percent of its $38,880,329 in deposits to the depositors of the Ohio Bank. In calculating this sum, the department lumped together the value of offsets, preferred claims, the deposits of other banks, deposit certificates surrendered, and public funds. Some time after the Ohio Bank closed, all the money that was deposited as a reserve from other banks, $1,504,445, was returned in full. All the money that was deposited on behalf of trust funds, $2,087,324, was also fully repaid. Then there was another $2,004,078 of public funds on deposit, mostly taxes, that was, after some litigation, counted as a preferred deposit and returned to various town, county, and city governments. A total of some $3,832,233 worth of deposits were offset by loans, and a whopping $7,053,801 worth of deposits were sold to the bank by people other than those who originally held them. That left less than a 50 percent dividend for the common depositor.

What all these numbers add up to was a class system at work in the liquidation. Roughly (and these calculations must be rough, given the destruction of more detailed bank records), 10 percent of deposits, claimed as protected trust funds but never actually invested in securities, were returned at nearly their full value. Another 10 percent was offset for loans at a rate more advantageous than that found in the open market for deposit certificates and in many cases close to par. About 20 percent of deposits were sacrificed to brokers at a severe discount. The remaining 60 percent of deposits realized below 50 percent of their value. Rates in each category differed for each bank, though each had the same stratification of classes who benefited unequally in the liquidation.[34]

While insiders clearly had an advantage in the course of liquidation and were able to liberate a higher percentage of their deposits from the closed banks than the average person, they also bore one unique legal burden that was not easily shaken. Every shareholder in a bank was obligated to pay an amount equal to his or her investment into the bank when it failed. This provision, commonly known as "double liability," was the most firmly established banking law in Ohio, having been written into the state's constitution of 1851. For many decades the double liability provision served as the only legal safeguard for the good conduct of bankers.[35] When Ohio legislated more specific regulations for corporations and banks, the constitutional provision of 1851 remained primary and could not be modified or limited without constitutional amendment. The double liability law was reaffirmed immediately after the Toledo bank crash by the Supreme Court of Ohio, which ordered that those owing banks a double liability payment could not have them set-off equally by their own deposits "except so far as dividends may be paid thereon."[36] In other words, there was no quick or privileged way for bankers to shed their liability, so they simply didn't pay them.

Three years after the collapse, only slightly more than half of bank shareholders who had been ordered to pay their liability had done so. Some, like a group of investors owing nearly a half million dollars to three of the closed banks, legally delayed payment for two years by contesting the right of the superintendent of banks to be the state's collector.[37] Others simply ignored their bills. Interestingly, the shareholders who had ponied up the most cash, about 10 percent more than the average, were those whose bank was under the most legal attack, the Security-Home. The Ohio Bank's shareholders were the most delinquent, probably because they had watered their stock more than most in the years before the crisis.

A peek underneath the totals reveals a predictable trend: the most responsible shareholders owned the fewest number of shares. The numbers are only available for the Commercial Bank, the smallest of the four big failures, but there is no reason to believe these trends were not true at the other banks as well. Only 39 percent of shareholders whose shareholdings amounted to more than $1,000 had paid their debts, while exactly half of those whose shares totaled less than $1,000 had done so. The three investors who were the principal owners of the bank, who held nearly a third of all shares in the bank, or a total of $205,300, or more than three times the holdings of all investors owning less than $1,000, had together paid off only 10 percent, or $21,178.24, of their liability.

Though the state Banking Department eventually won judgments against the largest recalcitrant shareholders, the complexity of their financial and business dealings provided many places for them to hide their money and stave off payment. F. E. Stewart, former vice-president of the Commercial Bank, had succeeded in paying only $45.55 of his $64,150 stock liability by the time he was dragged into Judge John McCabe's court in January of 1934. Stewart was quizzed by a private attorney, Nolan Boggs, hired to recover as much money as he could by the state on a commission basis. Though he didn't admit this to the judge, Boggs himself had once been a shareholder of the Commercial Bank; however, unlike Stewart, he had paid his own liability of $800 in full. Boggs was after several hundred shares of Kennecott Copper and Packard Motors that Stewart had squirreled away in a safe deposit box. Being a sharp banker, Stewart knew that trust funds were protected from being seized and claimed that he had privately pledged the stock to the support of his ninety-year-old, blind mother. Boggs then went after $2,800 in cash that Stewart then claimed was actually an inheritance given to his wife. Finally, Boggs zeroed in on a stash of government bonds, worth in the neighborhood of $7,880. Stewart claimed that these belonged to his wife and that she had loaned them to him in exchange for 50 shares of Commercial Bank stock as collateral. The idea that Stewart needed to secure a loan from his wife with collateral, if true, might have revealed a certain shakiness to their marriage. What is more strange is that Stewart did so just a few weeks before the Commercial closed, a tacit admission that he had swindled his wife. In the end Stewart's testimony didn't convince the judge, and most of the securities were awarded to the liquidators and Boggs made a fat fee which was also paid out of the Commercial Bank's assets, scratching a little bit more from the withering pile left to divide up among the depositors.[38]

Besides simply not paying, there was only one way for a shareholder to avoid paying the face value of their shares back to a failed bank. If the bank could be reopened or reorganized, double liability might be waived by the superintendent of banks. For this reason, even banks that had been thoroughly looted by their owners attempted to reopen. However, like every other question involved in bank liquidation, the decision of which banks would reopen and which would be dissolved lay not in the public realm, but was decided behind the scenes among a very small group of players. This select group of men did not base their decisions on considerations of public necessity or convenience but made the process a continuation of the competitive struggles for financial control of the city that had existed before the banks closed.

The only way a bank in as much trouble as Toledo's closed banks could possibly reopen was to secure some sort of outside loan guarantees and a quick infusion of cash. Only one of Toledo's four big closed banks, the Commerce Guardian bank, received such aid. It was the only one of the four that was a member of the Federal Reserve System, giving it easier access to federal loans than any other. The others looked to the Reconstruction Finance Corporation for help.

The RFC had been created late in Hoover's administration to provide loan guarantees to corporations and banks that were on the verge of sinking beneath the Depression's waves. Congress allocated $500 million of seed money to establish the RFC's loan fund and gave the quasi-public corporation permission to issue its own bonds worth up to three times that. Unwilling to make it a permanent wing of government, Congress also placed a one-year sunset provision into the bill, ensuring its demise after one year unless renewed by order of the president.[39]

From the start, President Hoover, who was uncomfortable with the very concept of the RFC, organized its structure so as to decentralize its functions out of Washington. Rather than having Washington bureaucrats reviewing applications for loans, the initial screening process devolved to thirty-three local agencies peppered throughout the nation. These review committees were staffed not by disinterested government professionals, but by local bankers. Such an organizational tree certainly avoided Hoover's fears of creating a mushrooming bureaucracy that would lord over private citizens from a distant capital city, but they allowed local rivalries, jealousies, and competitive pressures to enter the process of loan approval from the very start.

Such parochial considerations came into play when a group of activists attempted to secure federal aid to reopen the Ohio Bank. Composed of a number of small shareholders in the Ohio Bank along with a few others who had no direct financial stake themselves, the Ohio Bank Depositors Committee was initially optimistic that federal loans would be steered their way. They had good cause: their local party boss, Walter Folger Brown, was a member of Hoover's cabinet and one of the president's most trusted political advisors; a local man, W. W. Knight, was a member of the Federal Reserve Board for the region; Henry Thompson, president of the Toledo Trust bank, was a member of the RFC loan committee for the Cleveland district that included Toledo; and, finally, when President Hoover visited Toledo in September of 1931, he promised aid for the city. In less than a year of effort, the Ohio Bank committee had received a warm endorsement of their plan for reorganization from Governor George White and had begun collecting the thousands of consent forms from depositors pledging their deposits to the new venture.

In spite of, or perhaps because of, Toledo's political muscle in the state and even the nation, the Ohio Bank reorganization plan began encountering unexplained obstacles. Just before Christmas of 1932, one depositor, Eugene Rheinfrank, sued the state Department of Banking, asking a judge to order it to distribute an immediate dividend to the Ohio Bank's creditors. Superintendent of Banks Fulton then indicated his support for plans to reorganize the bank rather than to pay out more of its cash immediately, writing to the reorganization committee that were a dividend issued, there would be no chance of the bank ever reopening. But just three days later, Fulton reversed himself, saying that the existing plan was insufficient and that more cash would have to be infused into the bank before it could be restarted.

The historical record is disputed as to what happened in those three days to change Superintendent Fulton's mind. All sides admit that during one of those days, Fulton had a meeting with three important Toledo industrialists, Frank Collins, W. E. Levis, and E. J. Marshall, at the Deshler Hotel in Columbus. This meeting aroused suspicions among those pushing for the Ohio Bank's reopening because Collins and Levis were in charge of the reorganization of the Commerce Guardian Bank and Marshall was one of its former directors. The leader of the Ohio Bank's reorganization effort claimed that Collins returned to Toledo and openly boasted that the Ohio would never reopen. Fulton denied to an Ohio Senate investigating committee that he had discussed the Ohio Bank issue at the Deshler meeting, though his attorney later "revised" his statement for the record, admitting that Fulton had been informed that Collins and Levis opposed the Ohio Bank's reopening, but not by them directly (leaving open the question of whether Marshall lobbied against it on their behalf). Walter Baertschi, leader of the Ohio Bank depositors association that was spearheading the Ohio's reorganization drive, later charged that Collins and Levis had even threatened him.[40] Though there is not enough evidence to prove that the

Commerce Guardian faction was pulling strings to block the Ohio Bank's reopening, it is certain that these men would have had an interest in limiting the growth of competition to their fledgling bank.

Beyond the charges flung at the Commerce Guardian group, there was other evidence that someone was actively working to keep the Ohio Bank closed. Testifying before the Ohio Senate Banking Committee, Superintendent Fulton described how the Reconstruction Finance Corporation in Washington stonewalled his efforts to aid the Ohio Bank's opening. In spite of his lobbying, Fulton said, the RFC would only agree to give a loan to help liquidate the bank, not one to help it open. Fulton's attorney added that the depositors committee's complaint was "with the RFC. They evidently told [them] one thing and the department [of banks] another."[41]

If there was a cabal of Toledo financiers working to block the reopening of the Ohio Bank, what could have been their motive? Walter Baertschi had one theory: "We have felt right along that we could not open because the opening would be a loss by withdrawal of four million dollars of Ohio funds to the Toledo Trust Co. and the withdrawal of other monies by loyal depositors of the Ohio who would rush to return to that bank."[42] One outspoken editor of a small-circulation weekly newspaper also saw the evidence as pointing to a Toledo Trust conspiracy:

> The facts are these: Walter F. Brown, former Postmaster general, is a member of the Federal Reserve Board of this district; he is also director of the Toledo Trust Co. W. W. Knight, vice-president of a big hardware company, is a member of the Federal Reserve Board; he is also a director of the Toledo Trust Co. Henry L. Thompson, president of a big hardware concern, is also president of the Toledo Trust Co. and a member of the R.F.C. in Cleveland.
>
> You get the point? All three of them are naturally interested in the welfare of the Toledo Trust Co. . . . . These three men, with their financial associates, undoubtedly have great power and influence with the recommendations of the R.F.C.[43]

There is no doubt that Toledo Trust viewed the collapse of the other banks as its one great chance to gain unrivaled supremacy in what had long been a hotly competitive financial market. On August 20, 1931, less than a week after the bank closings, Superintendent Fulton ordered that all the cash and securities in all the shuttered banks be transferred to the Toledo Trust Bank, immediately increasing Toledo Trust's deposits by millions of dollars. The very next day, Toledo Trust opened its first branch bank, in an old location of its nemesis, the Security-Home Bank, on Starr Avenue.[44] The following day it opened the second branch bank in its history, at another Security-Home building on the busy commercial intersection of Monroe and Detroit. By the end of the week, Henry Thompson gleefully reported that his bank's deposits were up four million since the bank crisis began. By the end of the year, with all the added business, increased deposits, and expanded branches, Toledo Trust was forced to expand its payroll from 118 employees to 201.[45]

Interestingly, the first RFC loan to reach Toledo benefited a handful of directors of Toledo Trust. In early 1934, a $700,000 loan was approved to assist in the reorganization of the First National Bank, a small federal bank that capsized in the fall of 1931. As part of its reopening, the board room of First National was emptied out and a new slate of directors was put in place. Both vice-presidents, Rathbun Fuller and George R. Ford, were directors of Toledo Trust. Additionally, Fuller also served as Toledo Trust's corporate attorney. One other longtime director of Toledo Trust, Gordon Mather, took a chair with the First National's board. On the surface of things, this RFC loan seemed not only to assist in the reopening of a rival bank, but to engineer its quiet takeover by Toledo Trust interests.[46]

There can be no doubt that Henry Thompson and the other men deeply invested in the Toledo Trust were well positioned politically to have blocked federal loans to the Ohio Bank. Whether he or his associates did so in fact will for now have to remain an unanswered question. Thompson's group were not the only powerful players who might have worked to block the reopening of Toledo's other closed banks. Backers of the Commerce Guardian reopening, men who stood to lose their exemption from payment of their double liability if their project failed, were also alleged to have meddled in the process. If either of these well-connected and influential financial factions had intervened in the Ohio's bid to reopen, their political weight would have easily crushed that of the Ohio's reorganization committee, which was composed of men of modest means who had no chits to be called in with political parties and whose anger exerted no fear among policymakers. The few men associated with the Ohio Bank who could call in favors, who could command consideration of their wishes, and whose wrath carried consequences for anyone seeking office or appointment, such as the Ohio's president George Jones and his business partner, Willard Webb, reportedly had no interest in the bank's reopening once they had paid their liability assessments. Eventually they found it easier to simply buy a stake in a new bank, Citizens Savings, that was organized in the spring of 1932. In the end the Ohio Bank remained closed and was not finally liquidated completely until 1943.

On average, the liquidation of Toledo's closed banks stretched over more than a decade, and when it concluded it remained unclear just how much the average depositor was repaid. The liquidation of Security-Home Bank was officially declared complete two weeks after the bombing of Pearl Harbor. The state Banking Department triumphantly reported that nearly three-quarters of all the deposits in the bank had been repaid (73.5 percent). This number, however, seems to have been purposely inflated. One indication of this is that the total amount of deposits used as the denominator in figuring out this percentage was 25 percent smaller than that which the Department of Banking reported when the bank closed in 1931. By underreporting the total deposits and overreporting the dividends paid out, state officials were able to dress up the bleak record of their liquidation efforts in Toledo. When the figures are straightened out, the Security-Home depositors who held onto their claims until the bitter end actually recovered closer to 60 percent of their money.[47]

Of course, losses are computed not only in volume but in time, and Toledo's bank liquidation took longer than any other in the state. The longer it takes for money to be recovered, the more is lost in the unearned utility of that money. The time in which those frozen deposits could have been used to purchase tools, to open a small business, to finance an education, or to make investments, could never be recovered. Even had the money never been touched, but simply left in a bank account, it would have gradually accumulated interest and grown. Of the last 5 banks to be liquidated out of the 211 banks closed in Ohio during the Great Depression, 3 were located in Toledo. Liquidation in Toledo did not officially come to an end until the spring of 1943, when the Commerce Guardian and the Ohio banks mailed their last dividends to depositors.[48] Toledo's long span of liquidation was the financial equivalent of an investment losing all its principal. Had the banks stayed open and people's money simply sat in an account at an interest rate of 4.5 percent, compounding interest would have rewarded them with a 60 percent increase over their principal by 1941, about the same amount as the total recovered by general depositors of the Security-Home bank.

In the end, even using the Banking Department's optimistic numbers, $5,780,806 in Security-Home deposits alone were never repaid, a sum alone equal to 22.4 percent of the losses across all 158 banks that had been liquidated in Ohio during the decade of the 1930s. Even without the addition of the losses at the three other big banks to the Security-Home's total, Toledo's losses dwarfed those of any other city in the state.

While the size of Toledo's losses are explainable given the rottenness of the bank's foundations before they failed and the scale of last-minute insider loans and withdrawals, the incredible duration of the liquidation in the city is not. To some degree, the time it took to sell off the assets of banks was proportionate to their size. The mammoth state banks in Toledo simply had so many tens of thousands of lots, mortgages, securities, and buildings that to have dumped them all on the market at one time would have been impossible. But other large liquidations didn't take quite as long. The Union Trust Company of Dayton, a bank about the same size as Toledo's Commerce Guardian Bank, failed a month after the banks in Toledo but was fully dissolved nearly three years ahead of Toledo's first bank to wrap up its business.[49] One reason for the difference may have been that some people had an interest in prolonging the business of wrapping up the banks' affairs.

Each year Toledo's failed banks spent hundreds of thousands of dollars to pay for their own dismemberment. Some of this money went to cover the salaries of the hundreds of clerks, accountants, and secretaries retained by the banks. Other bills, such as for utilities, bank office mortgages, and administrative supplies, also had to be paid out of bank earnings and assets. But one of the biggest expenses was the legal costs incurred in both suing intransigent debtors and in fending off depositor and shareholder lawsuits. For a few well-placed legal firms in Toledo, the bank disaster was a huge source of revenue.

By one conservative estimate, about one hundred thousand dollars was paid to local law firms to handle various bank suits on behalf of the state during the first two years after the bank's failure. Most of this money poured into the coffers of a handful of politically connected law firms at the discretion of the liquidation supervisors and the state's Republican attorney general, Gilbert Bettman.[50] With no public review of these appointments or their costs, they proved a great source of patronage and political favoritism. The bulk of the legal contracts went to the firm of Brown and Sanger, whose senior partner, Walter Folger Brown, still reigned as state GOP boss. Brown's first lieutenant, N. J. Walinski, and the important chairman of the Lucas County Republican Central Committee, Nolan Boggs, also landed a share of fees. Smaller portions of the legal pie went to Lehr Fess, son of Republican Senator Fess, and to Duffey, Bryce and Duffey, the firm of Congressman Duffey. The attorney general's office was aware that this was an uneconomical method of liquidation, for in the days immediately following the collapse of the banks its spokesman was quoted as saying that the AG's office would "do everything possible to handle the legal work so that there would be no expense to depositors."[51]

With politics behind the commissioning of lawyers and no public accountability of their activities (as legal costs were not reported separately from all the other costs of liquidation) legal fees spiraled upwards. By the

second year of liquidation, even the attorney general's office began to complain that fees given to Toledo lawyers were inflated by half.[52] Bank suits
proved such a steady source of income that in many cases lawyers initiated
suits and won judgments on behalf of bank liquidators who would not bother
to actually collect on them.[53] In 1935, after depositors' groups denounced
the filing of phony cases against bankrupt debtors by politically appointed
law firms, incoming Democratic governor Martin Davey announced he was
appointing a special investigator to look into the charges. Davey, eager to
pounce on an issue that could embarrass the previous administration, said,
"In Toledo, I am told, one lawyer was paid $60,000 from the assets of a sin-
gle closed bank. In numerous other cases money which should have been
distributed to distressed depositors was dissipated in attorney's fees." In some
cases, Davey said, this practice "took on the aspects of a regular racket."[54]

Little came of the Davey investigation, and apparently little changed in
the legal bonanza of liquidation in Toledo. Five years later the same depositor activists were still denouncing the legal farming of banks for legal fees,
especially the practice of retaining lawyers who themselves owed large sums
of money to the banks. Judge John S. Pratt was paid a retainer by the Ohio
Bank of $500 per month although he owed the Ohio Bank $10,929.56. None
of Pratt's salary was credited to his debt.[55] This was particularly ironic as
it was reported that in the early months of the banks' liquidation a number of law firms offered their services to the state Banking Department, asking that their fees be applied to debts they owed the closed banks. These
offers were turned down.[56]

Because the Ohio Banking Department did not release itemized reports
of the expenses incurred in closing the banks in Toledo, it is impossible to
estimate the total amount overspent on legal expenses. However, the overall cost of liquidation in Toledo was so much higher than that in the state
as a whole that these expenses must have been quite large. By 1940, the
cost of liquidation of the four largest Toledo banks was $4,123,573. This
amounted to 6 percent of total deposit claims at these banks, a total twice
as large as the statewide average of 3 percent. Though Toledo accounted
for about one-tenth of all the deposits frozen in bank failures during the
decade of the 1930s, it used one-fifth of the total money spent to clean up
the mess.[57]

The task of closing Toledo's banks took more than a decade and millions
of dollars. Like the bank failures themselves, the bank liquidations were characterized by insider favoritism, class privilege, and political patronage. Though
by 1941 the banks may have eventually paid out nearly as much money to
their creditors as they froze in 1931, much of it was funneled upwards to
the already wealthy and powerful while most humble depositors only ever

recovered a small fraction of their savings. For some, the liquidation of Toledo's banks proved a boon rather than a bust. For most, the secrecy and unfairness that surrounded the process of liquidation merely confirmed all their worst assumptions about the lack of democracy in their community. While Toledo's elites pecked at its financial corpses, masses of everyday depositors organized to demand justice.

CHAPTER FIVE

PROSECUTIONS AND PROTESTS

Toledo's banking collapse created a social crisis that went far beyond its shattering impact on the region's economy. Toledo's economic losses could be calculated with a fair degree of precision, and over time, perhaps a long time, the lost capital would be recovered and reaccumulated. Fundamentally, the political and economic systems that had led to this disaster still functioned, though at a much lower level of activity and profitability (even the bank failures themselves proved sources of profit to a lucky few), and Toledo's elites still held a near monopoly of power in the city. As usual, most of the pain and cost of the disaster would be handed down the social ladder. The greatest danger posed by the bank failures was their impact on the consciousness of the public.

Overnight many of the powerful and reassuring symbols of capitalism were upended. When the great ornate doors that once symbolized the strength, durability, and safety of the banks were barred and guarded against the public they suddenly symbolized the privileges of wealth and the inequality of the law. The vain bank towers that were hailed as symbols of growth and prosperity now loomed as monuments to excess and folly. Even the humble bank book, once an icon of responsibility and planning for the future, became a token of failure.

Along with shifting the meaning of the everyday symbols of growth, prosperity, and security, the bank crisis undermined the authority of ruling elites. The figure of the banker, though eyed suspiciously for their covert power by the poor, had long benefited from an aura of cautious responsibility that legitimized their authority. When bankers died they were always eulogized in the press as careful stewards and builders of the city. Though this conservative banker identity served well to shield the financial elite from popular assaults on their privileges, it was immediately compromised by the inarguable fact of a bank closing. Banks that failed could not have been conservatively and responsibly run. Exposed without the benefit of their armor of probity, bankers became "banksters"—the lawless racketeering of

111

gangsters combined with the power and privilege of bankers.[1] The leader of the depositors protest movement struck this note at the first mass rally in September 1931, saying, "bank racketeering seems to be in vogue in Toledo."[2] After Toledo suffered from a gang turf war in 1933 when the Detroit "Purple Gang" muscled in to the Toledo mob's turf, many writers found Toledo's rackets an apt metaphor for Toledo's bankers. Edward Steinbeck wrote the editor of the *News-Bee* saying the Purple Gang were a "small-fry" compared to the "higher brackets, the closed bank racket."[3] One bankers' lawyer complained that "every man who has ever worked for a bank is [now] called a gangster."[4]

When Toledo's banks failed in the summer of 1931 the hidden dynamics of wealth and power in the city slowly came to light. While Toledo's banks operated normally the most important decisions determining the functioning of the city took place privately in board rooms beyond the scrutiny of the press and without public record. But after the banks failed, their records were placed in the hands of the state and were in jeopardy of being revealed by civil suits and overeager reporters. Rumors of banker misdeeds had swirled around town for months and with the final act of their closing began to take form as public allegations. But rumors feed on a lack of specifics. When state officials showed no interest in exposing any of the deals and actions that had brought the banks down, they fueled speculation that there was much to hide. When bankers themselves waited more than a month to issue a public statement, they confirmed the public's suspicion that they were guilty. The longer it took for any details of what had happened to the banks to emerge, the deeper was the shared sense that crimes had been committed.

Toledo's government and courts were restrained from investigating credible charges of bank fraud and malfeasance by their political entanglements with the bankers themselves. The real political muscle of Toledo's bankers was evident in the midst of their greatest crisis. A hotly contested mayoral primary was fought out over the summer of 1931 while the Security-Home Bank was in the midst of liquidation and three of the four largest banks in the city had suspended withdrawals. The election pitted incumbent Mayor Jackson against Addison Q. Thatcher, who was just the sort of eccentric insurgent that Toledo's political currents had a habit of throwing up from time to time, along with the usual number of minor candidates.

The grandson of a local judge and the son of the city engineer, Thatcher was born into Toledo's Republican machine and was a natural politician. The Thatchers were among Toledo's pioneer families, though their century in Toledo was less than half their time in America. Before moving west, the Thatcher clan were Massachusetts pilgrims, whose most famous member was Thomas Thatcher, the first pastor of Boston's South Church.

In between, both Thatcher's grandfather and father wore union blue in the War Between the States. Thatcher's political pedigree may have destined him for office, but his own upbringing better prepared him for the rocky road of Toledo political campaigns. When he was but twenty, his father died and left him and his brother in charge of the family marine engineering business. Working around the docks acquainted him with Toledo's underclass, the large transient population of men who floated from working the harbor to working the railroads and other odd jobs. It was a muscular world of flop houses, cheap saloons, petty gangs, communal ethics, straw bosses, blood sports, honor, loyalty, and ethnic rivalries. In 1919, Thatcher emerged as the foremost representative of this world by organizing a heavyweight boxing championship between Jesse Willard and Jack Dempsey fought in a makeshift stadium overlooking the river's piers. Every Christmas throughout the 1920s, Thatcher personally hosted a massive "no questions asked" dinner for the city's poor which he turned into a twice-daily feed when unemployment worsened in 1930. When he launched his political career, running for county commissioner in 1930, this tall, sharp-featured man with a hole in his right ear from a bullet he took subduing a gun-wielding man back in 1917 was seen as the champion of the man in the street.[5]

Perhaps because he did not have to worry about the support of the underworld, Thatcher could afford to run for mayor on an anti-vice and corruption campaign. He attacked William T. Jackson for continuing the spoils system and defending gamblers and bootleggers and ran on the slogan of "destroying the political machine." Jackson, a man who viewed himself as the mayor who swept the old Brown machine out of office, weakly defended himself by saying that he had fired "only 75 men" because they opposed him politically, while his predecessor, Mayor Brough, had turned out over a thousand of his own opponents.[6] Interestingly, though the biggest crisis facing the city was the bank disaster that had frozen several millions of the city's dollars and impaired its ability to collect future taxes as long as its citizens couldn't draw on their own accounts, neither Thatcher nor Jackson made an issue of the bank failures in their campaigns.

Jackson's silence on the bank issue was most understandable as he had long been the banker's voice in the city. Besides the numerous bankers and realtors that Jackson had sitting in his cabinet, Jackson's current campaign treasurer was John W. Koehrman, a director of the Security-Home Bank. The chairman of the city's Republican Central Committee was Nolan Boggs, a director of the American Bank. Five of Jackson's nine largest contributors were bank directors, while a sixth was a large real estate developer.[7]

Though Jackson was obviously the candidate of Toledo's captains of finance, his opponent could not easily attack him for this without the danger of a political ricochet. Thatcher's choice of friends also exposed him to charges of banker influence. Thatcher's campaign chairman was Percy Jones, the son of Toledo's famous progressive mayor, Samuel "Golden Rule" Jones, but also well known as a director of the Commerce Guardian Bank. One of his largest contributors was W. H. Haskell, who was also a director of the Commerce Guardian Bank. More potentially damaging, as well as being an entanglement he could not easily break, Addison Thatcher's own brother-in-law was Stacy McNary, the president of the Security-Home Bank.[8]

Toledo's bank collapse took place three days after the mayoral primary narrowed the field to Thatcher and Jackson. Four days after the bank closings, local municipal judge Ira R. Cole, a Democratic candidate for mayor in the just-concluded primary who polled less than 10 percent of the vote, attempted to restart his political career by getting out in front on the bank issue. Cole was the only Democratic judge in the county and also the one with the most flamboyant record. He had a troubled youth and was caught in the act of robbery and sentenced to the state pen, but somehow afterward avoided jail when his sentence was probated. This may have had something to do with the coming of the Great War, Cole distinguishing himself in service and coming home a hero among his friends in the American Legion. Since the war, Cole had built his career and reputation on his outspoken independence in a city run by bosses and lackeys.[9] So, it was probably in keeping with his character when Cole wrote a public letter to the county prosecutor, Carl Christensen, urging him to empanel a special grand jury to investigate the circumstances surrounding the closing of the banks. Though Cole gave a copy of his letter to all the three daily newspapers, none published it in full and only the Toledo *Times* even mentioned it, when it referred to "Judge Ira R. Cole urging a grand jury investigation of the recent closing of the five Toledo banks."[10] Toledo's Polish readers learned from the weekly *Ameryka-Echo* that Cole had charged that insiders had removed their own funds before the banks closed while accepting deposits on the other end.[11] The *Blade* chose not to mention Cole's letter, though it did find room to publish the full text of an open letter from the Chamber of Commerce praising Toledo's bankers for "industriously working on their problems."[12]

Carl J. Christensen was not the sort of man one would expect to shield bankers. Christensen was the child of poor Danish immigrants. When he was grown enough he went to work for the railroad, landing a job as a brakeman on the New York Central. On a snowy winter morning in 1914, Christensen was crushed between two boxcars and lost his arm. After that he made just enough selling real estate to enroll at Toledo's St. John's University. Following in the footsteps of his brother Wilfred, Carl took a law degree and together they hung out their shingle and began to work their way into politics. Wilfred eventually won election as president of the Lucas County Republican Club, and Carl began to move up the rungs of the Brown machine. Carl Christensen was appointed Toledo's police court prosecutor in 1922. Three years later he won his first election as municipal judge. In 1929 he was tapped by Walter Folger Brown to try and regain the mayor's office from William T. Jackson. He made a strong showing, losing by fewer than four points, and was rewarded with the prosecutor's nomination two years later.[13]

The fact that Christensen was Brown's pick for prosecutor was very telling. Only Brown's most trusted and loyal men were given a crack at this post, as control of the county prosecutor's office was a pillar of the Brown machine. Brown's first lieutenant, Harry Commager, had long run the office from the vantage of first assistant prosecutor. From this office flowed not only a significant amount of patronage, but also a powerful means to reward friends and punish enemies.[14]

Prosecutor Christensen rejected Cole's demand for a criminal investigation, but did so in a way that gave him room to claim he was in favor of one. Christensen expressed his reluctance to make any investigation while the state's commerce director was conducting an active investigation of his own.[15] However, at the very same time Ohio's secretary of commerce, Theodore Tangeman, indicated the opposite, saying that anything of a "criminal nature" was the responsibility of the county prosecutor.[16] Governor George White also passed the buck, saying that the issue was the responsibility of the Department of Banking and he would not get involved and order an investigation unless asked to do so by state banking officials.[17]

While the state Banking Department had in its possession storerooms of evidence of the self-dealing, fraud, and chicanery that had brought down Toledo's banks, it officially insisted that the ultimate blame for the banking disaster belonged to the depositors and not the managers of the banks. Superintendent Fulton's yearly report on the progress of liquidations began by blaming the victim. "Due to the general unrest and unfounded rumors circulated by irresponsible persons, the number of closings during the year of 1931 was considerably multiplied."[18]

In the face of official disinclination to view the bank failures as a "case" that needed to be investigated, private citizens mounted investigations of their own. Though Christensen did not instruct them to, the sitting county grand jury began questioning a person who reported that he "saw something carried out of the bank the day before the closing" which he presumed to be a bag of cash. Councilman Joseph Wawrzyniak, leader of the Polish working-class community, stirred up a hive when he introduced a resolution at the city council meeting demanding that the Ohio attorney general investigate the bank closings and determine if any laws had been broken. Wawrzyniak's resolution specifically instructed the attorney general to look into the giving of excessive loans to officers, the purchasing of prohibited securities, the payment of excessive dividends, a failure to maintain reserves, and the accepting of deposits when the banks were insolvent. Action on the resolution was blocked by a trio of councilman including Harry Irwin, an employee of the Commercial Savings Bank.

Then Manuel Zimmerman, a local attorney and head of a depositors association that formed back in June, filed a civil action demanding the return of $104,423 withdrawn by firms controlled by bank directors just before the Security-Home Bank closed. However weak the case Zimmerman brought to court, he had succeeded in exposing the first embarrassing detail, the pebble that starts an avalanche.[19] A couple of days later, Zimmerman filed more papers on behalf of depositors, demanding a full accounting of all the banks' loans and debts from the state Banking Department, all withdrawals made on June 16, and details of the bank's holdings of worthless German Republic bonds.[20] State officials did not appreciate Zimmerman's private investigation. Zimmerman's exposures prompted Superintendent of Banks Ira Fulton to warn, "Rash action on the part of depositors now will only hinder our work."[21]

In spite of the many government appeals to the public to be patient and trust their officials, many people began to take matters into their own hands. While Zimmerman exposed what he could through the local courts, another plain but extraordinary man, Walter Baertschi, the branch manager of the Virginia Life Insurance Company, stepped forward and began organizing a depositor movement. Baertschi's offices in the Second National Bank Building gave him a front row seat on the goings on in the banks.[22] Before August was out, Baertschi spoke before the Toledo post of the American Legion and convinced them to vote unanimously to form a committee to aid the creation of a citywide depositors' organization.[23] At that time the Legion was one of the largest social organizations in the area, with twenty "posts" in the county.

It did not take long for the combined pressure of Judge Cole's public letter, Baertshi's organizing of war veterans, Wawrzyniak's protest in the city council, and Zimmerman's publicizing bank misconduct through the county courts to provoke a response from state officials. Toledo's bank activists had forced their hand by making it politically dangerous to continue to do nothing. Within days of these events Ohio Attorney General Gilbert Bettman arrived in Toledo with most of his staff and announced to reporters that his office was preparing to file over a million dollars worth of civil actions against unnamed individuals, including some bank directors,

who had made last-minute withdrawals from the Security-Home Bank, saying " . . . I am convinced that action is needed here at once." Though no
reporters had the temerity to ask the attorney general why after ten weeks
of inaction he had suddenly grown so interested in the activities of bank
insiders, Bettman did unwittingly hint at where the pressure to act was coming from: Bettman promised that proper actions would be taken "if the Security-
Home bank has been sacked, as rumored in the street."[24]

His promises of action aside, Bettman was not yet prepared to publicly
indict the powerful industrialists who had "sacked" the banks. Before filing his recovery suits and thereby revealing the names of the sackers, Bettman
tried to reach a private agreement with each of these men. One by one
they were summoned to the Commodore Perry Hotel to his suite, which
was cluttered with stacks of papers and boxes of files and crowded with
legal assistants, secretaries, and a stenographer. Each was ordered to return
his money or face exposure in court. Reporters trying to eavesdrop from
down the hall could only hear occasional shouting through the night until
four in the morning. Telephone switchboard operators told the papers that
they noted a spike in long distance calls about that time. The airport reported
that there was a greater than usual number of flights booked out of town
on fast mail planes to New York, Cleveland, and Chicago.[25] Speculation
was that some of the men pressed by Bettman were attempting to get lines
of credit from big city banks. Though the large dailies portrayed
Bettman's conferences as tantamount to the third-degree, the editor of the
Ameryka-Echo was not so impressed: "Only when the Toledo citizens started
to be outraged that the prosecutors did not investigate any of the accusations made against the Toledo bankers did the Attorney General come down
to Toledo with his assistants and after a few days of staying here got on
some of the Security director's backs."[26]

If Attorney General Bettman had expected that his taking charge of the
situation in Toledo would defuse the growing protest movement, he was
quickly proved wrong. The day after Bettman's hotel negotiations, a meeting of the executive committee of the Security-Home Bank Depositors' Protective
Association drew two hundred people. The committee approved circulating a petition demanding that Governor White order a full state investigation of the bank closings and booked the largest hall in the city, Civic
Auditorium, for a mass meeting that coming Friday night. Most importantly,
the committee elected Leon E. Idoine, an insurance agent, as president,
and C. T. Rosenburg, a high school teacher, as treasurer and then drew up
a grass-roots organizational plan, dividing the city into a dozen subassoci-
ations, each corresponding to the neighborhood of a branch bank. The tone
of the group was rapidly moving in a radical direction as seen when

Manuel Zimmerman, now chair of the legal committee, took the podium and attacked state officials for stalling, charging that the "Ohio legislature is controlled by a banking lobby."[27]

The following day Prosecutor Christensen told reporters that he had been conducting an investigation of Security-Home Bank all along, promised to present the bank issue to the next grand jury, and said he believed there was a basis for bringing charges soon. As the next grand jury was not due to be sworn in until September 20, this bought the prosecutor nearly three weeks to see how the situation played out. Christensen even announced that he was forgoing his early fall vacation to devote all his energies to the bank cases.[28]

The trickle of tantalizing details about who grabbed the "smart money" and the height of the pile of insider loans suddenly became a torrent. After three days of attempts to cajole bank insiders to return their late withdrawals, Bettman and his staff gave up and returned to the capital. Before leaving, they filed four suits asking the return of about a half million dollars from two local corporations and one Security-Home bank director. That same day the Banking Department released an inventory of the assets of the Security-Home Bank, the result of an audit that the *Ameryka-Echo* complained had proceeded at a "turtle's pace" since June. The long delay combined with the timing of the release of the audit on the same day as the filing of Bettman's recovery suits hints at some connection between these events. If politics had been a reason for delaying release of the report, perhaps Bettman's spilling of the beans in his lawsuits provided cover for the timid bank bureaucrats. Whatever the case may have been, the Department of Banks inventory, an unadorned list of names and sums owed to the bank, was a devastating indictment of the bank's top officers. Though the figures were not elaborated upon, they were published, and those with an eye for numbers, like the lawyers involved with the depositors' organizations, could find scandal aplenty. For the first time in print was an official total of $2,332,301.94 in loans given to bank insiders, more than a fifth of them given with no collateral at all and much of the rest secured with second mortgages on lots or shares of bankrupt real estate companies. Many of the loans were dated within two weeks of the bank's closing, some even having been approved on Memorial Day, a day when the bank was closed to the public. The *Ameryka-Echo* was not shy in showing its outrage. Its article on the release of the bank audit began, "today a scandalous thing came out."[29]

For the first time since the beginning of the bank crisis three months earlier, the city's editorial pages turned from lecturing the public to be calm and have faith in their leaders to calling for that leadership's overthrow. The *News-Bee* editorialized, "When it becomes necessary for the attorney general to go into a city with his entire staff and force some of the leading citizens to obey the banking laws—the laws that have protected them while they made much of their money—it is time for the community to begin looking around for a new type of financial leadership." The more conservative *Blade* echoed the growing protest, heading its editorial "Let the Probe Go Deep."[30]

The new revelations came just in time for the first mass protest meeting held that night. Thousands of people packed the Civic Auditorium (the big dailies reported 2,500, while the little *Ameryka-Echo* claimed 4,000). Most attendees added their names to sheaves of petitions to the governor calling for the naming of a special grand jury. Governor White was clearly viewed by the anxious crowd as their last hope for justice. The rally's chairman focused his aim squarely on the governor: "we pray and beseech you . . . Governor White to instruct the attorney general to use every power within his command to probe to the limit every transaction in the operation of the Security-Home bank where there is any suggestion of fraudulent operation . . . and if any evidence is found, to prosecute with all firmness each and every individual proven guilty in such transactions."[31]

Over the next week the landslide of protest continued to build. Toledo's Association of Public Accountants implied their lack of confidence in the authorities by offering to monitor the work of the auditors that had been hired to go over the books of the Security-Home Bank by Prosecutor Christensen. The female members of the League of Polish Affairs organized a drive to gather signatures on the bank investigation petitions to Governor White. One of the city's strongest unions, the Brotherhood of Union Trainmen, voted to demand that Attorney General Bettman immediately release the names of all the directors and officers of the Security-Home Bank who made last-minute withdrawals. Across the city nightly district meetings attracted crowds by the hundreds. On Tuesday, meetings were held simultaneously at Close Memorial Hall, St. Anne's parish school, and the Polish Falcon's Hall. Wednesday, Zimmerman and Idoine shuttled between the Knights of Pythias Hall, Memorial Baptist Church, and the DeVilbiss Auditorium and kept up their exhausting pace the following evening when they addressed large audiences in the Municipal Auditorium, the Thatcher Auditorium, and Drella's Hall. Councilman Wawrzyniak, whose public statements were not reported by the large dailies, began intensifying his rhetoric, telling the four hundred mostly Polish men and women at Drella's Hall that "the small depositors took their cents to the bank and the large ones took them out by the back door."[32] One newspaper reported a popular joke making the rounds:

A stranger from out of town accosted a Toledo citizen as he was passing a bank and asked him this question:

"Pardon me, my friend, but what is that peculiar looking box hanging up
there on the side of the building with an alarm bell on it?"
"Oh, that is a bank burglar alarm!" replied the Toledo citizen.
"What is it doing on the outside?"[33]

While the major daily papers maintained a guarded neutrality toward the
growing depositor movement, the small neighborhood newspapers
jumped wholeheartedly onto the bandwagon. The Polish *Ameryka-Echo* laced
its reporting of the actions of state officials with sarcasm and gave prominent space for notices of upcoming depositor rallies. Across the river a weekly
shopper, the *East Side Sun*, whose politics had never strayed much from reporting on the meetings of the neighborhood businessmen's club and an occasional temperance editorial, passionately embraced the cause. The
newfound activism of the *Sun*'s editor, James Toppin, was driven by both
his relative isolation from the centers of downtown influence and the experiences of his youth, when he had worked as night compositor for Joseph
Pulitzer's New York *World* during the height of its muckraking. Even after
he purchased the *Sun* in 1920, Toppin continued to pay his union dues and
work the linotype machine. Toppin was no radical, but he lived by a personal credo, "Pay your bills and tell the truth," that clashed so fundamentally with the actions of the city's elite that he was compelled to devote his
newspaper to the cause of the depositors.[34]

By September Toppin had turned over the most prominent space in his
newspaper, front page center above the fold, to bold print editorials
demanding investigations, prosecutions, and even hinting at a desire for even
more drastic action. On the front page of his edition for September 24, Toppin
published a "joke" that was less a joke than a veiled threat:

A typical rancher from Arizona was visiting some friends in East Toledo
last week, and of course, he heard all about the banks closing their doors.
"We don't have any more bank failures down in our state," he said.
"How come?" asked the interested Toledoan (who, by the way, has his
funds tied up in one of the closed banks).
"Well, we had a big bank failure about ten years ago. We got kind-a tired
a-waiting for the President to make a statement, so we organized a little
depositors' party, "escorted" the President and the Board of Directors out
to the edge of town and strung 'em up on the telegraph poles on the main
road . . . Since then we ain't had any bank failures in Arizoney!"[35]

Such talk was common enough that Toledo's union newspaper felt compelled to warn its readers that "all of the threats of violent reprisals upon

any of those in charge or control of these banking institutions will not help relieve the situation one particle." Understandably, a few of the bankers in town became quite jumpy. Several bank officials hired private security guards to patrol their homes. Raleigh Mills, vice-president of the Security-Home Bank, employed the Metro Secret Service to watch his house. On a particularly moonless night, the Metro guard believed he had found a nitroglycerin bomb on the Mills' porch and called the police, who determined that it was just an ordinary bottle.[36]

The gauge of the effectiveness of any protest movement is the force of the reaction it provokes. By this measure, the depositors' movement was making rapid progress. Toledo's bishop, Karl Alter, warned Catholics "to act very carefully" and to make a wary choice of whom they choose as their leaders. The board of directors of the Security-Home Bank, who had kept their silence for nearly three months, rushed to issue their version of events in a strident statement that placed all the responsibility for the disaster on the public for running on their otherwise well-run bank. (Leon Idoine spoke for most depositors when he retorted, "It is insulting the intelligence of the public to make such futile and puerile statements as have been offered at this late day by a group of men supposedly qualified as bankers . . .")[37]

Prosecutor Christensen took the lead in attempting to stifle criticism of the handling of the bank crisis. On the day of the first mass depositor rally, Christensen warned that Ohio law made it a crime to spread malicious rumors about the state's banks. Christensen then repeated his warnings a few days later, reminding protesters that Ohio law imposes "huge penalties" on those who spread rumors about the banks. At the time, this seemed no idle threat. Just weeks before the collapse of a half-dozen Chicago banks earlier that year, Chicago officials arrested and charged D. E. Earley, an organizer for the Communist party, and charged him with sedition for making speeches denouncing the city's bankers along with capitalism in general.[38]

With little apparent encouragement from the county prosecutor's office, the grand jury began its investigation in October and for a week or so a stream of bank officials were summoned to testify. Months later, waiting until the very last days of its term to act, the grand jury handed down a sheaf of indictments. There is no clear indication of what caused the jury's delay. It may have been due to a conflict with Prosecutor Christensen, who reportedly opposed the grand jury's actions and secretly scolded them, telling them their charges were nothing but "nonsense."[39]

Assistant Prosecutor Arnold Bunge was given the job of drafting the legal paperwork. At thirty years of age, Bunge was the youngest and least senior member of Christensen's staff. Like his boss, Bunge's life was the sort that would have given him little sympathy for the privileges of the comfortable elite. Orphaned when he was six, Bunge grew up in the Lutheran Home for Boys in the working class east side of the city. After graduation from Waite High School, Bunge worked days at the Toledo Stamp and Stencil Company to pay his way through night school at the University of Toledo. Passing the bar in 1926, Bunge went straight into county service and earned a reputation as a workaholic. He was savvy enough to navigate the political tides of city elections and keep his job through a succession of bosses from different parties and factions within parties.[40]

Bunge put in long hours, and when he was done he had drawn up papers against six bankers. Together they shared a total of forty-eight charges representing the full spectrum of crimes defined by the Ohio banking statutes. Although it appeared to the public that the prosecutor had just thrown the book at a ring of banksters, only a few of the charges had a serious chance of success.

In all the one hundred and twenty articles of the banking code of 1908, only three carried criminal penalties. Violating any of the other laws merely carried the potential for the banking department to seize the assets of the bank—a jeopardy that contained no terror for bankers whose banks had already failed. One of these provisions, Section 33, penalizing the abetting of the passing of bad checks, applied primarily to employees. Another, Section 116, making it illegal to accept a deposit when the banker knew the bank to be insolvent, carried a standard of proof that any lawyer could see was nearly impossible to meet—after all, how does one prove that the banker "knew" the bank was insolvent? In such a case it is not enough to prove that the bank was insolvent at the moment the deposit was made, a difficult point given the mass of figures and assessments required, but it was also necessary to show that the banker believed the bank's collapse was inevitable. To beat such a rap, the banker merely had to show that he had hope. Worst of all, neither of these sections contained any specific penalties for violators, an omission that forced prosecutors to draw an analogy to related sections that did, a legal stretch that had never been tested in this realm of law.

A prosecutor's best bet lay in Section 44, the one that contained the most comprehensive definitions of banking crimes and one that contained specific penalties. Section 44 laid out two broadly defined prohibited actions: embezzling bank funds and making false reports. Embezzlement included everything from snatching coin from the cash drawer to complicated fraud schemes involving fake bills of exchange and fictitious loans. The variety of such schemes, their possible similarity to the normal complicated daily operations of the bank, and the need to show that they were performed not to save the bank but with the "intent to defraud" made embezzlement also difficult to prove in all but those cases involving desperate clerks. Higher bank officers practically needed to be caught with a sack of cash in the trunk of their car racing for the state line to prove their embezzling intent. That left one clause, an almost pro forma provision, that lay as the real bear trap waiting to be sprung. This was the clause stating that anyone "who makes any false entry in any book, report or statement of the corporation . . ." could also face the same penalty as the embezzler—up to thirty years in the state pen.

In spite of the obvious advantage of prosecution under the false entry clause, only two of the six defendants were charged with this offense. Though the star defendant, former Security-Home president Stacy McNary, was buried under dozens of charges, only two of them accused him of making a false entry with the intent to deceive an agent of the state. Clifford Whitmore, McNary's predecessor, also faced a tough false report rap. The bulk of the charges were drawn in the most difficult manner, alleging "willful" misapplication of funds with "the intent to defraud" the Security-Home Bank, the bank's shareholders, or a token depositor, a Mr. Paul Merker. If that wasn't tough enough, some of the defendants were charged with the "willful" acceptance of deposits with the intent to defraud poor Mr. Merker when they "knew" the bank to be insolvent.

As none of the principals in this drama are still alive and none of the prosecutor's papers have been preserved, it will never be known exactly why the prosecution chose such a difficult line of attack. Did political pressure make it necessary to play to the public rather than to chart the best legal strategy? Did the prosecutors suspect that by entering so many new and untested charges into the hamper, they would feed years of motions, appeals, and delays? Was that their hidden strategy—to give the legal machine so much fuel that it would chug along for years but always in circles? Or were they simply not clever enough to understand what they had done?

Within forty-eight hours the president, chairman of the board, and two out of three of the vice-presidents, as well as a former president and one other director of the Security-Home bank, were phoned and politely asked to appear in common pleas court the next morning. Though there was no real need to do so, given Christensen's reluctance to go forward with the prosecution, Judge Lemmon specifically ordered him not to arrest the bankers. At the appointed hour of 9:30 A.M., only four of the men ordered to show up, Will Gunckel, Frank Hoehler, Raleigh Mills, and Clifford Whitmore, had appeared, but rather than issue arrest warrants for the absent bankers, the court waited patiently for over an hour for the star defendants, Stacy McNary and LeRoy Eastman, to arrive. The judge showed no irritation at being kept waiting and released each man on a personal bond of $2,000.

Lawyers for the defendants asked for an unusual postponement of two weeks before entering their pleas, and without objection from the prosecutor or hesitation from the bench, all the bankers were allowed to go free without having to state whether they were guilty or innocent.[41]

This last courtesy, as it turns out, was of great consequence. Had the judge required the men to enter a plea that morning, as was routine, the legal battle would have swiftly moved onto questions related to the scheduling and procedure of the upcoming trials. But because of the long delay between indictment and arraignment, the defense was given an opportunity to bombard the court with motions relating to the indictment itself, points of law which would have been moot had the arraignment occurred. Before the week was out dozens of motions to quash the indictments on various grounds had been submitted. More time was granted to consider these motions, and then appeals of the rulings of the motions delayed the proceedings further. In March the Supreme Court of Ohio agreed to hear an appeal in the case and for much of the rest of 1932 there lingered an eerie silence on the banking issue. After LeRoy Eastman and Clifford Whitmore's appeal to quash their indictments had been taken up by the Supreme Court of Ohio, little more was heard out of the Lucas County prosecutor's office. It seemed as though they either wished to wait to see what the high court's precedent-setting ruling would be or they were glad to see the whole affair head downstate and out of their hair. The defense's strategy of delay and obstruction worked as planned, and the first of these six bank officers did not actually have to stand before the court and declare their guilt or innocence for another year, until March 30, 1933.[42]

Much of the reason for this long delay was the reluctance of Prosecutor Christensen to respond to a defense request for a "bill of particulars," a legal document that details the prosecution's scenario of how the crime was committed. Such a document was of immense benefit to the defense in that it provided a road map as to how the prosecution planned on establishing the facts of the case. Whether because he didn't want to give the defense such an advantage, or because he preferred to keep the case on ice while he ran for reelection, the prosecutor made one excuse after another to the court for why his office was so behind in drafting this document.

Christensen's snail's pace of prosecution became a minor issue in the election. One of his opponents in the May primary, former assistant prosecutor Cecil Stickney, challenged Christensen to answer a series of questions which he claimed were "on everybody's lips:"

Why did Mr. Christensen wait so long before starting a grand jury investigation of the closed Toledo banks?

Why did he entrust the responsibility of drawing the indictments against the bankers involved in Toledo bank failures to an office subordinate?[43]

Another candidate in the primary race, Joe Cannon, representing the goo-goo (period slang for "good government") reform wing of the Democratic party, centered his campaign on the bank issue and demanded that "there must be a full and complete disclosure to the public of the incidents leading up to a voluntary closing of the 'closed banks.' This shocking catastrophe must not be catalogued as another of Toledo's unsolved offenses—it must not be 'white washed.'" However much Cannon's rhetoric may have connected with the mood of the public, his quixotic campaign was ignored by the powerful daily press and easily brushed aside by the powerful political machines of the city.[44]

Christensen survived the primary challenge only to face a far more powerful Democratic foe in November, a young polished lawyer with a Tennessee drawl, Frazier Reams (figure 7). Reams picked up where Stickney left off and told reporters, "I have never been able to understand why these [bank] indictments have been allowed to lie for a year without trial. If I am elected, these will be the first cases to be tried."[45] Reams not only won election as county prosecutor; he polled more votes in Toledo than any other Democratic candidate for any office.[46]

Undoubtedly, some of Toledo's financiers breathed a sigh of relief upon the election of Frazier Reams as county prosecutor in 1932. To them, Reams was one of their own: a man who shared their experiences and their outlook. Like them, in the 1920s Reams plunged into the real estate game, becoming a partner and the secretary of the Toledo Civic Realty Company, the largest of seventy real estate companies chartered in 1926 in the city. Toledo Civic Realty's president was Stanley J. Hiett, heir to the Hiett realty fortune, and a partner in the law firm of Fraser, Hiett, Wall and Effler, that would later represent most of the banker defendants. Prior to his venture into politics, Reams was known as a "local banker" and was referred to as such when his name appeared in the papers. One of his first jobs upon arriving in town was as trust officer for the Commercial Bank, and before long he occupied the powerful chair of vice-president and director. Reams also moved smoothly in the elite circles of service and trade clubs: he was made a trustee of the Chamber of Commerce and was tapped as chairman of a committee of the American Institute of Banking. Just before the banking crisis, Reams stepped down as vice-president to devote more time to his law practice with the firm of Tracy, Chapman and Welles, though he kept his seat on the board of directors. Reams was claimed as their own by the country club set, some-

Figure 7
Frazier Reams, former vice-president and director of the Commercial
Bank and Lucas County prosecutor in the mid-1930s.
(Reprinted with permission of the *Blade*)

times quite literally as in the spring of 1931 when the newsletter of the Toledo
Beach Club boasted that one of their own members would be the city's next
mayor: "It is possible that a member of the Beach Club will be the next mayor
of Toledo. Frazier Reams, one of the newer members of the club, is being
advanced by his friends as a specially worthy candidate."[47]

From the moment Frazier Reams took office in January of 1932, the depositors movement pressured him to act on the moribund bank cases. Though
the days of mass protest meetings attracting thousands to denounce
bankers had waned with the passage of over a year's time, a meeting of Security-
Home depositor organizers held soon after Reams' swearing-in attracted
thirty or so activists. The meeting was chaired by Samuel Wittenberg, who
used his soapbox to denounce Reams and demand that the state appoint an
independent prosecutor. Reams, said Wittenberg, was disqualified from prosecuting the bankers as he himself had been a bank official at the time the
banks failed and had turned down his request to call a special grand jury
saying "he had other things to do." Wittenberg urged the depositor
activists to organize a mass protest rally around the courthouse to demand
a special, independent investigation.[48]

Wittenberg would not have had much difficulty organizing his protest
given the sheer desperation of the city at that moment. On New Year's Day

over eleven thousand people queued up for the holiday soup line. The line snaked across streets that were choked with snow because the city had suspended all snow removal and laid off all its plow crews. That same day the newly installed mayor was forced to fire five hundred city workers and cut all others to three-quarters wages just to meet his monthly payroll. City officials attempted to stretch relief rations by hiring dieticians to calculate the smallest allotment required to sustain life.[49]

Knowing the political sensitivity of the bank issue and the angry mood of the people, Reams immediately called reporters and gave his version of the story. "During the campaign," explained Reams, "Mr. Wittenberg, organizer of the movement to have a special counsel appointed, was one of my most ardent supporters. This outburst has been occasioned by his disappointment over my not appointing his prospective son-in-law on my staff."[50]

Reams, having been vividly reminded that it was political suicide to become known as the banker prosecutor who let the banksters off the hook, immediately swung into action. The day after the Security-Home depositors' association meeting and Wittenberg's outburst against him, Reams announced that he was preparing to take the cases of two of the bankers to the Ohio Supreme Court. The following week, he completed and filed the bill of particulars that had gone unfinished under Christensen's supervision for over a year.[51] This cleared the way for the quick arraignment of Stacy McNary, William Gunckel, and George Mills, though Judge John McCabe granted them yet another week's postponement, and then another, and then another. The first of this trio, Mills, would not actually be arraigned for two more months, while the others succeeded in delaying the proceedings for six months.[52]

Near the end of March, Ohio's high court ruled that Judge Stuart had erred in throwing out the indictments against Eastman and Whitmore the previous year. The decision was the first sign of progress in the cases in over a year and was cheered by the depositors' movement. "Nothing can wipe out the despair, sorrow and suffering that have been caused by the closing of this one bank," wrote Toppin in his *East Side Sun*, "but [the decision] will give the betrayed and sorely tried citizens of Toledo some hope that justice has not fled out of the world . . ."[53] Eastman's and Whitmore's cases were resubmitted to a grand jury, which reinstated the same charges and may have even issued a new secret charge against Marion Miller, former president of the Home Bank, who was now retired to the south of France. Judge Robert Gosline managed to fend off five defense motions to quash the new indictments and arraigned the bankers the next day.[54]

Twenty-seven months after he had been arrested Eastman was finally arraigned and pled not guilty to the charges. In a surprise move, Eastman waived his right to a jury trial, which was allowed under Ohio law. Clearly his lawyers had calculated that their chances of finding twelve men and women who had not lost their money in a Toledo bank were far worse than the wrath of a single judge, not that they ever really intended their defendant to go to trial. When the time came for deciding Eastman's bail, Judge Gosline surprised all observers by setting his personal bond at $10,000, five times what Judge Stuart had imposed the year before. Gosline then proceeded to demonstrate his impatience with the pace of these prosecutions by turning down five defense motions in a row.[55] The Eastman legal team finally succeeded in getting a hearing before the state supreme court, this time alleging that the new indictments represented double jeopardy and were therefore unconstitutional. As Eastman's original case had not actually gone to trial in the first instance, his complaint of double jeopardy was extremely weak, but as long as the case was before the high court, Eastman and the other bank defendants could request more postponements from the local judge.[56]

After seeing Gosline's backbone in handling Eastman's arraignment, the lawyers for Stacy McNary and Frank Hoehler, who were next on the judge's docket, scrambled to push Judge Gosline off his bench. Like most other Toledoans, Judge Gosline had lost a considerable sum when the banks closed. As it turned out, Gosline's money happened to have been deposited in McNary's Security-Home Bank. In a letter written to the chief of the Ohio Supreme Court, Gosline admitted his apparent conflict of interest, but promised he could conduct a trial free of bias. Chief Justice Carl J. Weygandt was not impressed and formally asked Gosline to recuse himself.

By stepping down, Gosline revealed two little-spoken-of facts that prevented the effective prosecution of the bankers. If any judge who had lost money in Toledo's banks was disqualified from hearing the bank cases, then the only alternative was to bring in a jurist from outside of the county. Chief Justice Carl J. Weygandt thought this the best course of action, but could not order that it be done. In order to bring a judge onto the case, that judge would have to be added to the county payroll, and the county did not even have enough funds to pay the back wages of its own employees. With the county in bankruptcy, there was a constant pressure on judges to expedite cases and for prosecutors to avoid costly trials. Thus, each day that the bankers could delay their trials added to the county's fiscal burden and increased the weight of the argument against prosecuting them at all.

Secondly, Gosline's departure highlighted the fact that no other county judge wanted anything to do with the bankers' cases. Not because they were unwinnable or legally uninteresting (they had by this time already won the distinction of being "the most skillfully involved criminal litigation in the history of Lucas County"), but because they were no-win cases politically.[57] There were but two political interests involved in the cases, and both could not be satisfied at the same time. If a judge, like Judge Gosline, showed the bankers a firm hand and ended their delaying tactics, he could expect to be ostracized by the moneyed elites and punished by the Brown machine. On the other hand, if he rolled over for the defense and the bankers walked away without any sanction for their actions, the voters of the city would never return him to the bench or any other office he sought.

That no elected judge wanted the job was made embarrassingly obvious when head judge Roy Stuart decided to draw lots to determine who would be given the assignment. All four common pleas judges, Prosecutor Frazier Reams, and Harold Fraser for the defense convened in Stuart's chambers, and four pennies were placed in a hat. Before they began Fraser affirmed that he would have no objection to either the procedure or the unlucky judge. Three of the coins had even dates and one was dated 1909. Each man took his turn plucking a coin out of the hat, hoping it was any year but 1909. Judge Martin ended up being the odd man out (or, in this case, in).[58] The unprecedented spectacle prompted the editor of the *News-Bee* to scold the members of the bench:

> There appears to have been a disinclination in the Common Pleas bench here to take jurisdiction in this trial . . . As long as judges are elected there may be a reluctance to preside in trials in which powerful influences on both sides are apparent . . . Hearing of such cases may be an unpleasant duty but it is a duty for which these judges were selected by their fellow citizens.[59]

Once the question of which reluctant judge would oversee the trial was settled, the defenses went back to their delaying tactics while the prosecutors seemed happy to have the trial indefinitely continue. After all, without a formal acquittal to raise the public's ire, an on-going trial allowed the prosecutor to perpetually flail the bankers and wrap himself in the mantle of the people's champion. McNary's counsel, Harold Fraser, rummaged through his bag to find any monkey wrench that he could toss into the gears. He moved to quash based on the claim that the actions alleged in the indictment were not a crime because the banking code specified no specific penalties for violations. He asked the judge to establish that the standard which the prosecution had to meet was proving that his client had profited by his actions and not just that he had intentionally done everything he was accused of. When Judge Martin turned those motions down, Fraser attempted to use the judge's ruling as grounds to demand a new bill of particulars. All the while, Fraser hinted at his grand strategy—drawing out the trial so long that the county could not afford to continue it: "It is so unfair to force these men [McNary and Hoehler] to undergo the expense of a trial that will last from a month to a year, or to put the county to this expense, without examining the demurrers carefully."[60]

These words were aimed at the county's political leadership; they were a clear threat to bleed the county budget white. That same week it was reported that tax collections had fallen 60 percent from the year before. County spending was down 25 percent from the year before, the largest cuts coming out of three judicial budgets: $13,000 from the prosecutor's office, $14,000 from the common pleas courts, and $11,000 from the clerk of courts. The men who had most contributed to wrecking the county's budget now stood to benefit from the county's inability to afford prosecuting them.[61]

Before Martin's court got around to selecting a jury for Stacy McNary, Harold Fraser had lodged 269 requests for revisions in the prosecution's bill of particulars.[62] Weeks later, when these motions had finally been swept aside and a date for a trial was about to be set, Fraser announced that he was going to file motions of prejudice against every judge in the county, the very thing he had promised not to do before Judge Martin drew his losing coin. As it turned out, Judge Martin did not lose much money in the banks and he was allowed to continue, though Fraser's ploy did delay the trial for another month.[63] By the time the trial opened in July of 1933 and jury selection began, the county was so short of money that it could not afford to pay jurors their small per diems and was postponing trials until September so as to put those costs onto the next fiscal year's budget.[64]

With the McNary trial under way, Fraser had many more opportunities for draining the county budget and pressuring the judge to quash the indictment or the prosecutor to give up. First there was the "slow and tedious" process of picking a jury. It began with Judge Martin calling both attorneys into his chambers and having them agree that since the trial would probably be a long one, they should excuse any juror whose business or employment could be jeopardized by a long absence. Anyone whose name was picked out of the jury wheel was allowed to leave if they claimed they had pressing business to attend to. By the end of the morning of the first day of jury selection, the entire venire of names had been exhausted and Judge Martin ordered another 120 names put in the jury wheel.[65]

McNary, somberly dressed in a dark grey suit, watched the examination of the prospective jurors from a chair positioned behind his lawyer. Harold Fraser took command of the room and demonstrated how he had earned a reputation as a "bulldog" in court. Fraser interrupted Reams frequently, objecting to even innocuous questions. When Reams asked one juror, "Do you believe the laws of Ohio should be enforced as to banks?" Fraser jumped up and shouted "Object! I can see no reason for singling these laws out." Judge Martin agreed and Reams was not allowed to ask other jurors whether they thought banking laws should be enforced. Meanwhile, Fraser was allowed to use his questions as a means of implanting into the jurors' minds a reason for acquitting his client: "Because the world has suffered from a depression, do you believe bankers should be prosecuted?" Fraser used his challenges to remove most Security-Home depositors, though he did not object to Edna Murphy, the young wife of a mailman, whose only child carried pennies to school to put in a Security-Home account. Reams raised only a few exceptions, objecting to E. J. Hotchkiss, a former director of the Sylvania Bank when that bank's largest shareholder was the Security-Home Bank, and George Koehler, an elderly music teacher who was a friend of the Gunckel family (William Gunckel was awaiting trial on another bank indictment) and a stockholder in the Ohio Bank.[66] Curiously, he didn't raise an objection to William Buckhout, whose son was married to the daughter of banker Thomas Tracy, his former law partner.[67]

The jury that was charged with deciding McNary's fate was most characterized by its lack of wage-earners. There were six women, all homemakers, half of whom were poor and at least one of whom was relatively well off. Among the men there was one retiree, two men out of work, and one accountant, one salesman, and one man who sold stationery out of his home. All listened attentively as Fraser delivered his opening statement, painting McNary as a "patriot who had toiled night and day to save his bank when the world-wide depression threatened its existence."[68]

Later that same day, a popular local bootlegger named Jack Kennedy was taking a summer stroll with his girlfriend when men emerged from a car and fired fourteen bullets into his body. Kennedy's killing marked the culmination of a simmering turf war between Kennedy's Toledo gang and Detroit's "Purple Gang" as the Purple's underboss, Thomas "Yonnie" Licavoli, muscled his way onto Kennedy's turf. Overnight Kennedy's murder stole the headlines and diverted the public's attention from McNary's bank trial. It also marked the beginning of a new phase in Frazier Ream's career. Where up to this time Reams seemed to be riding to the next election as the defender of the humble depositor against the rapacious schemes of greedy banksters, now he had a choice of steeds. Kennedy's murder presented the opportunity to become Toledo's version of Elliot Ness. Reams could, if he chose, focus all his resources on smashing the Purple Gang. Licavoli and his gang of outsiders had succeeded in taking over Toledo's liquor, gambling, extortion, and prostitution rackets from local gangs who had prospered under the protection of local political bosses; this development had now made it politically possible for the county prosecutor to profit from cracking down on vice.

Reams seemed to want a new horse. Once he was notified of the Kennedy murder, Reams put his office on an emergency footing. He and his assistants holed up in the prosecutor's offices the entire night, not emerging until 6:30 the next morning when they took a break to unwind at the local horse track.[69] For the rest of Reams' career as prosecutor, he would focus most of his energies at smashing the Purple Gang and shutting down the city's rackets.

When the trial reconvened, Fraser was ready with a new delaying tactic. He demanded that the prosecution provide him with a certified list of all assets in the Security-Home Bank on the date that McNary compelled the board of directors to vote a dividend while allegedly knowing the bank had not turned a profit. Fraser was betting that the prosecution had not really done much in the way of auditing the accounts of the bank for that particular day. If he was right and the judge ordered the prosecution to present an itemized inventory, it would force the prosecution to either rely on the bank's own inflated figures, which showed a profit and thereby dispelled at least one set of charges, or it would force the prosecutor to ask for a postponement so he could give his examiners time to work. Either way, the odds of McNary getting off were much improved.

Fraser's hunch was correct. In spite of having had six months to prepare his case, not counting the year his predecessor neglected it, Reams apparently had never ordered an audit of the bank. The fact that neither he nor Carl Christensen had anticipated the possibility that such evidence might be included in the discovery process reveals either gross incompetence or a lack of seriousness in prosecuting the cases in the first place. Such evidence did go to the heart of not only the dividend charge but also the false reporting charges, which had the lowest legal threshold of proof and would have been the ones to focus on for a swift conviction. (That false report charges were the easiest ones to pursue was widely known at the time. Even the *Saturday Evening Post* noted that "the published statement hangs over the head of the banker like a sword of Damocles. If the bank fails and the prosecutor can prove that the statement was false when made, which he not infrequently does prove, it is that much longer in prison for the banker."[70]) Subsequent history would show that the legal team Reams assembled in his years as prosecutor were as sharp as they come. Reams' first assistant, Joel Rhinefort, was a well-respected county prosecutor in Oklahoma before he was hired away to Toledo. Arnold Bunge spent long hours stooped over his books, and his subsequent lack of sleep was commented upon by reporters. Reams' own sharp juridical skills would soon become renowned as he quickly smashed the Licavoli gang and became the first prosecutor in the city's modern history to effectively shut down at least the most open casinos and brothels in the city. The only good explanation why Frazier Reams had to stand before Judge Martin, one month after arraignment and thirty months after indictment, and ask for a postponement because his office had not begun the most basic fact-checking in the case was that Reams was never really serious about going to trial. No wonder Judge Martin rolled his eyes and said "[I] had hoped to live to see the end of this trial, but at the rate it's progressing I never will." Martin granted a three-day recess for Reams to conduct his audit, but at the end of this time the accountants reported that they had not even finished adding up the figures in the files beginning with the letter "A" and Martin postponed the trial for sixty days.[71]

By September of 1933 the prosecution's audit of the Security-Home Bank was completed. The cost of accountants had bitten deeply into the already strapped prosecutor's budget, and still there was no clear end in sight for the trial. Just as the prosecution seemed, at last, to have their ducks in a row, Harold Fraser switched tactics and scattered them all again.

McNary's "bulldog" of a lawyer, having squeezed every day and every dollar out of his last stalling tactic, now asked Judge Martin to order the prosecution to first prove that McNary had actually "caused" the dividend to be paid. Fraser appealed to the judge's increasing sensitivity to the cost and length of the trial, saying that unless the prosecution could establish that point, all the audits and financial testimony in the world could not convict his client. The prosecutors were flabbergasted. Having focused for two months on establishing the financial state of the bank, they were now confronted with the idea that they could not actually present this evidence but instead had to prove McNary's own actions on the day in question. Arnold Bunge asked the judge, "Then we can't submit evidence on the condition of the bank till we show that its president knew about those conditions?" Judge Martin went along with Fraser's diversion and ordered the prosecutors to first prove that a dividend was paid, then that McNary had compelled this payment, then whether there were actually profits to pay for it, then whether McNary had criminal intent. In spite of this serious setback, Reams continued to tell reporters that this would be the test case for all the other banking cases. "We of the prosecution," he declared, "have an increasing curiosity to see whether banking laws mean anything or not. This is a case which can test their worth."[72]

Throughout the trial of McNary, none of the daily newspapers pointed out an obvious fact. Not only was the prosecutor a former bank director himself, but he had committed the very same crime he was now prosecuting McNary for. The principal charge against McNary was that he had voted a dividend at a time when he knew that his bank was insolvent, thereby indirectly stealing depositors' savings. Reams was present at the Commercial Bank directors' meeting that voted to issue a dividend after the bank had frozen all withdrawals. Sitting just across the mahogany boardroom table from him was fellow director Harold Fraser, now his opposite in the McNary trial.[73] The conflicts of interest that Reams carried throughout this prosecution could not have been more glaring—if Reams succeeded in establishing that the law could put McNary behind bars for voting a dividend when his bank was insolvent, then by the same token Reams could be indicted for his actions as a director of the Commercial Bank.[74]

This conflict of interest may have dictated the flawed legal strategy that Reams pursued in the McNary case. Reams attempted to distinguish between the actions of the president of the bank and the actions of its directors. Early on in McNary's trial, the prosecution team argued that McNary "compelled" the issuing of a dividend, while the directors merely rubber-stamped his decisions. This distinction made little sense in terms of the law, but it seems to have gone far in distancing Toledo's hundreds of bank directors, including Prosecutor Reams himself, from the reach of the law.

Jurors heard from two witnesses over as many days before Fraser succeeded in dropping the curtain on Reams' play. After the morning's preliminaries and twenty minutes of testimony, Fraser took the floor and asked the judge to excuse the jury while he argued some finer points of law. In a performance more fitting of the senate than the common pleas court, Fraser proceeded to cite precedent and statute continuously for the next seven hours. His point, when boiled down, was this: even if his client had compelled the payment of a dividend when no funds were available, that action, however intended, was not against the law in Ohio.[75] Judge Martin took the night to think it over and the next morning he opened court by suddenly ruling that McNary's charges did not constitute a crime under Ohio law. With a rap of the gavel Martin declared the charges overruled. McNary, who normally showed no emotion in the courtroom, was observed by one reporter who wrote, "[H]is eyes twinkled for the first time in days and a slight smile crossed his face. He arose from his chair, extracted a pipe from his pocket and lit it and smoked with apparent pleasure."[76]

The prosecutors were suddenly exposed. The weak hand they had dealt themselves was now an embarrassing fact, and they lashed out at the judge who had called their bluff. Arnold Bunge explained to the crush of reporters in the courtroom hallway, "Then, if directors want to steal from a bank, all they have to do is to declare a dividend whether there is money with which to pay it or not, and pay the dividend to themselves." Bunge went on to explain that Judge Martin had ruled that though the banking laws clearly prohibited the actions of McNary and other bankers, it did not attach particular penalties to those actions but did leave a catch-all penalty for "willful misapplication of funds." To not connect the one to the other, as Judge Martin did, was like not allowing the prosecution of someone for willfully running into your car, because the law of malicious destruction of property does not specifically mention the use of automobiles.[77]

While his assistant did a good job of making the case for the prosecution's interpretation of the law, Frazier Reams seemed overly eager to extend Judge Martin's ruling beyond its immediate relevance. Reams, in his denunciation of Judge Martin's ruling, actually expanded it: "This ruling goes to the very base of all pending indictments against bankers in Lucas County. If this is the law depositors are completely without protection in this type of offense, however flagrant." Given that there were still charges based not on the statute that Judge Martin had overruled but rooted in the very section of the banking code that Martin used as an example of a clause with force, why would Reams declare that all charges against all bankers were now in jeopardy?[78]

While Reams chose not to pursue the misreporting charges against the bank officials, he also could not afford to appear to give up on the bank cases altogether. At the moment that McNary's case was dismissed, Reams' name was being circulated in high party circles as a possible candidate for state attorney general in the next year's election. Politically, Reams' best course of action was to keep the bank cases on a low simmer by appealing them, giving him the opportunity to talk tough against banksters when needed, but also allowing him the excuse of not initiating another trial until a higher court ruled definitively. Meanwhile he could keep his name in the headlines by bravely beating down the "outsider" Detroit gangsters. Reams himself admitted that "It is easier to bring first degree murder cases to trial than bank cases . . ."[79]

While the prosecution of bankers stalled with the quashing of McNary's indictment, the movement for a state investigation of the bankers' actions continued. Earlier that year depositor activists Walter Baertschi and Edward Arnos convinced the publisher of the *News-Bee* to journey with them to Cleveland for a conference with state senator L. L. Marshall, who had seemed the most outspoken legislator on the bank issue. After their meeting, Marshall agreed to launch an official investigation. Soon after the McNary ruling, James Toppin, publisher of the *East Side Sun*, organized a coalition of the city's other editors of weekly shoppers, Raymond E. Hildebrand of the *South Side News*, and Albert C. Ward, editor of the *West Toledo Standard*, "to tell the truth about Toledo's bank situation." Toppin was receiving tips and "startling information" from unnamed sources, which he eagerly rushed into print.[80]

The Marshall committee began looking into Toledo's bank story in early November of 1933. E. J. Falkenstein, a former economics teacher, who had been hired by Marshall's committee as the special examiner, arrived in Toledo and got down to work reviewing the records compiled by the prosecutor's office. In just two weeks Falkenstein was prepared to reveal a more complete story of the events of the summer of 1931 than had ever been told to the people who suffered from them.[81]

The council chamber of the newly built Safety Building was as crowded as it had ever been when Marshall's bank investigation committee held its first hearing on November 23, 1933. Over two hundred people elbowed for standing room and filled the chamber with a murky haze from their nervous cigarettes. More packed the hallway beyond its doors, straining to hear. Beside the senators, the front table was thick with lawyers: a representative from the federal prosecutor's office, both assistant city law directors, an assistant U.S. attorney, Harold Fraser and one of his partners, E. G. Wall, as well as a representative from the Ohio attorney general's office. Lawyers and representatives of depositors associations were there. It seemed everyone who had a stake in the banks was there except Frazier Reams. The absence of Reams was noted by many, and the early exit of his two assistants raised suspicions in the morning's paper that they may have been disinterested in the proceedings.

The crowd was there to hear for themselves what the newspapers, bureaucrats, and politicians had kept from them for the past two years—the names of the bigwigs who had withdrawn their money ahead of the hoi polloi. It was past 7:30 in the evening when Senator Marshall calmed the echoing chatter with a wave of his hand and was met by a barrage of flashbulbs. When the popping subsided he introduced his fellow senators and announced that the purpose of the committee was to understand what had happened in Toledo so that they could recommend legislation to reinforce the state's banking laws. Then he introduced the star of the show.

Edward J. Falkenstein, a young, tall, slightly built man, took the lectern and began reading from his thirty-five page report. Falkenstein commanded attention without even trying. As one reporter observed, "Here was a man who knew his business. The crowd realized it right off. Lawyers in the room whispered to one another . . . Only once did he make an apparent error and then, for the most part, the crowd laughed with him—not at him. It was a different sort of laugh from the throaty, jeering laugh it loosed every so often as he testified to particularly amazing findings in the bank's affairs." [82] When he got to the point in his report where he detailed how officers and directors of the Ohio had borrowed 82 percent of the bank's capital for their own uses, the audience groaned. When Falkenstein revealed that the withdrawal suspension notice placed in the local papers was different from the one actually recorded in the bank's minutes, the public version omitting the fact that individual directors and tellers could make exceptions to this rule, the crowd erupted in derisive laughter.

Falkenstein pulled one skeleton after another from the Ohio Bank's closet: how six and a half million dollars was withdrawn from the Ohio during the supposed sixty-day "suspension period" by "favored insiders"; how George M. Jones dressed up the bank's reports to the state by depositing a million dollars cash just before the quarterly audit and then removing it once it was over; how the Dime Bank deal had watered the Ohio's stock; how illegal cash advances to an insurance company had kept it from calling in bad mortgages. By the time the big standard clock on the wall edged near eleven at night, Falkenstein had successfully confirmed most of the city's suspicions and implicitly condemned not only its bankers but also all the other institutions—the press, the bench, the prosecutors, the politicians—that had been shown unable to tell the people the truth about what had happened. Over the next four days the hearings continued into other banks, other deals, and more "smart money" revelations, and though the onslaught of figures and corporate names and dates were more than most people could keep track of, the overreaching grand fact could not be forgotten. A small privileged group had broken the public's trust, stolen their money, and plunged the city into the depths of the worst depression in history and had successfully retained their power and wealth and escaped any punishment for their actions.

One of the most dramatic and damaging revelations of the Marshall hearings occurred during the reading of an otherwise drab report. An elderly man stood up in the rear of the room and shouted that what had just been read was a lie. The gentleman introduced himself as Gerald K. Lombard and explained he had been an employee of the Commerce Guardian Bank for twenty years and that the bank's true condition had long been covered up. Lombard was asked why he had not come forward before that day, and Lombard said that he had tried on two other occasions—once before a grand jury whose foreman he recognized as the uncle of one of the Commerce Guardian directors and then a second time, before a federal grand jury among whose members he spotted one of the bank's former directors. Lombard claimed that he had been fired from the bank when he tried to raise concerns about its management, after which the president of the bank, Ed Kirby, suggested that he move to Florida or California.[83]

The Marshall committee hearings reignited protest against the bankers and, by implication, the political structure that had either protected them or been ineffective in bringing them to justice. Toledo's newly elected socialist mayor, Solon Klotz, became the first mayor to speak out against the city's bankers, noting that when the rainy day the depositors had planned for came at last, it was found that "the bankers had all the umbrellas." A week later it was learned that a county grand jury had begun calling banking officials and other experts, starting with investigator Edward J. Falkenstein. Subpoenas went out to George M. Jones, ordering him to appear with all his bank records, and to William M. Konzen, the state official in charge of liquidation. Then Edward Kirschner, Toledo's postmaster and former vice-president of the Ohio Bank, was summoned, and many expected fresh indictments to be handed down soon. The crusading *East Side Sun* reported, "The Lucas County Grand Jury is just now beginning an investigation of certain bank officials' actions in the fateful days of 1931—which have been known to some people all along, but which could never reach official ears until the explosion came . . ."[84]

One of those "officials" the *Sun* editor James Toppin referred to was undoubtedly Frazier Reams. The following week Toppin stepped up his rhetoric a notch, reprinting in full Reams' promise made a year before to investigate and prosecute the bankers.

> Does any of our readers know—(we confess, we don't)—of any investigation of the closed banks by Prosecutor Reams? . . . The people of Toledo are waiting to see what Prosecutor Reams is going to do to fulfill his election promises . . . Mr. Reams has abundant material at hand to tear things wide open—and the people of Toledo are looking to him for immediate action in this exceedingly important matter. We have waited long enough![85]

Toppin's impatience was not without cause. A month had passed since the dramatic revelations of the Marshall committee, and in that span of time Reams had made no public statements on the issue of the banks. Once it had been reported that a county grand jury had been calling witnesses, there was a growing public expectation that more indictments would soon be handed down.

Almost from the moment that the grand jury turned its attention to banking matters, its relationship with the prosecutor's office became stormy. Though the workings of a grand jury are shrouded in official secrecy, a surprising amount of information about the growing conflict between the jurors and the prosecutors leaked out. It is known that around the time that the jury began actively investigating the relationship between the Ohio Savings Bank and its shell subsidiary company, Vistula Investment, the fireworks began. One juror, William J. Morrow, had an argument with First Assistant

Prosecutor Joel Rhinefort that became so heated it was feared the two would come to blows. From that point on, Rhinefort did not step into the jury room, and his duties were assumed by his associate, Arnold Bunge.[86]

Later that week the jurors met with Prosecutor Reams and agreed to take a break from Tuesday, December 19, until first thing Saturday morning, December 23, and understood that Reams would present certain unnamed witnesses at that time. But the day after the jury questioned Edward Kirchner, the politician who held the patronage-rich office of postmaster but who was called to testify as the former vice-president of the Ohio Bank, Frazier Reams announced to reporters that he would not call the jury back into session until December 29, a week later, leaving the jury little time to complete the investigation they had started before their term ended on January 8. The prosecutor's office told the reporter for the *Blade* that "it had been intended to call the jurors back into session . . . but it was determined today that there are not enough routine matters for them to consider." Actually, it was later revealed by one of the jurors that during that intervening period the jury had scheduled the testimony of Claude Campbell, a former director of the Ohio Savings Bank, and others. In an unprecedented move, the jurors at that point resolved to bypass the prosecutor and take matters into their own hands. The day after Christmas the foreman of the jury, Harry Burkhart, showed up at the prosecutor's office and demanded a list of the addresses of all the other jurors. He then summoned them himself and later that day the grand jury had an unusual private meeting with Judge Roy Stuart. Among the topics discussed was their legal ability to continue their bank investigation on their own.[87]

In the last days of their term, the jurors completed two reports. They handed up a report and the usual sheaf of indictments to the judge, and then they submitted a separate report in which they commented on the conduct of the prosecutor's office: "We believe these [banking] matters should be investigated in the public interest and regret that the prosecuting attorney, for some reason unknown to us, not only refused to aid us in such examination, but by canceling our sessions prevented us from doing so."[88] Later Harry Burkhart, pressed by a reporter to elaborate, explained, "We wanted to investigate the bank matter thoroughly, we wanted to give the prosecutor a break. But we did not get any cooperation from him."[89]

Reams was now exposed to criticism from all sides. The *News-Bee*, a natural ally of Reams as the city's nominally Democratic newspaper, was first to express its disappointment with Reams' handling of the bank cases. "The prosecutor has made a truly commendable record during his first term in office," the *News-Bee* editor wrote, "but little has been done about banks. Here is the place, and now is the time to do something."[90] Toledo's newly inaugurated mayor, Solon T. Klotz, denounced Reams in one of his first

public speeches, saying: "If you are a gangster, God help you, you'll get the
electric chair, but if you starve and rob thousands, you are O.K."[91]

In response, Reams charged that the grand jury's actions were actually
a "political trick of disgruntled Republicans," insinuating that the jurors had
been hand-selected by Republican bosses and used to sully his reputation
so as to keep him from becoming the Democrat's nominee for Ohio attorney general in the upcoming election. Certainly, such a scheme was not unprecedented in the rough-and-tumble history of Toledo municipal politics. But
such an accusation carried less weight than it might have in previous years,
as the grand jury he had accused of political intrigue was the first in which
a number of the jurors had been selected at random rather than being all
hand-picked by the presiding judge. Of the fifteen members of the jury, nine
had been selected by Judge Stuart and six were chosen by the jury wheel.
The letter condemning Reams was signed by all fifteen jurors.[92]

The process of selecting a new grand jury began the day after Reams made
his dramatic accusations against the retiring jury. This time it was Judge
Stahl's turn to be head judge, and he was determined to avoid a repeat of
the embarrassments of the previous week. Judge Stahl drew the entire jury
from the random pool and, as a result, for the first time in county history,
ended up with a jury that included women. After the usual examinations
and oaths, Stahl lectured his jurors sternly: "Your function is not to render
opinions but to return indictments if you feel the evidence before you so
justifies. You are not detectives." Clearly, Stahl did not want this grand jury
poking its nose where it was not led, like the last one had.[93]

While the new grand jury looked into new indictments, the by-then three-
year-old indictments of five different bankers still languished in legal pur-
gatory. In early February, the first big break in those cases came when an
Ohio appellate court overruled Judge Martin's dismissal of the charges against
Stacy McNary, clearing the way for trial in all the pending cases. A week
later, the U.S. Supreme Court refused to hear the appeal of LeRoy
Eastman, stating its lack of jurisdiction in the matter. For the moment, at
least, all impediments to prosecution were overcome.[94]

Within a fortnight of this decision, Reams stood before Judge Stahl and
asked him to schedule an "early date" for the trials. "Any time you say,"
replied the judge. "We'll start within a few days, then," Reams stated. Three
weeks later, Reams had still not placed the bankers' cases on the docket.
James Toppin of the *East Side Sun* had had enough and posted this open
letter to Reams on page 1 of his paper:

> You promised immediate, vigorous prosecutions of all the bank cases!
> That was almost a month ago! We haven't seen much that is new in the

daily press since you made that promise. What is being done in these bank prosecutions? . . . [You have] done an impressive job in investigating activities of the Licavoli gang . . . Now, Mr. Reams, how about the bankers?[95]

Ten more days passed and still there was no word from the prosecutor's office as to when the bankers' trials would be held. Though there were no remaining legal impediments to trial, the prosecutor's office did not move to schedule a trial for over a year.[96]

At the same moment, with stunning suddenness, the grand jury that had been working since early January hearing evidence of misappropriations in the city's distribution of food to the hungry, summoned Edward Falkenstein, the chief investigator of the Senate Banking Committee, signaling the opening of yet another bank investigation. Later that day, Frazier Reams checked himself into the Toledo Hospital, suffering from what his spokesman described as "fatigue and nervous exhaustion." It was later learned that the grand jury's target that day was the Commercial Savings Bank, which counted among its directors in 1931 its rising star, Frazier Reams.

While Reams took his hospital rest, the grand jury heard testimony from both Commercial Bank officials and bank customers. Mrs. Percy B. Williams testified that she purchased a home in the Westmoreland development and took out a $6,000 mortgage with Commercial Bank but found out later that that the bank had recorded her note as being worth $12,000. William Rundell told how he paid off some personal loans in May of 1931, less than a month before the bank collapsed, but though the bank took his payment, it didn't cancel his notes. August Streicher said he purchased participation certificates in mortgage trusts marketed by Commercial Bank and was infuriated when he discovered that the bank was continually shuffling mortgages into and out of the trust, a practice known as "pyramiding" that allowed the bank to hide its bad assets at the certificate-owners' expense. Williams, Rundell, and Streicher were unusual not because they testified to the jury—many others did as well—but because they again told their stories to reporters milling in the courthouse corridor.[97]

As the queue of Commercial Bank witnesses lengthened outside the closed jury room doors, Frazier Reams decided to flee south "for his health." For the next six weeks his exact whereabouts were not disclosed, some saying he had gone to Florida, others claiming he was in his home state of Tennessee. In either case, he was conveniently beyond the reach of Lucas County's grand jury. Moreover, in their boss's absence, the assistant prosecutors made no move to schedule the bankers' trials.[98]

Though none of the daily newspapers made an issue of Reams' timely vacation, the *News-Bee* did hint that something was amiss when a reporter asked Assistant Prosecutor Rhinefort, "Why did Prosecutor Reams leave Toledo just when the Commercial bank investigation started?" but chose not to push further when Rhinefort replied "The reason as already stated in the press—his illness."[99] Once again, only the spunky *East Side News* was bold enough to lay its suspicions before the public:

> Just about, or shortly after the Commercial Savings Bank and Trust Co. Bank investigation got under way, Prosecutor Reams (or Banker Reams—take your choice; anyway one and the same gentleman) had to "go South for his health!" according to the daily papers. The article did not say whether it was for the "tummy ache" or for a more serious ailment! . . . In light of what has been brought out by the Senate investigations, and the documentary evidence that substantiates the facts . . . for the life of us we cannot see why the Prosecutor of Lucas County, Frazier Reams, does not concentrate on these bank cases and put them on trial.[100]

After a month of testimony from over twenty witnesses, the grand jury found itself buried under an accumulated mound of evidence and statistics on the condition of the Commercial Bank and the behavior of its directors. Drawn from every walk of life, the jurors had no particular expertise in banking or the law. Throughout their hearings they remained dependent on the advice and opinions of the assistant prosecutors to make sense out of a daunting mass of evidence. With just a few days to go in their term, Assistant Prosecutor Rhinefort expressed his opinion that there wasn't enough time for the jury to complete their work and the work left unfinished by this panel would have to be taken up by the next. In spite of Rhinefort's pessimism, the jurors sincerely tried to complete their work, deliberating for five straight hours on the last legal day of their term. Several times they paused and requested clarification of the bank laws from the prosecutors, but in the end, in spite of their heroic efforts and their flouting of Judge Stahl's warning to not act like "detectives," the jurors were unable to agree and adjourned without voting fresh indictments.[101]

The failure of yet another grand jury fueled more rumors and whispers among political observers. Assistant Prosecutor Rhinefort was even compelled to publicly deny that he had received instructions from superiors to handle any bank case "with gloves," to state that he didn't believe that the grand jury had "passed the buck," and to claim, "I do not know the reasons which prompted the grand jury in its findings and report . . .," which was odd given that he had been closely involved in all aspects of their hearings.[102]

Another new grand jury was empanelled, and it was soon announced that it too had begun to look into bank matters, but it had chosen not to pick up where the old jury left off, with the Commercial Bank, but instead to examine the Commerce Guardian Bank. A few weeks later a "deeply-tanned, robust, and radiant" Frazier Reams returned to Toledo from the rustic cabin in the hills of Tennessee where he had hidden out in seclusion.[103]

Judging by letters from readers published in the daily papers, frustration against Reams and the lack of progress in the bank cases reached an all-time high in the spring of 1934. "What is the prosecutor doing about it? Is he listening to shyster lawyers to protect bankers?" wrote one. Another complained: "Our wonderful new deal prosecutor was going to do something great, according to the speeches he made before he was elected to office. He was going to put the bankers in jail in no time. But what has he done? Fooled his time away on slot machines and beer rackets. When finally a banker did come up for trial he got cold feet and had to go to Florida for his health and get his feet warm . . . Toledo is one of the worst towns in the United States, if not the worst, the bankers and politicians play hand-in-hand—what one can't get the other does . . ." One anonymous reader wrote: "The prosecutor should not be allowed to shelve the bank cases any longer in favor of any other case, lest they grow so stale that they be forgotten and thereby certain parties who want them forgotten be satisfied. The public is sick and tired of the flaunting of murder cases, gambling investigations and other matters as a screen to hide the bank purveyors . . ." "Why can't we have an honest, sincere probe of the failed banks . . . ?" another letter-writer pleaded, "Is it because County Prosecutor Reams is mixed up in the Commercial bank situation?"[104]

When the year 1934 began, the *East Side Sun* observed that the powerful mass movement of depositors that formed in the fall of 1931 had vanished while the issues they fought for remained alive. "Where are all the people of Toledo who have [been] robbed of their money by these "smart money" manipulators? Are they just dumb and dense, or are they afraid?" In what would prove to be an eerily prophetic passage, the *Sun* attempted to spur the movement to life:

> Remember, no matter how hopeless and forlorn a cause might have appeared, history records hundreds of instances where an enraged populace have risen en masse and have secured justice and punished wrong-doers! It can be done in Toledo in 1934 if the citizens of Toledo have any "guts" left! What are YOU going to do about it? Are YOU going to let them rob you and get away with it?[105]

Though three years of investigations, hearings, and legal proceedings had not produced any convictions of bankers, they had proved very effective in deepening the public's contempt for their criminal justice system. One week after the spring grand jury adjourned without taking action in the bank cases, Judge Stuart issued an injunction against leaders of a fledgling automobile workers union who were organizing mass picketing in support of a strike that was unfolding less than a mile from his courtroom. The judge ordered the union to allow no more than twenty-five picketers at one time in front of the massive brick Auto-Lite factory. In response, a group of radicals who had spent the last several years organizing unemployed workers and demanding a more humane system of relief sent a letter to Judge Stuart stating that they would "deliberately and specifically" violate his order which was "an abrogation of our democratic rights." On the morning of May 7 police arrested four leaders of the strike for picketing, and they all returned to the picket line as soon as they posted their bail money. A few days later forty-six men were hustled into paddy wagons, and by the time the men were lined up before Judge Stuart's bench, the courthouse was jammed with hundreds of protesters who cheered and sang union songs and demanded they be charged with contempt too. Over the next week, hundreds of people were arrested for contempt of Stuart's injunction and contempt it was—contempt for a system of justice that the growing crowds in front of the Auto-Lite factory had come to believe served only the city's bankers and bosses.[106]

What began as a strike aimed at winning recognition of a new-found auto-workers union grew by the end of May into a full scale urban riot. On a Monday afternoon, the spirited crowd in front of the Auto-Lite factory grew to include over a thousand people who listened to speeches before a large banner that read "1776, 1865, 1934." The crowd doubled in size by supper time and kept doubling each day until on Wednesday there were at least six thousand protesters walking the picket line. Inside, a skeleton crew of scabs tried to keep the plant running while hastily deputized company guards fixed tear gas launchers to the roof and barred the doors. The spark was an iron bolt thrown out of an upper story window that struck a young female picketer in the head, knocking her unconscious. City police moved in and arrested the strike leaders they could find and beat an elderly striker in full sight, provoking the riot that would envelop the neighborhood for the next three days. It took the largest peacetime deployment of Ohio's national guard, the arrest of hundreds, the declaring of martial law throughout the city, the wounding of hundreds, the shooting deaths of two protesters, and finally the intervention of the federal and state officials who pressured Auto-Lite owner Clement O. Miniger to recognize the union, to put down the rebellion. The Auto-Lite riot marked the beginning of the eventual unionization of the automobile industry and gave impetus to passage of the

landmark National Labor Relations Act that put unions on a solid legal footing for the first time.

The links between the Auto-Lite strike and the banking crisis seemed
very direct to the protesters in the street. The owner and president of the
Auto-Lite Corporation was none other than Clement O. Miniger, a
director of the Ohio Bank and a leading shareholder in both the Ohio and
the Security-Home banks. The Marshall bank investigation committee revealed
in January that Miniger had withdrawn every last penny left in his savings
account, $141,504.55, on the Security-Home's last day of operation, June
16, 1931.[107] His Auto-Lite company withdrew $46,050. In light of these
facts, alongside the frequent analogy drawn between the behavior of bankers
and gangsters, the most popular signs carried by picketers outside the gates
of the Auto-Lite plant make sense. They read: "We Don't Need
Dillinger—We Have Miniger." Interestingly, police confiscated many protesters' signs and introduced them as evidence of violation of Judge
Stuart's injunction, though company lawyers chose not to bring signs with
that particular slogan to the courtroom.[108] The correspondent for the *New
Republic* explained the Auto-Lite strike as a "civil war" that "surged up from
a long series of abuses against the workers in this hitherto open-shop town,"
specifically, "broken pledges by the management of the Electric Auto-Lite
Company" and the "connection of C. O. Miniger, president of that company, with the Toledo bank collapse which ruined thousands."[109]

Though Toledo's workers won the Auto-Lite strike, their violent
protest against an important symbol of the city's financial oligarchy did little to propel the prosecution of Toledo's bankers. Without explanation, Frazier
Reams had quietly chosen not to schedule LeRoy Eastman's trial as he had
claimed he was going to do quickly months earlier. One disheartened depositor, who described himself as "one of the many victims of misplaced confidence," was prophetic: "Remember this prediction. Not one of the many
known guilty plunderers will ever serve a day for their crimes . . ."[110]

Later that month, the Ohio Supreme Court kicked the props out from
under the state's case. In a split four-to-two decision, Ohio's high court ruled
that bankers voting themselves a dividend when a bank is insolvent was a
"bad practice," but because the statute forbidding it stated no specific criminal penalties, it was not a crime. The state's argument that this practice
amounted to the same thing as "misappropriation of funds," and was therefore punishable, did not impress the majority of formalist judges.[111]

The supreme court's ruling quashed twenty-six of the remaining fifty charges
pending against the six bankers. All that remained were those two charges
that relied on statutes that specified clear penalties for violators: making
false reports and accepting deposits into a bankrupt bank. In one sense, the

court had wiped out years of litigation and prosecutorial work in a stroke. In another, though, the court had forced the prosecutor's office to do what it perhaps should have done from the start—to prioritize the false report and deposit cases where they always had the best chances of conviction and firmest legal ground to fight appeals.

But instead of proceeding swiftly to trial on the remaining counts, the prosecutor's office wavered and delayed again. Rather than moving to trial, the prosecutor's office spent its time filing rejoinders to a train of motions by the bankers moving to dismiss the cases on various grounds. Had a date been set down in the docket, these motions, none of them having any merit and many of them merely carbon copies of motions already overruled years before, would have been expedited. As it was, from the summer and fall of 1934 until the summer of 1936, Reams seemed content to react, which allowed the defense to establish the snail's pace of the prosecution. For example, in September of 1934 George Eastman successfully tied things up by getting Judge Stahl to accept his claim of double jeopardy and dismiss him. It took until February of 1935 for the appeals court to reverse Judge Stahl and until April of the following year before the Ohio Supreme Court upheld the appeals court decision. During this long period, the prosecutor's office claimed it could not proceed against any of the other five defendants until these issues were cleared up, though neither Gunckel, Hoehler, Mills, or Whitmore had ever been to trial and therefore could not possibly, not even by the most tortured legal reasoning, claim the same double-jeopardy defense as Eastman. When next the banker defendants stood in a courtroom facing arraignment in late April of 1936, their lawyers objected and with straight faces argued that the charges should be dismissed because their clients had been denied their constitutional rights to a swift and speedy trial.[112]

Finally, the trial of McNary, Gunckel, Mills, and Eastman was scheduled to begin on Monday, May 11, 1936. Just as it got under way, defense counsel asked the judge to order the prosecutor's office to present them with copies of all the relevant documents that their evidence was derived from. Since the prosecutors had several years before commissioned audits of banking records and planned on using the summaries of that research in their case, the defendants demanded copies of all the original bank records those broad audits were compiled from. The number of records requested amounted to many tens of thousands of pages which, given the technology of the day, would have taken weeks, perhaps months to reproduce at an expense of thousands of dollars that the prosecutor's office did not have. Curiously, rather than responding that they would simply make the original records available to the defense at an appropriate location and convenient times, the prosecutor's office fought the motion, carrying their objection to this discovery through another serpentine road of appeals all the way up to the Ohio Supreme Court. By the time the motion was upheld, nearly another year's time had flowed by. Along the way, Frazier Ream's term as prosecutor had expired, and he moved on to become the chair of the Democratic party in Ohio and to the patronage post that went with it, collector of internal revenue.[113]

Toledo's new prosecutor, Thomas J. O'Connor, a longtime Democratic boss, showed no more eagerness to start the banker trials than his predecessor. Though he took office on New Year's Day, 1937 and the last pending appeals court decisions were handed down a month later, O'Connor didn't initiate any action in the cases until July. Then he took action and asked the local court to nullify all the remaining charges still hanging, ever so lightly, over the surviving five bankers (Frank Hoehler died in 1935).

O'Connor based his request on his view that the charges against the bankers were too difficult to prove and that the financial burden that would be placed on the county in attempting to prove them was prohibitive, estimating it would cost about $100,000, more than the entire annual budget of his office. O'Connor claimed that each of these cases required that the state prove that the Security-Home Bank was insolvent though the bank's own statements claimed it to be millions in the black. To do this, he believed that the rules of evidence required him to "introduce each note, mortgage, bond or other instrument" of the bank for consideration.

However, O'Connor failed to mention that the difficult task of proving the insolvency of the bank was only present in two of the remaining six indictments, namely, number 21051 that charged McNary, Mills, Gunckel and Eastman with accepting deposits while the bank was insolvent and number 20404 that charged McNary alone with reporting the bank solvent when it was actually bankrupt. However, there remained two indictments against Stacy McNary and two against Clifford Whitmore, the highest bank officials, where the state would not be required to establish the overall health of the bank. Indictments 20399 and 20400 alleged McNary illegally purchased shares of prohibited stocks and then forged a fictitious note to hide this fact from state bank inspectors. Whether the bank as a whole was bankrupt or profitable made no difference in determining whether McNary purchased these stocks or filed these false reports. Whitmore's indictments likewise charged him with illegally borrowing protected trust funds to finance a real estate scam involving the Security Bank's headquarters and then covering up these transactions in false reports to the state. Clearly, if O'Connor had wanted to continue to pursue McNary and Whitmore, he could have without having to hurdle the high evidentiary bar he complained of. From the beginning of the bankers' cases it had always been true that these charges were the easiest to prove and most legally secure, though curiously all of O'Connor's predecessors chose to pursue them last.

On July 10, 1937, the longest criminal trials in Ohio history came to an end when Judge Scott Stahl, the judge who three years earlier had warned a grand jury intent on investigating bankers that they "were not detectives," nullified all the remaining charges against the five bank officers. Stahl also erased secret indictments against two other bankers that had never been arrested because one of them had left the country, and it was said that arresting the one would tip off the other that he was wanted. As a result, their identity remains a secret to this day. In releasing the bankers, Judge Stahl said not one word about the merits of the cases or the legal issues involved in the banking laws, but merely said he was granting permission to nolle the indictments because "I have the utmost faith in his [O'Connor's] integrity and feel sure that no consideration other than an honest desire to serve the public could in any way color or influence his official act."[114]

Besides lawyers for the defendants, there was no one in the courtroom to witness this historic moment except for one observer who asked permission to address the court. (Prosecutor O'Connor had some other engagement.) Walter Baertschi, one of the original organizers of the depositors' movement after the banks failed, stood and launched into a cascade of complaints, denouncing how the bankers had raided the savings of thousands, how witnesses had seen a bank president leaving the bank with a bag full of money, how insiders and their pet corporations were allowed to drain their deposits while the common person was locked out. He accused the judge and the prosecutor of holding a double standard, saying that they would never complain of the cost of bringing an armed bank robber to trial.

After six years, a half-dozen grand juries, one state senate investigation, two Ohio Supreme Court decisions, and three county prosecutors, none of the original seventy charges stuck. Toledo's bankers escaped punishment not simply because the laws of Ohio were weak, but because the political and juridical systems that controlled the administration of justice were all structured in their favor. Bankers were able to use the very profits that they were charged with accumulating illegally to finance a limitless succession of delays and appeals. The economic chaos wrought by the failure of their banks bankrupted the county and sharply limited the resources available to their legal adversaries. But perhaps their greatest power lay in the fact that upon the success of these six bankers in beating their raps hinged the fate of scores of other powerful men. These six represented just one of the four major banks that collapsed. The crimes with which they were charged were very similar, in some cases even less audacious, than practices that appear to have been common among Toledo's bankers prior to June of 1931. Throughout those many years of litigation dozens of other powerful and politically influential men knew their own fate was clouded as long as charges continued against the Security-Home Six. Even the prosecutor during most of those years was certainly aware that his political career and even his own liberty were at risk if some of the charges he pursued were successful. The record of these cases strongly suggests that due to these pressures, due to the political power of the class of men whose actions placed them in the same legal categories as the bankers in the dock, local judges contorted themselves to accommodate the defendants, all parties dragged their feet, and the prosecutors hindered grand juries and chose their weakest legal options over their strongest.

Immediately with the quashing of all the charges, the meaning of these events began to be reinterpreted in a way that came to view them as transcending the individual. Prosecutor O'Connor, reflecting on the history of the bankers' case, argued that society could at last understand the events of the summer of 1931 in their proper perspective:

> These indictments were reported . . . at a time when the public mind was inflamed, and intense feeling existing [sic] in the community, owing to the widespread closing of the Toledo banks. The grand jury considered the evidence under the circumstances then existing and the real situation, worldwide in character, could not be adequately appraised and the fundamental issues involved were obscured.[115]

With the passage of time the inflammatory passions of the mob had died down, O'Connor argued, and all could properly appreciate that what happened in Toledo in the summer of 1931 was merely part of a worldwide economic phenomenon known as "The Great Depression." Thus, there were no individual agents of this disaster, only victims. While businessmen would not likewise credit Adam Smith's invisible hand for their success, they were quick to blame their failures on the equally disembodied workings of the business cycle. The Great Depression, like a terrible storm that rips through the town, was of nobody's making and no one's fault. This pattern of thinking would come to dominate popular and academic views of the Depression and made possible the quick reassertion of the customary status and privileges of Toledo's bankers.

EPILOGUE

In 1932 a Polish grocer leased the old Security-Home Opeika Bank branch on Lagrange Avenue. He removed the wooden shutters from the large front windows, swept out the dust, installed new counters, and applied a coat of whitewash to turn the lobby into a corner store. Before he was finished several people shuffled in and handed him their old Security-Home bank books and asked for their money back. Sadly he told them that this was no longer a bank, that he only rented the space for his store.

A couple of months after the supreme court ruled in 1934 that it was not illegal for bank directors to vote themselves dividends when their bank was bankrupt, a group of men and women, sweating in the August heat, crammed into the elevator at the courthouse. The genial operator pulled closed the metal gate and turned the handle to descend. Suddenly there was a metallic grinding sound and those inside let out an involuntary shout as the car plunged. Luckily they had dropped only one floor and no one was badly hurt. For the second time that month the operator wrenched back the door and helped his passengers to safety. The county's own elevator was no longer safe.

Three years before, after the banks failed, the county commissioners were forced to make hard choices in the face of a gaping deficit. Among the hundreds of county employees laid off and never rehired were the elevator inspectors.[1] Later that week, the judges, lawyers, secretaries, clerks, and LeRoy Eastman took the stairs to get to the courtroom where Judge Stahl vacated all the charges against the banker who had done his part to ensure that they would all be walking rather than riding up to the courtroom that day.[2]

In early December of 1935, Franklin Roosevelt's presidential train made a stop at Toledo's crumbling Union Station, which was so decrepit and uncomfortable that crowds had watched and cheered as a portion of it burned down in 1930. It was the first time a president had come to the city since Hoover swung through at the time of the city's bank crash of 1931.

Since that time, Toledo had sunk to the distinction of having more of its population on government relief programs than any other of the thirty-seven cities surveyed by the Federal Emergency Relief Agency. More than one in six of all Toledoans depended on government handouts to survive, compared with the national average of one in ten. In spite of the chill in the cloudy evening air, several thousand people crowded around the rear of his Pullman car to see him. Roosevelt spoke for less than five minutes, telling the crowd they had a friend in Washington, before traveling on.[3]

As the President's train pulled away it passed the scars of a city in collapse. In spite of repeated police attempts to clear squatters out from along the Maumee River, its banks were crowded with shacks. That night, Roosevelt may have noticed how dark the city was, as the city had long before rationed the replacement of light bulbs in street lights and many of the theatres along St. Clair street, the city's theatre district once dubbed the "great white way" for its brilliant marquee lights, were boarded up. By day it may have looked as if the city was being gradually reclaimed by the countryside, for many people plowed up their lawns to plant vegetables and the city gave permission for 3,234 vacant lots to be claimed for gardens. Even that wasn't enough to prevent an old-fashioned bread riot with hundreds of people breaking into a grocery store in September of 1932 and then audaciously parading to the county courthouse to demand more relief.[4]

As the train crossed over the river, just to the north stood the bent and torn members of the Fasset Street Bridge, which had collapsed back in September and stood in shambles for lack of money to repair it. When Roosevelt returned to Toledo two years later, had he looked out his window he would have seen the Fasset Street Bridge in the same sorry shape. Even though it was one of only three spans connecting the city across the river, Toledoans had to wait until 1938 for the WPA to repair it.[5]

Other scars left by the city's bankruptcy were less visible. By 1932 the city was forced to pay its employees with IOUs, paper scrip that local grocers, and, reportedly, even local bootleggers, accepted at a discount. Each succeeding year saw more layoffs until what had once been considered essential personnel were also let go. Ironically, it was Toledo's one socialist mayor, Solon Trembely Klotz, who finally cut fifty policemen and fifty firemen from the city payroll and closed four fire stations in 1934, a year that happened to see a record number of fires ravage the city. Maintenance and replacement of old fire equipment was deferred so long that half the fire equipment in the department's inventory was in need of repair. The city's director of finance reported that "owing to mechanical failures fire companies often could not respond to alarms or, having reached the site, were unable to function properly, causing heavier fire losses due to delays in attacking fires."[6]

The depression that gripped the city disrupted the normal patterns of life in ways far beyond the locked factory gate and the shuttered bank. Couples choose to delay or forgo marriage in tough times. In the three years prior to the bank crisis there were 28,855 marriages. In the three years after the banks failed roughly a quarter as many lovers (7,676) took vows. On the other hand, divorces fell by more than half, in part due to the expense of litigation and, apparently, in part due to the need to keep families together as an economic unit. The cold numbers printed in the annual reports of court dockets illustrate how mass unemployment and long bread lines served to cruelly limit the options of couples trapped in unhappy relationships. While the numbers of those filing for divorce on the grounds of "willful absence" and "gross neglect"—causes which suggest no economic incentive to remain coupled—remained steady, the number of those suing because of "adultery" dropped by two-thirds, for "drunkenness" by half, and for "extreme cruelty" by six-sevenths. Apparently, privation forced many to endure a philandering or abusive spouse who paid the rent, but not one who didn't.[7]

Many facing the choice of hunger or crime chose the latter. Petty larcenies averaged 212 per month in the quarter that began in April 1931 and jumped to 254 for that beginning in August. Prior to the summer of 1931, the highest number of complaints for petty theft was 252 recorded in October of 1930. Nine out of the twelve months for which records were kept following Toledo's bank failures exceeded that record.[8] One entire neighborhood on the city's east side organized the systematic looting of passing railroad cars, with some participants soaping the tracks to slow the cars, others forcing doors, and others hurriedly carting grain or coal away. One mugger was quoted as apologizing to his victim, "I wouldn't be doing this if I could get a job."[9]

Statistical measures of socially aberrant behaviors peaked at the time of Toledo's bank failures. The 51 murders committed in that year were a 31 percent jump from 1930 and proved to be the most recorded in the city between the world wars. In spite of Prohibition, deaths from cirrhosis of the liver also jumped 43 percent; falling just one body short of the interwar high set in 1935 after Congress opened the taps again. However, a Depression economy did have one positive effect on public health—because of the closing of factories and a decline in railroad traffic, industrial accidents declined to rates not seen in twenty years.[10]

The breadth of the dislocation and destruction wrought by the Depression on Toledo is evident in the gross figures reported by the U.S. Census Bureau. Between the decennial censuses of 1930 and 1940, the city that had a generation before been one of the fastest growing in the nation saw its population decline from 290,718 to 282,349. Disaggregating the num-

Figure 8
A Toledo cartoonist lampoons the secrecy of local bankers, 1935. (Reprinted with permission of the *Blade*)

bers reveals that the bulk of this drop was among the foreign-born, who composed over 10 percent of the population in 1930. More than a quarter of this community, long the foundation of the city's industrial workforce, had left Toledo by 1940.

Beginning in 1940, the Ohio Department of Banks began petitioning Lucas County judges for permission to destroy all the remaining records of Toledo's failed banks. Claiming that it was acting to "obviate the necessity of expending several hundred dollars in connection with the removal and storage of these records," state officials moved to burn truckloads of files as each failed bank's liquidation was concluded. Even before these furnaces were stoked, much of the most incriminating evidence had already been destroyed. In 1933, during the trial of Stacy McNary, a bookkeeper employed by the state liquidation officials testified that he could not audit the bank's balance sheets because many of the Security-Home's bank files were missing. Frank J. Klauser, who was put in charge of liquidating the Security-Home's trust department, told state investigators that Joseph Eppstein, the special counsel representing the Ohio attorney general's office in Toledo, visited his office and demanded all records relating to the McCondin Heights Addition. Klauser reluctantly turned these over and grew even more suspicious when Eppstein refused to give him a receipt. Joseph Eppstein was the brother of Isadore Eppstein, who was a partner in the Security-Bond Company, which reportedly sold forged mortgage certificates of McCondin Heights Addition properties to the Security-Home Bank. Before the decade was out all the bank records of this tragedy were nothing more than smoke (figure 8).[11]

Due to a dearth of historic banking records, it is difficult to assess how typical the Toledo bank run episode was. State regulators worked in secret, sometimes covering up their own lackadaisical enforcement of bank laws. State legislatures, at the urging of their state's financial industries, later sealed or destroyed their banking records. Today, none of the economically most important states of the banking crisis of the 1930s (New York, Pennsylvania, Michigan, Ohio, or Illinois) have, or allow access to, the records of their state banking departments.[12]

Without such detailed financial records, researchers must rely on more general evidence that points to a broad pattern of fraudulent banking practices during the 1920s and 1930s. The historical record of this era is filled with vague references to the "inappropriate" actions and "mismanagement" of banks. Naturally, when pressed to explain the financial crisis at all, conservative politicians and state regulators preferred to describe the actions of powerful bankers and businessmen as incompetent rather than criminal; the former category was water under the bridge, while the later demanded justice. Yet behind such unspecific language lurked a wide range of behavior, which, while often not technically criminal under the lax statutes of the day, certainly revolved around placing the interest of the banks' officers and investors ahead of the public's. When a bank run threatened, this likely included removing their money, or otherwise sheltering their assets from being distributed through state liquidation, before any worried crowds could press through the doors.

Because the withdrawal of "smart money" took place out of the public's view, the extent of the practice can only be guessed at. Only occasionally, as in the case of Toledo's bank failures and a few others, do these back-door bank runs surface in the historical record. For example, the former bank commissioner of Connecticut, recounting his experiences trying to stem the tide of bank failures in his state during the Depression, took credit for intervening quickly to prevent "attempts made to give preference to certain depositors just previous to the closing of a bank" though he was not so impolitic as to name any names.[13]

Though the historical record of smart money runs is thin, it was nonetheless the case that the temptation for bankers to tip off their relatives, friends, and business associates about the likely failure of their bank was strong in all cases. Clarence Budington Kelland was a director of a bank that failed in 1931 and later wrote down his insider's story for a popular monthly magazine. Kelland describes well the pressures on a banker in that situation: "When we in our bank realized we were at the last ditch it wasn't a pleasant time. We had money in the bank ourselves. I had numerous friends, even relatives, who had in it sums they could ill afford to lose. And when the bank closed I felt they would come to me and say, 'Hey, Bud, what's the idea? You were a director. You knew what was coming. A swell friend you were not to tip us off!'"[14]

Likewise, the New Republic observed, "the people who work in banks are human and they behave like human beings when they discover that their bank is about to blow up. They tell their uncles and aunts and brothers-in-law to withdraw 'quietly' and then the fat is in the fire."[15]

The underlying factors that doomed Toledo's banks—the accumulation of excessive real estate paper, lax enforcement by state regulators, insider loans, and bank management's unwillingness to charge down actual losses—were all commonly mentioned as being causes of bank failures. T. Bruce Robb, who conducted an intensive study of bank failures in Nebraska, generalized that lax enforcement, an excessive proliferation of banks, and incompetent bank management were the major factors in the bank failures of the 1930s. Robb pointed in particular to the problem of the interlocking business interests of bankers: "One of the great curses of a decentralized system of unit banks as developed in this country is the opportunity it affords to men of affairs to enter the banking business and use the community's deposits to lubricate their private ventures. No man can successfully serve two masters, and the spectacle of a banker in the role of a credit man making loans to his own enterprises is grotesque."[16]

In his own study of Nebraska banks, Robb found that nearly all of the one hundred and sixteen failed banks that he examined routinely broke state banking laws that capped the amount of loans to any one person at 20 percent of a bank's capital and surplus. The practice was so widespread that Robb reported, "there was scarcely a bank among those audited that did not violate this rule—many of them flagrantly and brazenly."[17]

Such interlocking interests of bankers and developers were also cited as one of the root causes of the Chicago bank panic of 1931. In one widely read post-mortem, it was noted that the banks that tended to fail first in Chicago were those "organized by real-estate men" who used the bank to promote their own businesses.[18]

Many contemporary economists placed great weight on the human factor in Depression bank failures. Robert Weidenhammer, an economist with the University of Minnesota who headed a survey of fifty failed banks in that state in the early 1930s, concluded that external factors were not nearly as important as the actions of their managers: "all banks failed for well-defined reasons that were the reflection of poor management methods. Overextended loan portfolios and no secondary reserves, these two main evidences of faulty operating policies, are after all only the result of the same managerial sin." Weidenhammer, however, chose not to probe the reasons why bankers recklessly overextended themselves in this way.[19]

Former bank regulator George Bassett found that much of the weakness of banks in his state of Connecticut was also due to "many cases of loans made on unsound credit or inadequate collateral, some indications that certain borrowers had 'pull' . . ."[20] Economist Walter Spahr, who attempted the first national analysis of bank failures in the United States, estimated that an overwhelming number of them were due to "poor management," by which he meant "officers are of an inferior sort" who "permit sentiment to play too large a part in the making of local loans" and "directorates usually . . . filled with local businessmen who know little about banking and often are indifferent regarding the bank's affairs." Economist C. D. Bremer, whose 1935 study of bank failures is still frequently cited, concluded that "the immediate causes of many failures may be directly traced to grossly injudicious as well as illegal practices." Robert G. Rodkey, whose study of Michigan bank failures appeared the same year, concluded that in spite of the depression, "there was nothing fundamental in conditions in Michigan which made it relatively difficult to conduct banking on a sound basis" and that the data "indicates incompetence as the fundamental cause of failure of these banks . . ."[21]

Recent studies have revealed that withdrawals by bank officers and directors, either directly or through offsetting unsecured loans, were a cause of the collapse of the banking industry in Florida in 1926 and the later collapse of the Manley banking chain in Georgia.[22] Chicago's neighborhood banks fell like dominos after some chain bankers were tried for giving unsecured loans to friends and political associates.[23] A number of banks that contributed to the Michigan banking holiday, including Detroit's huge First National Bank, engaged in financial shell games, stock kiting schemes, or book falsification.[24] The most important bank failures of the first years of the Depression, the collapse of Caldwell and Company of Nashville and New York's Bank of the United States, involved a long list of fraudulent practices.[25] Even Milton Friedman and Anna Jacobson Schwartz (though they do not analyze the meaning of "bad management") conclude from their reading of Fed meeting minutes that "[members of the Federal Reserve Board] tended to regard bank failures as regrettable consequences of bad management and bad banking practices, or as inevitable reactions to prior speculative excesses, or as a consequence but hardly a cause of the financial and economic collapse in process." Given that such was the case, "The relatively few large member banks that failed at the end of 1930 were regarded by many Reserve officials as unfortunate cases of bad management and therefore not subject to correction by central bank action."[26]

A study commissioned by an industry lobby group in 1932 investigating the causes of bank failures admitted that "general all-around poor management," "large loans to officers and directors," "defalcation and embezzlement," and "excessive loans to businesses in which officers or directors are interested," all played a major role.[27] The California superintendent of banks concluded in 1928 that over one-quarter of the bank failures in his state "resulted solely from the dishonesty of an officer . . ." The "predominating cause" of the rest skated the ill-defined borderland between criminal and irresponsible behavior, including "mismanagement, which manifested itself in a wide variety of ways, chief among which were excessive loans to individuals, poor investment, failure to secure proper collateral, payment of unwarranted dividends, a general inability to retain sufficient liquid assets to meet extraordinary demands of depositors, and finally, actual inability to maintain a cash reserve equal to that provided for in the Bank Act of this state."[28] J. F. T. O'Connor, the U.S. comptroller of the currency during the New Deal, also laid the blame for the banking industry's shaky foundations on the corrupt insider dealing of the bankers themselves.[29] His predecessor had previously estimated that 9 percent of the failures that occurred in 1930 were directly due to "dishonesty," on top of 38 percent that were due to "incompetent management."[30] (Given that incompetence was one legal defense against the charge of dishonesty, these figures probably need to be considered together rather than separately.) Former comptroller John W. Pole "touched off a few fireworks in Washington" in the spring of 1933 when he told a Senate committee that "Defalcations are common matters . . ." Interrupted by an Indiana senator who blustered, "Do you mean to say that defalcations by bank presidents are common?" Pole affirmed that they were and agreed with the senator that for that reason it was "no wonder at all" that the public had no confidence in the banks.[31]

Likewise, in 1929, officials from the Federal Reserve testified before Congress that insider loans were an important cause of banking failures in the United States.[32] In 1933 an assistant attorney general of the United States told Congress that occasions where bank officials had placed false entries in their books were so common that it no longer attracted his official attention.[33] Interestingly, the only state in the nation that suffered no bank failures between 1930 and 1932, Rhode Island, was also the state with the toughest laws criminalizing insider bank loans.[34]

Because few state banking officials were willing to tackle their state's powerful banking lobbies, few states thoroughly investigated the microeconomic behavior of officers of failed banks. Though this makes it difficult for historians to piece together the full story of the banking collapse, the outline can be discerned. While state officials rarely pursued indictments against bank officials for violations of state banking laws, the U.S. attorney general made something of an attempt to uphold federal laws. The AG's prosecutions provide one benchmark for the level of flagrant criminality in the banking community. In 1931, the AG's office prosecuted 427 individuals for breaking federal banking laws, double the number from just the year before.[35] On average in this period, about one in five of those convicted were executive officers of banks. Given their considerable resources with which to mount a defense, this is a large number indeed.[36]

Many fragments of the story are to be found in the avalanche of private lawsuits that began to cascade into the court system in the late 1920s. Counting just the suits that reached the appellate level between 1926 and 1942, over 450 separate suits alleged some sort of financial chicanery on the part of bankers.[37] In 1932, the *Notre Dame Lawyer*, a respected law journal, noted that "Thousands of bankers and 'figure head directors' have fallen heir to civil litigation by virtue of their titular offices."[38] Among the offenses commonly charged were the making of false entries, illegal insider loans, fraudulent investment schemes, and illegal withdrawals. Needless to say, many of the institutions in question failed in this period.

The men who led the city of Toledo to ruin in 1931 claimed to have been exonerated by the courts, and their control and influence over the city's affairs did not significantly decline for another generation. Of the men who stood charged with crimes for their actions while officers of Toledo's banks, only Stacy McNary felt he had more opportunity elsewhere and moved away to Cleveland and then in 1951 to southern California where he lived to the age of ninety-nine. George Mills stayed on as the vice-president of the reorganized Commerce Guardian Bank until his death in 1946. Leroy Eastman chose not to reenter the banking field, though he did continue on as chairman of the board of City Auto Stamping and as a director of

City Machine and Tool Company, both among the city's largest employers. His connection with the shady dealings of Toledo's banks seemed not to have long tainted his reputation, as he was elected president of the Chamber of Commerce in 1951 and in 1953 was put in charge of organizing a prayer service on Flag Day to commemorate Ohio's sesquicentennial.[39]

Indeed, in some ways the power of Toledo's industrialists grew by the mid-1930s, when a highly marketed lobbying effort succeeded in convincing enough voters to abolish the mayor's office, limit the power of the city council, and establish an appointive city manager. This solved the power elite's problem of Toledo's penchant for electing independent mavericks as their mayors, from Samuel "Golden Rule" Jones at the turn of the century to socialist Solon T. Klotz in 1933. This removed much of the potential political profit to be turned in attacking the city's industrial elite by reminding voters of past misdeeds and cover-ups. When the city boomed again, buoyed by a flood of war contracts, most Toledoans received their paychecks from and paid their mortgages to the very same industrialists who had failed in 1931.

A narrowing of media outlets limited the opportunity for nonestablishment voices to repeat the scandalous details of the bank story. In 1934 Toledo's Polish-language daily newspaper, *Ameryka-Echo*, folded. Four year later the newspaper read by more working families in town than any other, and the paper that had done the bulk of the investigative work in uncovering the facts behind the banking failures, the Scripps-Howard chain's *News-Bee*, called it quits. This left only two dailies, the Republican Toledo *Blade*, and the *Blade*-owned Toledo *Times*. Toledo supported a lively union weekly, though by the early 1940s it increasingly adopted the business-unionist focus of Toledo's most conservative labor leaders. None of them showed the slightest interest in revisiting the financial scandals of a bygone era.

In the end, the facts underlying the worst urban banking collapse of the Great Depression faded away while the image of panicked depositors reading the notices pasted to the doors carried on. What the camera did not see and what society has not remembered was the quiet bank run going on behind those doors.

Many years later, in the 1950s, when Toledo's banks were back on their feet and the city was once again growing, one elderly man would walk into his bank on the first banking day each year and empty his entire account. Each year he would return later that same week and redeposit the same amount. One year, a banker observing his odd behavior could not contain his curiosity and he asked the old man why he closed his account one day and opened it again a few days later. The old man, old enough to remember well the great bank run of 1931, answered, "I just want to be sure I can get my money."[40]

Notes

Notes to Introduction

1. Milton Friedman and Anna J. Schwartz, *A Monetary History of the United States, 1867–1960* (Princeton, N.J.: Princeton Univ. Press, 1963), p. 308. Friedman and Schwartz's interpretation of the banking failures is simplified even further in its retelling by other academics. "The stock market crash was followed one year later by a banking crisis lasting from October to December 1930. As deposits in failed banks rose, a contagion spread to convert demand and time deposits into currency . . .," p. 20. Ronnie J. Phillips, *The Chicago Plan & New Deal Banking Reform* (Armonk, N.Y.: M. E. Sharpe, 1995).

2. Elmus Wicker, *The Banking Panics of the Great Depression* (Cambridge, England: Cambridge Univ. Press, 1996), pp. 4–5.

3. *The Nation* 145:3503 (Aug. 24, 1932), p. 154; *Saturday Evening Post* 205:19 (Nov. 5, 1932), p. 64; H. Parker Willis, "Who Caused the Panic of 1929," *North American Review* 229 (Feb. 1930), p. 181; *Vital Speeches of the Day* 2 (July 15, 1936), p. 648.

4. *North American Review* 234 (Oct. 1932), pp. 243–246.

5. *American Mercury* 27 (Sept. 1932), p. 20.

6. James Truslow Adams, "The Responsibility of Bankers," *The Forum and Century* 86 (Aug. 1931), p. 86.

7. Joseph McCulley, "Thumbway Tham's Bank Account," *Best Detective Magazine*, 3:2, Dec. 1930; Victor Lauriston, "Double Liability," *Best Detective Magazine*, 3:6, Apr. 1931; Roy W. Hinds, "Simon Trapp Opens a Bank," *Best Detective Magazine*, 11:2, Dec. 1934; Robert Winton, "Buried in a Bank," *Best Detective Magazine*, 13:4, Feb. 1936, (Street & Smith, New York); Ralph Milne & A.P. Nelson, "The Bank that Robbed Itself," *True Gang Life*, 1:2, Jan. 1935 (Associated Authors, New York); Dave Barnes, "Death on the Credit Side," *Ace-High Detective Magazine*, 1:2, Sept. 1936, (Popular Publications, Chicago); "Bank Night in Hell," *Complete Detective*, Feb. 1939.

8. *Fortune* 13 (January 1936), p. 144; Ferdinand Pecora, *Wall Street under Oath: The Story of Our Modern Money Changers* (New York: Simon & Schuster, 1939), passim; Thomas F. Huertas and Joan L. Silverman, "Charles E. Mitchell: Scapegoat of the Crash?" *Business History Review*, 60 (1), 1986, pp. 81–103.

9. Gary M. Walton and Hugh Rockoff, *History of the American Economy* (New York: Harcourt Brace Jovanovich, 1990), pp. 485–486.

10. Ernest L. Bogart and Donald L. Kemmerer, *Economic History of the American People* (New York: Longmans, Green and Co., 1942), p. 744.

11. Randolph C. Downes, *Industrial Beginnings: Lucas County Historical Series 4* (Toledo: Historical Society of Northwestern Ohio, 1954), pp. 70–98; Gregory R.

Zieren, "The Propertied Worker: Working Class Formation in Toledo, Ohio, 1870–1900,"
Ph.D. diss., University of Delaware, 1982.

12. Glenn McLaughlin, *Growth of American Manufacturing Areas: A Comparative Analysis with Special Emphasis on Trends in the Pittsburgh District* (Westport, Connecticut: Greenwood Press, 1970, originally published 1938), p. 117.

13. Jerry W. Markham, *A Financial History of the United States*, vol. 2 (Armonk, New York: M. E. Sharpe, 2002), pp. 160–165; Wicker, *The Banking Panics of the Great Depression*, passim.

14. Data gathered from Ohio Department of Banks and Banking *Annual Reports* for 1931–1933; *Banking and Monetary Statistics* (Federal Reserve, 1943), pp. 284–285; *Federal Reserve Bulletin*, 18:1 (Jan. 1932), p. 75; Paul B. Trescott, "Bank Failures, Interest Rates, and the Great Currency Outflow in the United States, 1929–1933," *Research in Economic History* Vol. 11 (1988), p. 58; Wicker, *The Banking Panics of the Great Depression*, p. 69.

15. *Federal Reserve Bulletin*, 23:9 (Sept. 1937), p. 891.

16. Data gathered from the *Annual Report of the Comptroller of the Currency*, Dec. 1, 1930, pp. 764–768; Dec. 7, 1931, pp. 1034–1041; Dec. 5, 1932, pp. 568–574; Jan. 3, 1934, pp. 648–663; Oct. 31, 1934, pp. 776–793; Campbell Gibson, "Population of the 100 Largest Cities and Other Urban Places in the United States, 1790–1990," Population Division Working Paper, No. 27 (U.S. Bureau of the Census, 1998), Table 16; *Annual Report of the Division of Banks* (Ohio), Dec. 31, 1930, pp. 18–21, 34–39; Dec. 31, 1931, pp. 112–113; Dec. 31, 1932, p. 49; Dec. 31, 1933, pp. 32; Dec. 31, 1934, pp. 55.

17. Data gathered from the *Annual Report of the Comptroller of the Currency*, Dec. 1, 1930, pp. 759–763; Dec. 7, 1931, pp. 1029–1033; Dec. 5, 1932, pp. 563–567; Jan. 3, 1934, pp. 643–647; Oct. 31, 1934, pp. 772–776. Toledo's totals do not include the roughly $50,000,000 frozen in the city's eleven savings and loan companies that also failed in the summer of 1931.

18. *News-Bee*, June 10, 11, 1930. "Informal Extemporaneous Remarks of the President, Toledo, Ohio, Dec. 9, 1935," Franklin D. Roosevelt Papers, President's Personal File: Speeches, Franklin D. Roosevelt Library, Hyde Park, New York. *News-Bee*, Dec. 10, 1935.

19. *News-Bee* (Toledo), Aug. 17, 1931.

20. *Twenty-fourth Annual Report of Division of Banks . . . for Fiscal Year Ended December 31, 1931* (Cleveland: Consolidated Press & Printing Co., 1932), pp. 8–9.

21. Charles H. Schroeder, "Some Aspects of the Toledo Bank Failures of 1931," M.A. thesis, University of Toledo, 1939.

22. Tana Mosier Porter, *Toledo Profile: A Sesquicentennial History* (Toledo Sesquicentennial Commission, 1987), p. 84.

23. For example, see Toledo *Blade*, Feb. 2, 1993.

24. See George Brown Tindall and David Emory Shi, *America: A Narrative History*, Fifth Edition (New York: W.W. Norton & Co., 1999), pp. 1236–1237; John W. Murrin et al., *Liberty, Equality, Power: A History of the American People* (New York: Harcourt Brace, 1999), pp. 838–839; Alan Brinkley, *The Unfinished Nation* (New York: McGraw Hill, 1993), pp. 654–656.

25. Toledo *Blade*, Nov. 23, 24, 25, 26, Dec. 1, 8, 1933; Jan. 5, 6, 1934.

26. Toledo *Blade*, Jan. 5, 1934, p. 1.

27. Toledo *Blade*, Nov. 24, 1933, p. 1

Notes to Chapter One

1. Toledo *Blade*, Mar. 12, 1950, p. 22.

2. E. H. Close obituary, Toledo *News-Bee*, Aug. 7, 1924.

3. *Annual Statistical Report of the Secretary of State* . . . (Springfield, Ohio: State Printers), 1919–1932.

4. William E. Fairfield, *Fire and Sand: The History of the Libbey-Owens Sheet Glass Company* (Cleveland: Lezius-Hiles Co., 1960); Joyce Shaw Paterson, *American Automobile Workers, 1900–1933* (Albany: State University of New York Press, 1987); Gregory M. Miller, "A Short History of Automobile Workers in Toledo, 1907–1935," M.A. thesis, University of Toledo, 2000.

5. Toledo *Blade*, Apr. 9, May 13, 1920.

6. Toledo *Blade*, May 10, 27, July 19, 1920.

7. Toledo *Blade*, Sept. 14, Nov. 29, 1921.

8. Geo. Ricaby Co. Brochure (1923), Business and Industries of Greater Toledo Collection, MSS Coll. 36, Box 1, Folder 164, Local History Department, Toledo–Lucas County Public Library.

9. Ibid.; see also "List of Stockholders in Toledo Banks" (Bell and Beckwith, 1921), in Bank Collection, Mss. 39, Folder 2, Toledo–Lucas County Public Library.

10. Killits, *Toledo and Lucas County*, vol. 2, 605.

11. *The Welles-Bowen Company, 1908–1968* (Unpublished manuscript, n.d.), p. 3, Toledo–Lucas County Public Library.

12. "Westmoreland Declaration of Restrictions," *Register of Deeds*, vol. 503, pp. 1–7, Lucas County Recorder's Office.

13. "Toledo Real Property Survey: Final Report," WPA Project #17971 (Toledo Metropolitan Housing Authority, 1939), pp. 23–25, Toledo–Lucas County Public Library.

14. *The Welles-Bowen Company, 1908–1968*, pp. 3–4, Toledo–Lucas County Public Library.

15. These eleven were: Claude Cambell, Zale and Al Reuben, Theodore Schmitt Jr., Elmer Gerson, Walter Stewart, Elmer Close, Walter Hoskin, Mark Bricker, William Welles, Louis Ottenheimer. See John M. Killits, *Toledo and Lucas County, Ohio, 1623–1923* (Chicago and Toledo: S.J. Clarke Publishing Co., 1923) vol. 3, pp. 67, 115, 132, 184, 238, 283, 385, 473, 490, 605, and 682.

16. *The Welles-Bowen Company, 1908–1968*, p. 2, Toledo–Lucas County Public Library.

17. Toledo *Blade*, Jan. 5, 1934.

18. Killits, *Toledo and Lucas County*, v. 2, pp. 480, 483.

19. Toledo *Blade*, Mar. 17, 1951.

20. *East Side Sun*, Nov. 15, 1933.

21. Data collected from *Index to Mortgages: Mortgagor*, 1921–1930, Lucas County Recorder's Office, Toledo Ohio; Killits, *Toledo and Lucas County;* Business Incorporation Records, Secretary of State of Ohio; and Business and Industries of Greater Toledo Collection, MSS Coll. 36, Local History Department, Lucas County-Toledo Public Library; *Annual Report Department of Banks and Banking of Ohio*, 1920–1931.

22. "Declaration of the People's Bank & Trust Company, Banking Department Requirements . . . ," Nov. 21, 1927, reprinted in the *Blade*, Jan. 5, 1934, p. 12.

23. "Examiner's Report, July 31, 1929, Loans to Officers and Directors," *Blade*, Jan. 5, 1934, p. 13.

24. Killits, vol. 3, p. 578.

25. "Security Home Trust Company, Liability of Officers and Directors," *Blade*, Jan. 5, 1934, p. 13.

26. "Subdivisions in Lucas County," *A Comprehensive Report on a Proposed System of Major Highways and Parkways for Lucas County, Ohio* (St. Louis: Harold Bartholmew and Assoc., 1928), p. 27.

27. Gregory R. Zieren, *The Propertied Worker: Working Class Formation in Toledo, Ohio, 1870–1900*, Ph.D. diss., University of Delaware, 1981.

28. "Heatherdowns Country Club," MSS Coll. 41, "Organizations of Greater Toledo," Box 1, Folder 34, TLCPL. One of Reuben Realty's extensions of the Homedale subdivision depended on the city's construction of a viaduct over rail lines. *News-Bee*, Nov. 30, 1929.

29. H. C. McClure, "The Story of the Summit Street Extension, Toledo, Ohio," *The American City*, 23:1, (July 1920), pp. 8–10.

30. "Business Agents' Report," January 9, 1919, Box 14, Folder 1, Central Labor Union Papers, Center for Archival Collections, Bowling Green State University; Toledo *Blade*, April 5, 1919.

31. For a survey of the business perspective see the Toledo *Blade*, Mar. 30, 1920, p. 6; May 24, 1921, p. 6.

32. Toledo *Blade*, Mar. 10, 1920, p. 14; June 7, 1920, p. 2; July 24, 1920, p. 1; Apr. 9, 1921, p. 13.

33. Eric J. Karolak, "'Fighting Autocracy at Home': The Willys-Overland Strike of 1919," Senior honors thesis, University of Toledo, Dept. of History, 1986 (copy housed at the Carlson Library), p. 24.

34. *The Automobile and Automotive Industries*, Oct. 4, 1917, p. 600.

35. *The Automobile and Automotive Industries*, Sept. 6, 1917, p. 427.

36. Letter of Quinlivan to all Local Unions, April 1, 1920, Central Labor Union Papers, Box 14, Folder 1, Center for Archival Collections, Bowling Green State University.

37. For general background on this era of labor conflict see Eric J. Karolak, "Fighting Autocracy at Home"; David A. McMurray, "The Willys-Overland Strike, 1919," *Northwest Ohio Quarterly*, 36:4 (Autumn 1964), pp. 171–181 and 37:1 (Winter 1964–65), pp. 33–43; Lorin Lee Cary, "The Bureau of Investigation and Radicalism in Toledo, Ohio: 1918–1920," *Labor History*, 21:3 (Summer 1980), pp. 430–440. Allegations of the collusion of the Merchants and Manufacturers Association and the Ku Klux Klan can be found in the Negly Cochran Papers, Cochran to E. W. Scripps, Jan. 24, 1923, Toledo–Lucas County Public Library. For glimpses of Toledo's K.K.K. see Toledo *Blade*, Aug. 20, 1921, p. 1; Sept. 19, 1921, p. 6.

38. Richard A. Rajner, *The Comprehensive History of Plumbers and Steam Fitters U.A. Local No. 50* (Toledo: Plumbers and Steamfitters No. 50, 1998), pp. 151–164; Toledo *Blade*, Jan. 21, 1921, p. 17; Quinlivan Reports for Aug. 5, May 26, 1921, Central Labor Union Papers, Box 9, Folder 1, Center for Archival Collections, Bowling Green State University; Toledo *Blade*, Nov. 30, 1921.

39. Quinlivan Reports for Sept. 30, 1921, Central Labor Union Papers, Box 9, Folder 1, Center for Archival Collections, Bowling Green State University.

40. Toledo *Blade*, May 27, 1921, p. 2; Timothy Borden, "Labor's Day: Public Commemoration and Toledo's Working Class," *Northwest Ohio Quarterly* 70:1/2 (Winter/Spring 1998), pp. 4–27.

41. *Industrial Survey* (City Plan Commission: Toledo, 1924), p. 11.

42. Data derived from the *Toledo Real Property Survey*, 1939, op. cit., p. 166. A survey of the construction trades showed that although construction employment increased by a third from 1926 to 1928, the construction payroll fell 3.3 percent. Spurgeon Bell et al., *Industrial and Commercial Ohio Yearbook, 1930* (Columbus: Bureau of Business Research, Ohio State University, 1930), pp. 15, 39.

43. Marnie Jones, *Holy Toledo* (Lexington: Univ. Press of Kentucky, 1998), passim.

44. Bill Roche, "My Thirty Years in Toledo," Toledo *News-Bee*, Jan. 1, 1929.

45. "The Background of City Government and Politics in Toledo" (University of Toledo: Department of Political Science, 1954), pp. 21–26, Canaday Center for Special Collections, Univ. of Toledo.

46. Randolph Downes, *The Rise of Warren Gamaliel Harding, 1865–1920* (Columbus: Ohio State Univ. Press, 1970), pp. 346–350, 420–422.

47. Ralph E. Phelps, *Profiles of Toledo Mayors* (Toledo: Blade Publishing Co., 1957), p. 34; "The Background of City Government and Politics in Toledo," pp. 26–29.

48. Wendell F. Johnson, *Toledo's Non-Partisan Movement* (Toledo: H.J. Chittendon Co., 1922), p. 47.

49. On Stewart see Toledo *Blade*, Mar. 15, 1951. On Jackson see Ralph E. Phelps, *Profiles of Toledo Mayors* (Toledo: Blade Publishing Co., 1957), p. 36.

50. On Hiett see Toledo *Times*, Apr. 28, 1939.

51. Toledo *Blade*, Sept. 13, 17, 19, 1921.

52. "History of the Toledo Chamber of Commerce," Chamber of Commerce Collection, MSS 84, Box 1, Local History Room, Toledo–Lucas County Public Library.

53. Toledo *Blade*, Feb. 27, 1922; Allen D. Albert, "Toledo—The City Young Blood Built," *Colliers'*, Jan. 8, 1921, pp. 10–11.

54. Toledo *Blade*, Oct. 5, 1920.

55. All proposals in the Toledo *Blade* for 1921: docks: Sept. 22, 1921; canal: Nov. 18, 1921; St. Clair St.: Feb. 19, 1921; opposition to income tax: Mar. 12, 1921; general policy on city improvement: Jan. 3, 8, 1921; schools: Allen D. Albert, "Toledo—The City Young Blood Built," *Colliers'*, Jan. 8, 1921, pp. 10–11.

56. *The Toledo City Journal*, June 26, 1926, pp. 309–311.

57. Toledo *Major Street Report*, 1924, p. 14; figures on annexations compiled from the *Index to the Toledo City Journal*, 1916–1930.

58. Toledo *Blade*, Sept. 7, 1921.

59. Toledo *Blade*, Aug. 7, 11, 1922.

60. Toledo *Blade*, Aug. 8, 1922.

61. William J. Nancarrow, "The Voters Speak: The Ohio Judicial Election of 1910 and Progressive Era Jurisprudence," *Proceedings of the Ohio Academy of History* (2001), pp. 37–38.

62. Editorial, "The City Hall Issue," Toledo *News-Bee*, Aug. 10, 1922.

63. *Toledo City Journal*, Aug. 29, 1925.

64. *The Background of City Government and Politics in Toledo*, p. 30. *Blade*, Nov. 24, 1926.

65. Virgil Sheppard, *William T. Jackson, Mayor, City of Toledo, 1928–1931* (unpublished manuscript, Canaday Center, Univ. of Toledo), p. 30.

66. Ibid. See also "Results of a Year's Activities of the City and County Planning Committee of a Chamber of Commerce," *The American City*, March 1930, pp. 105–106.

67. "The City Manager Campaign in Toledo," *American Political Science Review*, August 1929, pp. 735–737.

68. Virgil Sheppard, *William T. Jackson, Mayor, City of Toledo, 1928–1931* (unpublished manuscript, Canaday Center, Univ. of Toledo), pp. 6–8.

69. Sheppard, *William T. Jackson*, pp. 22–23; Frank R. Hickerson, *The Tower Builders: The Centennial Story of the University of Toledo* (Univ. of Toledo Press, 1972), pp. 190–191; Toledo *Blade*, Feb. 6, 9, 1929.

70. A. Theodorides, "Construction in the United States and Toledo Through Booms and Depressions: A Study of the Industry Covering the Period 1899–1939" (Bureau of Business Research, University of Toledo), Bulletin 13, May 25, 1939, p. 31.

71. Data derived from the *Toledo Real Property Survey*, 1939, op. cit., pp. 158–159.

72. Survey drawn from the *Lucas County Plat Map*, vol. 1, 1930, Toledo–Lucas County Public Library. A complete survey was not possible as vol. 2 of this edition has been lost.

73. Data derived from the *Toledo Real Property Survey*, 1939, op. cit., p. 165. See also S. J. Barrick, "The Cost of Government in Toledo, 1918–1931" (Toledo: Chamber of Commerce, 1932).

74. Ibid.; *Toledo City Journal*, June 26, 1930, pp. 445–446.

75. A. Theorides, "Construction in the United States and Toledo . . . ," p. 32.

76. "A Comprehensive Report on a Proposed System of Major Highways and Parkways for Lucas County . . ." (St. Louis: Harold Bartholomew and Assoc., 1928), pp. 7–8.

77. N. J. Walinski to New Thurston, June 26, 1939, "In re: Security Bond & Mortgage Company Loans," and "State ex. el. vs. Eppstein," Lucas County Common Pleas Case #156270, in Box 1, "Bank Cases, 1939–1940," Attorney General Papers, Ohio Historical Society, State Archives Series 498. Quote from "Examination of Frank J. Klauser," p. 12, "Bank Cases, 1939–1940," Ibid.

78. "Examination of William M. Konzen," pp. 6–7, Box 1, "Bank Cases, 1939–1940," Attorney General Papers, Ohio Historical Society, State Archives Series 498; Toledo *Blade*, Aug. 22, Sept. 1, 1931.

79. Toledo *Blade*, Mar. 17, 1951; Killits, vol. 2, p. 184.

80. Toledo *News-Bee*, Nov. 25, 1933. The figure of $90,000 was calculated from the value of the unsold share offer tendered by the Commercial Bank of $225 in December of 1927.

81. Peoples' Bank was also in the habit of purchasing nonperforming land parcels off the hands of its officers but not recording the deeds to gain lawful ownership of them. See Deed #182116. It contains a "correction" of a previous unrecorded deed that should have been executed four years earlier. *Register of Deeds*, vol. 508, p. 302, Lucas County Recorder's Office.

Notes to Chapter Two

1. Scripps-Howard reporter Paul Jones's profile of Brown in the Toledo *News-Bee*, Feb. 20, 1934.

2. "Second Annual Report of the Department of Banks and Banking for the Year ending 1909," *Ohio Executive Documents* 1909, vol. 3, #37 (Springfield, Ohio: State

Printers, 1909), pp. 531–536; "Third Annual Report of the Department of Banks and Banking for the Year ending 1910," *Ohio Executive Documents* 1909, vol. 1, #D (Springfield, Ohio: State Printers, 1910), pp. 204–205.

3. *Fifth Annual Report of the Department of Banks and Banking for the Year ending 1912* (Springfield, Ohio: State Printers, 1913), p. 3.

4. Ibid., p. 21.

5. Ibid., p. 6.

6. *Thirteenth Annual Report of the Department of Banks . . .* (Springfield, Ohio: State Printers, 1920), p. 11.

7. *Nineteenth Annual Report of the Department of Banks . . .* (Springfield, Ohio: State Printers, 1926), p. 8.

8. Examination of Robert T. Sewell, p. 8, Box 1, "Bank Cases, 1939–1940," Attorney General Papers, State Archives Series 498, Ohio Historical Society.

9. Robert G. Rodkey, "State Bank Failures in Michigan," *Michigan Business Studies,* vol. 7, #2 (Ann Arbor, 1935), p. 60.

10. J. M. Whitsett, *Banking Operations in Ohio, 1920–1940* (Columbus: The Ohio State Univ. Press, 1941), p. 156; Garet Garrett, "A Story of Banking," *The Saturday Evening Post,* Aug. 8, 1931, p. 78.

11. Whitsett, pp. 32–33.

12. Toledo *Blade,* Jan. 5, 1934, p. 2.

13. Testimony of Security-Home Bank assistant treasurer, James Newell, *Blade,* Sept. 23, 1933.

14. Toledo *Blade,* Nov. 24, 1933, p. 17.

15. Toledo *News-Bee,* Oct. 15, 1936.

16. Lucas Cty. 20399, *Ohio vs. McNary et al.,* Lucas County Clerk of Courts Office, Toledo, Ohio.

17. Toledo *News-Bee,* July 17, 1934; Toledo *Blade,* July 17, 1934; *East Side Sun,* Aug. 2, 9, 1934; *Toledo Legal News,* July 14, 1934, p. 2.

18. Immediately after the grand jury's revelations, Lucas County Prosecutor Frazier Reams promised to enter civil suits for recovery against the individuals who illegally sheltered taxes in this way, though a few months later he chose to instead write a letter to the county auditor urging him to investigate and nothing further was heard of the matter. Toledo *News-Bee,* Sept. 27, 1934.

19. Herbert Hoover to Walter Folger Brown, Mar. 25, 1933, Aug. 14, 1933; Walter Folger Brown to J. R. Nutt, June 20, 1934, *Walter Folger Brown Papers,* Ohio Historical Society, Columbus, Ohio.

20. *Nineteenth Annual Report of the Department of Banks . . .* (Springfield, Ohio: State Printers, 1926), p. 9. For a national context to these mergers, see Eugene Nelson White, "The Merger Movement in Banking, 1919–1933," *Journal of Economic History,* 45:2 (1985), pp. 285–291.

21. "Comparative Table of Toledo Banks" (Toledo: Stacy & Braun, 1913–1925), in Bank Collection, Mss. 39, Folder 1, Toledo–Lucas County Public Library.

22. The Jones syndicate made a small effort to cover their financial tracks by buying and selling the Dime Bank stock through a front company called the Vistula Holding Company. Toledo *News-Bee,* Nov. 24, 1928. A list of the directors of the Ohio Bank is found in the *Twenty-First Annual Report of the Division of Banks* (Columbus: 1928). Shareholders of the Dime and Ohio banks are detailed in the "List of Stockholders in Toledo Banks" (Bell and Beckwith, 1921), Bank Collection, Mss. 39, Folder 2,

Toledo–Lucas County Public Library. Bainbridge biographical information is from *Memoirs of Lucas County and the City of Toledo*, Ed. Harvey Scribner (Madison, Wisc.: Western Historical Association, 1910), vol. 2, p. 238, and Toledo *Blade*, Sept. 2, 1929.

23. See *Moody's Manual of Investments—Banks* for 1929, 1930, 1931.

24. Toledo *Blade*, Sept. 19, 1934; Toledo *News-Bee*, Nov. 24, 1933, p. 2, 5.

25. Toledo *News-Bee*, Nov. 25, 1933.

26. Toledo *News-Bee*, Jan. 4, 1926, p. 9; Oliver S. Bond died just two weeks after he relinquished control of his bank. Toledo *News-Bee*, Jan. 16, 1926, p. 1.

27. *Moody's Manual of Investments—Banks*, 1929, p. 414; 1930, pp. 655–656.

28. Toledo *Blade*, Jan. 5, 1934, pp. 2–3; Toledo *News-Bee*, Nov. 10, 1927.

29. In 1920, Home Bank had $5,071,387 total deposits and $526,155 of earned surplus and undivided profits. In 1929, Home had $9,499,435 in total deposits and $480,720 in earned surplus and undivided profits. *Moody's Manual of Investments— Banks*, 1930, p. 109; 1929, p. 126.

30. Figures on staff and branches compiled from *Moody's Manual of Investments—Banks*, 1927–1931; *Toledo Topics*, 5:7 (June 1930), p. 3.

31. Whitsett, pp. 84–85.

32. "The Second National Bank of Toledo, Ohio," Banks of Greater Toledo Collection, Box 1, Folder 20, Toledo–Lucas County Public Library.

33. Toledo *Blade*, Dec. 30, 1921.

34. Toledo *News-Bee*, Mar. 8, 1924.

35. Toledo *News-Bee*, Dec. 23, 1924.

36. Toledo *Blade*, Aug. 10, 1922.

37. Toledo *News-Bee*, Sept. 19, 1927.

38. Toledo *News-Bee*, Sept. 16, 1925.

39. *Toledo's Finest Office Building: The New Ohio Bank Building* (The Ohio Savings Bank, 1930), Banks of Greater Toledo Collection, Box 1, Folder 18, Toledo–Lucas County Public Library.

40. Toledo *News-Bee*, June 29, 1927, Feb. 21, 1928,

41. Toledo *News-Bee*, Sept. 7, 1934. It should be noted that Thomas Tracy already owned some Boody stock long before the Ohio deal was on the horizon. Tracy purchased $20,000 worth of Boody stock in 1911. Toledo *Blade*, Sept. 21, 1934.

42. In 1930 the Ohio Bank's capital and surplus amounted to $8,000,000. This allowed for a maximum of $4,800,000 of banking facilities. Prior to the building of the Ohio Bank tower, the bank claimed $1,890,363 worth of banking properties. With land and furnishings, the new building's cost was about $3,000,000, approximately one hundred thousand dollars more than the legal limit. When the Ohio Bank failed in 1931, the appraised value of its headquarters was $4,735,500. *Moodys*, 1931, p. 340; Toledo *Blade*, Nov. 24, 1933, p. 17.

43. Toledo *Blade*, Nov. 24, 1933, p. 18. See figures listed under "Banking House and Lot" and "Other Liabilities" in *Twentieth Annual Report of the Division of Banks for the Fiscal Year Ending Dec. 31, 1927* (Cleveland: State Printers, 1928) and *Twenty-Third Annual Report of the Division of Banks for the Fiscal Year Ending Dec. 31, 1930* (Cleveland: State Printers, 1931), p. 345.

44. Toledo *Blade*, Jan. 6, 1934, p.3.

45. Toledo *Blade*, Jan. 6, 1934, p. 4.

46. Figures derived from State Banking Reports for 1920, 1926, and 1930.

47. Toledo Real Property Survey, 1939, p. 166.

48. *Moody's Manual of Investments*, 1931, p. 339.
49. *Ulmer v. Fulton, Supt. of Banks, Et Al.*, Ohio Supreme Court, Nos. 24996 & 24997, Decided Apr. 24, 1935 (129 O.S., pp. 320–343).
50. Ibid.; Toledo *Times*, Jan. 6, 1934.
51. *Moody's Manual of Investments*, 1932, p. vii.
52. A listing of the delinquent properties can be found in the Toledo *Blade*, Nov. 7, 1933.
53. *Annual Report of the Department of Banks and Banking*, 1931, p. 26.
54. Toledo *News-Bee*, April 6, 1931.
55. Toledo *Blade*, Jan. 5, 6, 1934.
56. Letter of Judge Ira R. Cole in *Toledo Union Leader*, Sept. 18, 1931.

Notes to Chapter Three

1. Toledo *Times*, June 7, 8, 10, 1931; Toledo *Sunday Times*, June 7, 1931
2. Toledo *Times*, June 6, 1931; Toledo *News-Bee*, Dec. 17, 1931. Employment reports can be found in the Toledo *Blade*, Feb. 6, Mar. 13, 21, 28 and Apr. 20, 1931.
3. Toledo *Times*, June 7, 8, 10, 1931; Toledo *Sunday Times*, June 7, 1931.
4. Gunckel's note was never repaid and the property was eventually sold at a sheriff's auction in 1938. As late as 1964, the property sold for just $5,740. For property record see the transfer card for Lot 33, Revised Plat of Birkhead Place, Lucas County Auditor's Office, Toledo, Ohio. For Gunckel's loan, see Record of Mortgages, vol. 998, p. 387, Lucas County Recorder's Office.
5. Toledo *News-Bee*, June 23, 1931. Toledo's Polish-language paper, *Ameryka Echo—Toledo Daily Edition*, was first to carry news of Szymanski's arrest on June 20, 1931, p. 4.
6. *Current History*, 38 (May 1933), pp. 152–158.
7. *World's Work*, Dec. 1931, p. 40.
8. *Annual Report: Department of Banks and Banking*, 1926. Toledo *Blade*, Jan. 4, 1934.
9. Toledo *Blade*, Sept. 1, 1931.
10. Toledo *News-Bee*, Sept. 3, 1931.
11. Toledo *Blade*, Sept. 3, 1931.
12. Lucas County Clerk of Courts, Case # 20399, *Ohio vs. McNary et al* . . .
13. Statements of condition of Security-Home can be found in Toledo *Blade*, Sept. 3, 1931; Toledo *News-Bee*, Sept. 3, 1931; and Toledo *Blade*, Jan. 5, 1934.
14. Toledo *Blade*, Jan. 5, 1934.
15. Toledo *News-Bee*, Sept. 22, 1933; Toledo *Blade*, Sept. 22, 1933.
16. Toledo *Blade*, Jan. 5, 1934. A profile of Ira J. Fulton can be found in the Biographical abstracts of the Citizen's Historical Association, Ohio Historical Society.
17. Toledo *Blade*, Sept. 3, 1931.
18. Toledo *Blade*, Sept. 3, 1931.
19. *Fulton, Supt. of Banks, v. Rundell*, Ohio Supreme Court, Case No. 24208, April 11, 1934 (128 O.S., pp. 205–211).
20. Toledo *Blade*, Sept. 3, 1931.
21. *Ameryka Echo—Toledo Daily Edition*, Sept. 3, 1931 p. 1.
22. Toledo *Times*, June 12, 1931; Toledo *Blade*, May 3, 1929.

23. Toledo *Blade*, Jan. 5, 1934, p. 1.

24. Commerce Guardian Trust and Savings Bank, *A Catalog of Departments* (Commerce Guardian Trust and Savings Bank, n.d. (probably 1920s); Toledo–Lucas County Public Library, Banks of Greater Toledo Collection, Box 1, Folder 5).

25. Toledo *News-Bee*, June 18, 1931.

26. Toledo *Blade*, Nov. 24, 1933.

27. Toledo *Blade*, Nov. 24, 1933.

28. Toledo *Blade*, Nov. 24, 1933; Toledo *News-Bee*, Nov. 24, 1933; Toledo *Blade*, June 18, 1931. For Campbell mortgage, see Record of Mortgages, vol. 1005, p. 95, Lucas County Recorder's Office, Toledo Ohio.

29. Toledo *Sunday Times*, June 14, 1931.

30. Toledo *Blade*, Jan. 6, 1934, Nov. 25, 1933.

31. Toledo *News-Bee*, June 18, 1931.

32. Toledo *News-Bee*, Nov. 25, 1933.

33. Toledo *Blade*, Jan. 5, 1934.

34. Toledo *Blade*, June 17, 18, 19, 1931; Toledo *News-Bee*, June 18, 1931.

35. Toledo *News-Bee*, June 18, 19, 1931; *Sylvania Sentinel*, June 18, 1931.

36. Toledo *News-Bee*, June 18, 1931.

37. Toledo *Blade*, June 19, 1931; data compiled from *Mortality Statistics* (Bureau of the Census, Vital Statistics), 20th–37th Annual Reports.

38. It might be noted that if such "smart money" withdrawals were common in America, and there are indications that it was (see Epilogue), then this pressure to liquefy bank assets to pay off insiders might have been a major factor in the general decline of prices at certain critical times in the 1930s. This "smart money" effect on equity values has yet to be studied.

39. Toledo *News-Bee*, Nov. 25, 1933, pp. 1, 3; Toledo *Blade*, Nov. 24, 1933, p. 18.

40. Toledo *Blade*, Jan. 5, 1935.

41. Toledo *Blade*, Nov. 25, 1933.

42. Commercial held $5,122,076 in real estate mortgage loans in 1930. *Moody's Manual of Investments*, 1931, p. 145. Volume of mortgage transfers calculated from the Record of Mortgages, vol. 1001, 1004, 1010, Lucas County Recorder's Office, Toledo, Ohio. Interestingly, during the 1920s the Toledo representative of the Prudential Insurance Co. was George Ricaby, one of the leading real estate developers in the city. John M. Killits, *Toledo and Lucas County, 1623–1923* (Chicago: S.J. Clarke Co., 1923) vol. 3, p. 660.

43. Toledo *News-Bee*, Nov. 24, 1931.

44. Toledo *Blade*, Nov. 24, 1933, Toledo *Blade*, June 2, 1973. On Killits's banking activity, see *East Side Sun*, Dec. 6, 1933.

45. Toledo *News-Bee*, Nov. 24, 1931.

46. Though it was reported that the Ohio Bank granted 54 loans totaling $152,000 during the suspension period with no other collateral than offsetting bank deposits, this was only about 2 percent of the total withdrawn. Toledo *Blade*, Nov. 24, 1933.

47. Don Wolfe in his book *Frazier Reams: His Life and Times* (s.1.:s.n), 1978, reports that Reams secured a collateral-free loan with which he purchased radio station WTOL in 1931. WTOL would eventually become the center of a multimillion dollar broadcasting conglomerate controlled by Reams.

48. Second Mortgage Security Co. finally declared bankruptcy in 1945. (Ohio

Secretary of State Corporation Filings, Document A112_1093.) The City Hall Realty Co. was a shell organized by Edward G. Kirby, president of the Commerce Guardian Bank (Ohio Secretary of State Corporation Filings, Document V170_0013).

49. Auto-Lite traded around $40 per share in the summer of 1931. (Toledo *News-Bee*, Aug. 17, 1931.) Fraser loan detailed in Toledo *Blade*, Nov. 25, 1933.

50. Toledo *Blade*, Nov. 25, 1933.

51. Toledo *Blade*, Jan. 6, 1934; *American Examiner* (Columbus), Apr. 29, 1933.

52. Toledo *News-Bee*, Nov. 25, 1933; Toledo *Blade*, Nov. 25, 1933.

53. Toledo *Times*, Aug. 16, 1931; Toledo *News-Bee*, Aug. 18, 1931.

54. Mauritz A. Hallgren, "Bankers and Bread Lines in Toledo," *The Nation*, Apr. 6, 1932, pp. 395–397; *Business Week*, Sept. 27, 1931, pp. 26, 28.

55. Toledo *Blade*, Aug. 17, 1931.

56. *Ameryka Echo*, Aug. 17, 1931; Toledo *Blade*, Aug. 17, 1931.

57. *Ameryka Echo*, Aug. 17, 1931; Toledo *Blade*, Aug. 17, 1931.

58. *Ameryka Echo*, Aug. 17, 1931; Toledo *Blade*, Aug. 17, 1931.

59. *Business Week*, Sept. 1931, pp. 26, 28; *The Nation*, Apr. 6, 1932, pp. 395–397.

60. *Ameryka Echo*, Aug. 18, 1931;

61. Toledo *Blade*, Feb. 2, 1993, p. 15; *Barron's*, Sept. 7, 1931, p. 16.

62. Toledo *Times*, Aug. 20, 1931.

63. *Ameryka Echo—Toledo Daily Edition*, Sept. 1, 1931, p. 4.

64. *Time*, Aug. 24, 1931; *Business Week*, Sept. 1931, p. 26

65. New York *Herald Tribune*, Aug. 18, 1931; *Barron's*, Aug. 24, 1931, p. 2; Joseph B. Hubbard, "Hoarding and the Expansion of Currency in Circulation," *The Review of Economic Statistics*, 14:1 (Feb. 1932), pp. 31–34.

66. *Blade*, Aug. 17, 1931; *Barron's*, Aug. 24, 1931, p. 4, Sept. 7, 1931, p. 16; *Sylvania Sentinel*, Oct. 8, 1931.

67. Toledo *Blade*, Jan. 6, 1934; *Toledo Times*, Aug. 23, 1931. See also H. Bruce Throckmorton, "A Note on Labor Banks," *Labor History*, 20:4 (1979), pp. 573–575.

68. *Toledo Union Journal*, Aug. 21, 1931.

69. *Toledo Union Journal*, Oct. 2, 9, 1931; unemployment data from Allan H. Ballinger, "Methods of Relief and the Present Unemployment Emergency in the City of Toledo," (M.A. thesis, University of Toledo, 1933), pp. 29–36; wage data from "Wage and Salary Payments and Average Wages in Lucas County, Ohio, 1925–1934," *Employment Studies of Lucas County*, Part 2, Bureau of Business Research, Univ. of Toledo, Bulletin 3 (Dec. 16, 1936), p. 8.

70. *Toledo City Journal*, 17:8 (Feb. 20, 1932), p. 1.

71. Toledo *News-Bee*, Sept. 9, 1931.

72. Ballinger, "Methods of Relief and the Present Unemployment Emergency in the City of Toledo," pp. 29–35; "Wage and Salary Payments and Average Wages in Lucas County, Ohio, 1925–1934," *Employment Studies of Lucas County*, Part 2, Bulletin #3, Dec. 16, 1936 (Bureau of Business Research, University of Toledo); Richard D. Dorn, "The Works Progress Administration in Toledo, Ohio: Local Initiatives for Federal Aid during the New Deal, 1935–1943," *Northwest Ohio Quarterly*, 67:4 (Autumn 1995), p. 201.

73. Toledo *News-Bee*, Oct. 10, 1931, Dec. 2, 1931. Richard D. Dorn, "A New Deal for the Glass City: Local Initiatives for Federal Aid during the Great Depression in Toledo, Ohio" (M.A. thesis, University of Toledo, 1992), p. 36.

74. Toledo *News-Bee*, Sept. 21, 1931; Bernhard Ostrolenk, "Why the Banks Collapsed," *Current History* 38 (May 1933), p. 154.

Notes to Chapter Four

1. Toledo *Tribune*, June 3, 1932, p. 2.
2. Toledo *News-Bee*, Aug. 17, 1931.
3. Toledo *Blade*, Aug. 26, 1931.
4. Toledo *Blade*, Aug. 19, 1931; *Toledo Times*, Aug. 19, 1931.
5. *Toledo Times*, July 27, 1940.
6. Testimony of J. C. Van Pelt, pp. 2–3, Box 1, "Bank Cases, 1939–1940," Attorney General Papers, State Archives Series 498, Ohio Historical Society.
7. Testimony of James W. Eckenrode, p. 36, Box 1, "Bank Cases, 1939–1940," Attorney General Papers, State Archives Series 498, Ohio Historical Society.
8. Testimony of William M. Konzen, p. 5, Box 1, "Bank Cases, 1939–1940," Attorney General Papers, State Archives Series 498, Ohio Historical Society.
9. Testimony of William J. Dunn, p. 29; Testimony of James W. Eckenrode, pp. 36, 31, Box 1, "Bank Cases, 1939–1940," Attorney General Papers, State Archives Series 498, Ohio Historical Society.
10. Testimony of William M. Konzen, p. 7, Box 1, "Bank Cases, 1939–1940," Attorney General Papers, State Archives Series 498, Ohio Historical Society.
11. *Amerika-Echo*, Sept. 2, 1931; Toledo *Blade*, Sept. 3, 1931.
12. Toledo *Blade*, Aug. 22, 1931.
13. Toledo *Blade*, Aug. 25, 1931.
14. Toledo *Times*, Aug. 26, 1931; *Amerika-Echo*, Aug. 22, 1931.
15. Toledo *Blade*, Aug. 24, 1931.
16. Toledo *Blade*, Jan. 6, 1934, p. 4.
17. Of course, it is impossible to determine from these numbers the proportionate rate of asset retirement represented by cash realizations, though in order for the offsets to have leveraged 66 percent, the cash realizations would have had to average just 36 percent of the value of the assets realized.
18. Data taken from a liquidation report published in the Toledo *Blade*, Feb. 1, 1932. Figures computed by: Offsets/(Asset Reduction–Cash Realization) × 100.
19. Toledo *Times*, Nov. 29, 1931.
20. Toledo *Blade*, May 21, 1934. On W. L. Ross see John M. Killits, *Toledo and Lucas County, Ohio, 1623–1923* (Chicago: S.P. Clarke Co., 1923), v. 2, pp. 118, 121.
21. Data from Toledo *Blade*, Nov. 24, 1933 and *Annual Report of the Dept. of Banks for 1934*, p. 72.
22. Data derived from the *Annual Report of the Department of Banks*, 1931, pp. 112–123.
23. Richard A. McClure, "The Toledo Guaranty Corporation" (unpublished manuscript, 1977), p.1, Toledo–Lucas County Public Library.
24. Toledo *News-Bee*, Sept. 7, 1933.
25. Ibid.
26. Toledo *Blade*, Nov. 24, 1933; Toledo *News-Bee*, Nov. 24, 1933.
27. *Toledo City Directory*, 1931, 1932; "Re: The Toledo Citizens System Company," Toledo Better Business Bureau, n.d., Toledo–Lucas County Public Library.
28. *East Side Sun*, July 28, 1932.

29. McClure, "The Toledo Guaranty Corporation.."

30. Figures from *Annual Report of the Department of Banks*, 1935, pp. 72, 80.

31. Toledo *Blade*, Mar. 8, 1933; Apr. 21, 1933.

32. Toledo *News-Bee*, June 6, 12, 1934.

33. Toledo *Times*, Mar. 8, 1933.

34. Data derived from both the report of the bank's accounts on the date of its closing, *Blade*, Nov. 24, 1933, and the *Annual Report of the Division of Banks for 1934* (Columbus, 1935), p. 72.

35. *The State, Ex Rel. Fulton, Supt. of Banks v. Bremer, Admx.* Ohio Supreme Court, No. 25260, Dec. 4, 1935, (130 O.S., pp. 227–239).

36. *Andrews v. The State, Ex Rel. Blair, Supt. of Banks*, Ohio Supreme Court, No. 22955, Nov. 4, 1931 (124 O.S., pp. 359–360).

37. Toledo *Blade*, Dec. 7, 1933.

38. Toledo *Blade*, Jan. 5, 1934. Boggs' shareholder liability is documented in *Blade*, Oct. 12, 1934.

39. James Stuart Olson, *Herbert Hoover and the Reconstruction Finance Corporation, 1931–1933* (Ames: The Iowa State Univ. Press, 1977), pp. 38–39.

40. Toledo *News-Bee*, Nov. 24, 1933; *Blade*, Dec. 8, 1933.

41. Toledo *Blade*, Dec. 8, 1933.

42. Toledo *News-Bee*, Nov. 24, 1933.

43. *East Side Sun*, Nov. 8, 1933.

44. *Ameryka-Echo*, Aug. 20, 21, 31, 1931.

45. *Moody's Manual of Investments: Banks*, 1931 and 1932.

46. Toledo *Blade*, Feb. 25, 1934.

47. It appears that the department of banking included all offsets and purchased bank claims with actual cash dividends to arrive at their total amount of dividends rather than subtracting offsets from deposits before calculating the percentage of dividends paid. See "Schedule 2" *Annual Report of Banks and Banking for 1941*, pp. 96–97; "Statement Dec. 31, 1940—Banks in Liquidation," *Annual Report of Banks and Banking for 1940*, pp. 92–93; Toledo *Blade*, Sept. 22, 1941. See Appendix A for corrected figures.

48. Toledo *Times*, Apr. 14, 1943. The Commerce Guardian eventually paid out close to 75 percent of its overall deposit claims.

49. "Schedule 2," *Annual Report of Banks and Banking for 1941*, pp. 96–97.

50. Attorney General to Charles F. Carr, n.d. Attorney General Administrative Correspondence, 1933, p. 921, State Archives Series 501, Ohio Historical Society.

51. Toledo *Times*, Aug. 19, 1931.

52. Attorney General to Major C. W. Miller, Mar. 20, 1933. Attorney General Administrative Correspondence, 1933, p. 825, State Archives Series 501, Ohio Historical Society.

53. Joseph O. Eppstein to Herbert Duffey, Mar. 23, 1938, "Toledo Closed Banks Cases Papers," Box 1, "Ohio Savings Bank . . ." folder, Attorney General Papers, State Archives Series 498, Ohio Historical Society.

54. Toledo *Blade*, Jan. 21, 1935.

55. Toledo *Times*, July 14, 1940; John S. Pratt to Clemens R. Frank Jr., Feb. 7, 1940; Rodney P. Lein to Thomas J. Herbert, A.G., Jan. 22, 1940, "Toledo Closed Banks Cases Papers," Box 1, "State ex. el. vs. Eppstein" folder, Attorney General Papers, State Archives Series 498, Ohio Historical Society

56. Toledo *News-Bee*, Sept. 7, 1933.

57. See *Annual Report of the Division of Banks for 1936, 1940;* Whitsett, *Banking Operations in Ohio*, pp. 18–20.

Notes to Chapter Five

1. "It's all right to be prejudiced against bankers—or banksters as some people call them. We'll have to face that. I don't know what this world is coming to." Harold Fraser, defense lawyer for Stacey McNary, former president of the Security-Home bank. Toledo *News-Bee*, July 6, 1933. See also the *East Side Sun*, Dec. 27, 1933; Jan. 3, 10, 1934.

2. Toledo *Times*, Sept. 5, 1931.

3. Toledo *News-Bee*, Aug. 18, 1933.

4. Toledo *News-Bee*, May 19, 1933.

5. Ralph E. Phelps, *Profiles of Toledo Mayors* (Toledo: Blade Publishing Co., 1957), p. 37. "Pulling Thru the Crisis: How Toledo Leadership Met the Emergency of 1932 and 1933," pamphlet, Center for Archival Collections, Bowling Green State University; *News-Bee*, May 4, 1917.

6. Clipping dated July 30, 1931, source unknown, in Toledo–Lucas County Library, MSS Coll. 40, Box 2, Folder 18.

7. *Ameryka-Echo*, Aug. 22, 1931.

8. Ibid. See also the collection on "Politics" at the Toledo–Lucas County Public Library, MSS 40, Box 2, Folder 18.

9. Virgil Sheppard, *William T. Jackson, Mayor of Toledo, 1928–1931* (Unpublished manuscript, 1964) p. 32, Canaday Center for Archival Collections, University of Toledo.

10. Toledo *Times*, Aug. 20, 1931.

11. *Ameryka-Echo*, Aug. 20, 1931.

12. Toledo *Blade*, Aug. 21, 1931.

13. Toledo *Blade*, Nov. 26, 1928; Nov. 1, 1948; Mar. 25, 1961; Toledo *Times*, Sept. 21, 1930.

14. Toledo *News-Bee*, Feb. 20, 1934; Sheppard, *William T. Jackson*, pp. 42–45.

15. Toledo *Times*, Aug. 20, 1931.

16. Toledo *Blade*, Aug. 20, 1931.

17. Toledo *Times*, Aug. 29, 1931.

18. (Ohio) *Annual Report of the Department of Banks and Banking*, 1931, p. 30.

19. Toledo *Blade*, Aug. 25, 1931.

20. Toledo *Blade*, Aug. 28, 1931; Toledo *Times*, Aug. 28, 1931.

21. Toledo *Times*, Aug. 29, 1931.

22. Toledo *Times*, Mar. 1, 1931.

23. Toledo *Blade*, Aug. 29, 1931.

24. Toledo *Blade*, Sept. 1, 1931.

25. Toledo *News-Bee*, Sept. 2, 1931; Toledo *Blade*, Sept. 2, 3, 1931; *Ameryka-Echo*, Sept. 2, 1931.

26. *Ameryka-Echo*, Sept. 3, 1931.

27. Toledo *News-Bee*, Sept. 2, 1931; *Ameryka-Echo*, Sept. 2, 1931.

28. Toledo *Blade*, Sept. 8, 1931.

29. Toledo *Blade*, Sept. 3, 1931; *Ameryka-Echo*, Sept. 4, 1931.

30. Toledo *Blade*, Sept. 4, 1931.

31. Toledo *Times*, Sept. 5, 1931.

32. *Ameryka-Echo*, Sept. 10, 11, 1931; Toledo *Blade*, Sept. 8, 1932; Toledo *Times*, Sept. 6, 1931.

33. *East Side Sun*, Sept. 17, 1931.

34. Toledo *Blade*, June 27, 1949.

35. *East Side Sun*, Sept. 24, 1931.

36. *Ameryka-Echo*, Sept. 16, 1931; *Toledo Union Leader*, Aug. 21, 1931, p. 4.

37. Toledo *Blade*, Sept. 8, 1931.

38. *Ameryka-Echo*, Sept. 4, 8, 1931; *New York Times*, April 28, 1931.

39. Toledo *Blade*, Sept. 5, 1933.

40. Toledo *Blade*, Nov. 22, 1934.

41. Toledo *News-Bee*, Jan. 2, 3, 1932.

42. Toledo *News-Bee*, July 7, 1937.

43. *East Side Sun*, May 5, 1932.

44. Toledo *Tribune*, Apr. 22, 29, 1932.

45. Toledo *News-Bee*, Nov. 2, 1932.

46. Toledo *Times*, Apr. 14, 1933.

47. Undated clippings from the Toledo *News-Bee*, the Toledo *Blade*, the Toledo *Times*, and the *Beach Club*, in the Frazier Reams Collection, MSS 55, Box 3, Folders 7, 10 (Center for Archival Collections, Bowling Green State University). For information on the Toledo Civic Realty Co. see *Secretary of State of Ohio Annual Report for 1926* (Springfield, Ohio: State Printers, 1927), p. 64.

48. Toledo *News-Bee*, Jan. 17, 1933; Toledo *Times*, Jan. 17, 1933; Toledo *Blade*, Jan. 17, 18, 20, 1933.

49. Richard D. Dorn, "A New Deal for the Glass City: Local Initiatives for Federal Aid during the Great Depression in Toledo, Ohio" (M.A. thesis, University of Toledo, 1992), pp. 41–42, 57.

50. Toledo *Times*, Jan. 18, 1933.

51. Toledo *News-Bee*, Feb. 8, 1933; Toledo *Times*, Feb. 15, 1933.

52. Toledo *Times*, Feb. 18, 1933; Toledo *Blade*, March 18, Apr. 18, 1933; Toledo *News-Bee*, April 7, 1933.

53. *East Side Sun*, Mar. 27, 1933.

54. Toledo *Blade*, Mar. 29, 30, Apr. 1, 5, 1933; Toledo *News-Bee*, Apr. 3, 4, 1933.

55. Toledo *News-Bee*, Apr. 3, 4, 11, 1933.

56. Toledo *News-Bee*, Apr. 11, 14, 18, 1933.

57. Quote from editorial in the Toledo *News-Bee*, July 4, 1933.

58. Toledo *News-Bee*, May 16, 1933.

59. Toledo *News-Bee*, May 18, 1933.

60. Toledo *Blade*, May 22, 1933.

61. Toledo *News-Bee*, May 23, 1933.

62. Toledo *Blade*, July 6, 1933.

63. Toledo *News-Bee*, June 10, 1933; Toledo *Blade*, June 12, 15, 1933.

64. Toledo *Blade*, July 4, 1933.

65. Toledo *News-Bee*, July 5, 1933.

66. Toledo *News-Bee*, July 5, 1933.

67. Toledo *Times*, July 18, 1933.

68. Toledo *News-Bee*, July 7, 8, 1933.

69. Toledo *News-Bee*, July 15, 1933.

70. Albert W. Atwood, "Protecting Bank Depositors," *The Saturday Evening Post*, July 11, 1931, p. 95.

71. Toledo *Blade*, July 13, 17, 1933; Toledo *Times*, July 14, 17, 18, 1933.

72. Toledo *Times*, Sept. 21, 1933; Toledo *News-Bee*, Sept. 21, 1933.

73. Toledo *News-Bee*, Sept. 27, 1931.

74. Toledo *News-Bee*, Nov. 25, 1933, p. 3.

75. Toledo *News-Bee*, Sept. 26, 1933; Toledo *Blade*, Sept. 25, 1933.

76. Toledo *News-Bee*, Sept. 27, 1933.

77. Toledo *Times*, Sept. 27, 1933.

78. Toledo *News-Bee*, Sept. 27, 1933.

79. *Columbus Citizen*, Oct. 30, 1933; Toledo *News-Bee*, Jan. 22, 1934.

80. Toledo *News-Bee*, Apr. 23, 1935; *East Side Sun*, Nov. 1, 1933.

81. Toledo *News-Bee*, Nov. 9, 1933.

82. Quotes from "Curious Crowd . . ." *News-Bee*, Nov. 24, 1933.

83. Toledo *Times*, Jan. 6, 1934.

84. Toledo *Blade*, Dec. 4, 12, 13, 19, 1933; Toledo *Times*, Dec. 13, 1933; Toledo *News-Bee*, Dec. 13, 1933; *East Side Sun*, Dec. 13, 1933.

85. East Side *Sun*, Dec. 20, 1933.

86. Toledo *News-Bee*, Jan. 6, 1934.

87. Toledo *Blade*, Dec. 19, 20, 22, 27, 1933, Jan. 9, 1934; Toledo *Times*, Dec. 21, 1933.

88. Toledo *News-Bee*, Jan. 6, 1934.

89. Toledo *Blade*, Jan. 9, 1934.

90. Toledo *News-Bee*, Jan. 6, 1934.

91. Toledo *Blade*, Jan. 8, 1934.

92. Toledo *Blade*, Jan. 9, 1934; Toledo *Times*, Jan. 7, 1934.

93. Toledo *News-Bee*, Jan. 10, 1934.

94. Toledo *News-Bee*, Feb. 5, 1934.

95. *East Side Sun*, Mar. 7, 1934.

96. Toledo *News-Bee*, July 7, 1937.

97. Toledo *Times*, Mar. 21, 23, 1934.

98. Toledo *Blade*, Mar. 24, May 10, 1934.

99. Toledo *News-Bee*, Apr. 10, 1934.

100. *East Side Sun*, Apr. 26, 1934.

101. Toledo *Blade*, Apr. 2, 4, 5, 6, 1934; Toledo *News-Bee*, Apr. 7, 1934.

102. Toledo *News-Bee*, Apr. 10, 1934.

103. Toledo *Blade*, Apr. 10, 1934; May 10, 1934.

104. Toledo *News-Bee*, May 5, 1934; Toledo *News-Bee*, Apr. 28, 1934; Toledo *Blade*, Mar. 20, 1934; Toledo *News-Bee*, Apr. 24, 1934.

105. *East Side Sun*, Jan. 3, 1934.

106. Philip A. Korth, *I Remember Like Today: The Auto-Lite Strike of 1934* (East Lansing: Michigan State Univ. Press, 1988), p. 181; A. J. Muste, "The Battle of Toledo," *The Nation*, June 6, 1934, pp. 639–640.

107. Toledo *Blade*, Jan. 5, 1934.

108. Muste, "The Battle of Toledo," pp. 639–640.

109. "What is Behind Toledo," *The New Republic*, June 6, 1934, pp. 86–87.

110. Toledo *News-Bee*, June 5, 1934.

111. *McNary v. The State of Ohio*, No. 24687, June 20, 1934 (128 O.S., pp. 496–519).

112. Toledo *News-Bee*, July 7, 1937; Toledo *Blade*, Apr. 18, 1936; See also the records of cases 20399, 20400, 20401, 20402, 20403, 20404, 21051, Lucas County Clerk of Courts.

113. Toledo *News-Bee*, May 5, 8, 11, 1936.

114. Toledo *Blade*, July 10, 1937.

115. Ibid.

Notes to Epilogue

1. *News-Bee*, Aug. 4, 1934.

2. *Blade*, Aug. 23, 1934.

3. Federal Emergency Relief Agency, *Unemployment Relief Census* (Washington, 1934), Oct. 1933, p. 6. "Informal Extemporaneous Remarks of the President, Toledo, Ohio, Dec. 9, 1935," Franklin D. Roosevelt Papers, President's Personal File: Speeches, Franklin D. Roosevelt Library, Hyde Park, New York. *News-Bee*, Dec. 10, 1935.

4. Richard D. Dorn, "A New Deal for the Glass City: Local Initiatives for Federal Aid during the Great Depression in Toledo, Ohio" (M.A. thesis, University of Toledo, 1992), pp. 49–50. On closed theatres, see *News-Bee*, Feb. 2, 1933, Mar. 3, 1933.

5. Toledo *News-Bee*, Sept. 30, 1935, Feb. 9, 10, 1937, June 23, 1938.

6. *News-Bee*, Jan. 7, 1933, Mar. 13, Apr. 24, May 11, June 4, 1934. Toledo's 3,071 fires in 1934 were the most ever recorded, much higher than the 2,582 recorded in 1929. *History of the Toledo Fire Division, 1837–1977*, vol. 1, William O'Connor, ed. (Marceline, Missouri: Wadsworth Publishing, 1977), p. 146. D. E. A. Cameron, "Toledo Rehabilitates its Fire Division," *The American City*, vol. 56, June 1941, p. 65.

7. Data compiled from Annual Report of the Secretary of State . . . Ohio Statistics, 1928–1934 (Columbus, Ohio).

8. Data compiled from monthly police reports, *Toledo City Journal*, vols. 15–17, May 1930–Dec. 1932.

9. Dorn, "A New Deal for the Glass City," pp. 48.

10. Data compiled from *Mortality Statistics* (Bureau of the Census, Vital Statistics), 20th–37th Annual Reports.

11. *News-Bee*, July 13, 1933; Superintendent of Banks to N. R. Thurston, July 19, 1940; Testimony of Frank J. Klauser, pp. 13–15, Box 1, "Bank Cases, 1939–1940," Attorney General Papers, State Archives Series 498, Ohio Historical Society.

12. Raymond B. Vickers, *Panic in Paradise: Florida's Banking Crash of 1926* (Tuscaloosa: The Univ. of Alabama Press, 1994), pp. xi–xiv.

13. George J. Bassett, "Bank Closings in Connecticut," *Connecticut Law Journal* 16 (July 1942), p. 213.

14. Clarence Budington Kelland, "Ex-Banker," *American Magazine* 113 (Apr. 1932), p. 91.

15. *New Republic*, 98 (Mar. 1, 1939), p. 101.

16. T. Bruce Robb, "Safeguarding the Depositor," *American Academy of Political and Social Science*, 171 (Jan. 1934), pp. 54–62. Also see Robb, *State Bank Failures in*

Nebraska, Nebraska Studies in Business, No. 35 (Lincoln: Univ. of Nebraska Press, 1934).

17. Ibid.

18. Arthur Van Vlissingen, Jr., "Chicago's Minnow Banks," *World's Work*, 60 (Nov. 1931), pp. 41–44.

19. Robert Weidenhammer, "Better Bank Management: An Analysis of Fifty Bank Failures," *American Academy of Political and Social Science* 171 (Jan. 1934), pp. 47–53.

20. George J. Bassett, "Bank Closings in Connecticut," *Connecticut Law Journal* 16 (July 1942), p. 213.

21. Walter E. Spahr, "Bank Failures in the United States," *American Economic Review* 22 (Mar. 1932), p. 220; C. D. Bremer, *American Bank Failures* (New York: Columbia Univ. Press, 1935), p. 101; Robert G. Rodkey, "State Bank Failures in Michigan," *Michigan Business Studies*, 7:2 (1935), p. 2.

22. Vickers, *Panic in Paradise*; J. B. McFerrin, *Caldwell and Company* (Nashville: Vanderbilt Univ. Press, 1969; originally Univ. of North Carolina Press, 1939); David E. Hamilton, "The Causes of the Banking Panic of 1930: Another View," *Journal of Southern History*, 51:4 (November 1985), pp. 581–608.

23. *Business Week*, July 6, 1932, p. 6.

24. John T. Flynn, "Michigan Magic: The Detroit Banking Scandal," *Harper's Magazine* 168 (December 1933), pp. 1–11. Susan Estabrook Kennedy, *The Banking Crisis of 1933* (Lexington: Univ. Press of Kentucky, 1973), ch. 5.

25. Milton Friedman and Anna Jacobson Schwartz, *The Great Contraction, 1929–1933* (Princeton, N. J.: Princeton Univ. Press, 1967, ©1965), ch. 3; Elmus Wicker, *The Great Banking Panics of the Great Depression* (Cambridge, England: Cambridge Univ. Press, 1996), 33–37.

26. Friedman and Schwartz, *The Great Contraction*, pp. 62, 63.

27. National Industrial Conference Board, Inc., *The Banking Situation in the United States* (New York, 1932), p. 44.

28. John Philip Wernette, "Branch Banking in California and Bank Failures," *The Quarterly Journal of Economics* 46:2 (Feb., 1932), p. 369.

29. J. F. T. O'Connor, *The Banking Crisis and Recovery Under the Roosevelt Administration* (Chicago: Callaghan & Co., 1938), p. 8.

30. Walter E. Spahr, "Bank Failures in the United States," *The American Economic Review* 22:1 (March 1932), p. 220.

31. *News-Week* 1 (May 20, 1933), p. 25.

32. *Hearings on H.R. 141: Branch, Chain and Group Banking* (71st Cong., 1st session), I, Part IV, 444–45.

33. H. Parker Willis, "Are the Bankers to Blame?" *Current History*, Jan. 1934, p. 391.

34. Joseph E. Goodbar, *Managing the People's Money* (New Haven: Yale Univ. Press, 1935), p. 156; Kenneth Lewis Trefftzs, "The Regulation of Loans to Executive Officers of Commercial Banks," *The Journal of Political Economy* 50:3 (June, 1942), p. 374.

35. *Annual Report of the Attorney General of the United States for the Fiscal Year 1931* (Washington, D.C., 1932), p. 81.

36. *Annual Report of the Secretary of the Treasury . . . for the Fiscal Year 1930* (Washington, D.C., 1931), pp. 884–888; *Annual Report of the Secretary of the Treasury . . . for the Fiscal Year 1931* (Washington, D.C., 1932), pp. 808–818.

37. Compiled from the *Fourth Decennial Digest . . . 1926–1936*, Vol. 4, and *Fifth*

Decennial Digest . . . *1936–1947*, Vol. 6 (St. Paul, Minn.: West Publishing Co., 1937; 1947).

38. John A. Skiles, "Individual Personal Liability of Bank Directors for Negligent and Excess Loans," *Notre Dame Lawyer*, Vol. 7 (January 1932), p. 185.

39. The Social Security Death Index (SSN 273–03–2691) notes that Stacy McNary died in Sept. 1980 in Santa Clara, California. On Mills see Toledo *Times*, Jan. 10, 1946; Toledo *Blade*, Jan. 9, 1946. On Eastman see Toledo *Blade*, June 3, 1956 and *Ohio Sesquicentennial, Toledo–Lucas County 1803–1953* (Toledo Chamber of Commerce, 1953), Ward M. Canaday Center for Rare Books and Special Collections, University of Toledo.

40. Anecdote told by Homer Brickey, *Blade*, Feb. 2, 1993.

Bibliography

Newspapers

American Examiner (Columbus)
Ameryka–Echo—Toledo Daily Edition
Columbus Citizen
New York *Herald Tribune*
New York Times
Sylvania (Ohio) *Sentinel*
Toledo *Blade*
Toledo *Legal News*
Toledo *News-Bee*
Toledo *East Side Sun*
Toledo *Sunday Times*
Toledo *Times*
Toledo *Topics*
Toledo *Tribune*
Toledo *Union Leader*

Magazines

The American City
American Magazine
American Mercury
The Automotive and Automotive Industries
Barron's
Business Week
Colliers'
Current History
Federal Reserve Bulletin
The Forum and Century
Fortune
Harper's Magazine
Moody's Manual of Investments (Banks)
The Nation
The New Republic
News-Week
North American Review

Saturday Evening Post
Survey
The Toledo City Journal
Vital Speeches of the Day
World's Work

Government Publications

A Comprehensive Report on a Proposed System of Major Highways and Parkways for Lucas County, Ohio (St. Louis: Harold Bartholomew and Assoc., 1928), Toledo–Lucas County Public Library.
Annual Report of the Attorney General of the United States for the Fiscal Year 1931 (Washington, D.C., 1932).
Annual Report of the Comptroller of the Currency (Washington, 1929–1938)
Annual Report of the Ohio Division of Banks (Cleveland: State Printers), 1908–1948.
Annual Report of the Secretary of State . . . Ohio Statistics, 1928–1934 (Columbus, Ohio).
Annual Report of the Secretary of the Treasury . . . for the Fiscal Year 1930 (Washington, D.C., 1931).
Annual Statistical Report of the Secretary of State . . . (Springfield, Ohio: State Printers), 1919–1932.
Banking and Monetary Statistics (Federal Reserve, 1943)
Federal Emergency Relief Agency, *Unemployment Relief Census* (Washington, 1934).
Gibson, Campbell. "Population of the 100 Largest Cities and Other Urban Places in the United States, 1790–1990," Population Division Working Paper, No. 27 (U.S. Bureau of the Census, 1998).
Index to Mortgages: Mortgagor, 1921–1930, Lucas County Recorder's Office, Toledo Ohio.
Hearings on H.R. 141: Branch, Chain and Group Banking (71st Cong., 1st session), I, Part IV, pp. 444–45.
Industrial Survey (City of Toledo Plan Commission: Toledo, 1924).
Ohio Department of Mortality Statistics (Bureau of the Census, Vital Statistics), 20th–37th Annual Reports.
Ohio Secretary of State Corporation Filings, Secretary of State's Office, Columbus, Ohio.
Register of Deeds, vols. 503, 508, Lucas County Recorder's Office, Toledo, Ohio.
Record of Mortgages, vols. 998, 1001, 1004, 1005, 1010, Lucas County Recorder's Office, Toledo Ohio.
"Toledo Real Property Survey: Final Report," WPA Project #17971 (Toledo Metropolitan Housing Authority, 1939), Toledo–Lucas County Public Library.

Legal Records

Andrews v. The State, Ex Rel. Blair, Supt. of Banks, Ohio Supreme Court, No. 22955, Nov. 4, 1931 (124 O.S., pp. 359–360).
Fulton, Supt. of Banks, v. Rundell, Ohio Supreme Court, Case No. 24208, April 11, 1934 (128 O.S., pp. 205–211).

McNary v. The State of Ohio, No. 24687, June 20, 1934 (128 O.S., pp. 496–519).

Ohio vs. McNary et al., Lucas County No. 20399, Lucas County Clerk of Courts Office, Toledo, Ohio.

The State, Ex Rel. Fulton, Supt. of Banks v. Bremer, Admx. Ohio Supreme Court, No. 25260, Dec. 4, 1935 (130 O.S., pp. 227–239).

Ulmer v. Fulton, Supt. of Banks, et al., Ohio Supreme Court, Nos. 24996 & 24997, Decided Apr. 24, 1935 (129 O.S., pp. 32–343).

Manuscripts

COLUMBUS, OHIO

Ohio Historical Society

Attorney General Administrative Correspondence
Attorney General Papers
Biographical Abstracts of the Citizens' Historical Association.
Walter Folger Brown Papers

TOLEDO, OHIO

Toledo–Lucas County Public Library

Banks and Banking Collection.
Business and Industries of Greater Toledo Collection
Chamber of Commerce Collection
Index to the Toledo City Journal 1916–1930
Lucas County Plat Map, vol. 1, 1930
Negly Cochran Papers
Organizations of Greater Toledo

Ward M. Canaday Center for Rare Books and Special Collections, University of Toledo

Central Labor Union of Toledo and Vicinity Collection
John Hughes Collection
Lion Dry Goods Co. Financial Records
Toledo Edison Collection
Toledo Police Department Misc. Records
Ward M. Canaday Collection

BOWLING GREEN, OHIO

Center for Archival Collection, Bowling Green State University

Central Labor Union Papers
Sam Pollock Collection
Frazier Reams Collection

HYDE PARK, NEW YORK

Franklin D. Roosevelt Library

Franklin D. Roosevelt Papers

Articles

"The Background of City Government and Politics in Toledo." University of Toledo:
    Department of Political Science, 1954 (Canaday Center for Special Collections,
    University of Toledo).
Bassett, George J. "Bank Closings in Connecticut." *Connecticut Law Journal* 16 (July
    1942), pp. 208–222.
Borden, Timothy. "Labor's Day: Public Commemoration and Toledo's Working Class."
    Northwest Ohio Quarterly 70:1/2 (Winter/Spring 1998), pp. 4–27.
Cary, Lorin Lee. "The Bureau of Investigation and Radicalism in Toledo, Ohio:
    1918–1920." *Labor History*, 21:3 (Summer 1980), pp. 430–440.
Chari, V., and Ravi Jagannathan. "Banking Panics, Information and Rational
    Expectations Equilibrium." *Journal of Finance* 43 (1988), pp. 749–761.
Coyle, Eunice S. "A Review of Recent Failures." *The Review of Economic Statistics*
    14:1 (Feb. 1932), pp. 38–41.
"The City Manager Campaign in Toledo." *American Political Science Review*,
    August 1929, pp. 735–737.
Cooper, Russell, and Thomas W. Ross. "Bank Runs: Liquidity and Incentives." *NBER
    Working Papers Series No. 3921* (National Bureau of Economic Research,
    November 1991).
Diamond, Douglas W., and Philip H. Dybvig. "Bank Runs, Deposit Insurance, and
    Liquidity." *Journal of Political Economy*, 91:31 (June 1983), pp. 401–419.
Dorn, Richard D. "The Works Progress Administration in Toledo, Ohio: Local Initiatives
    for Federal Aid during the New Deal, 1935–1943." *Northwest Ohio Quarterly*, 67:4
    (Autumn 1995), pp. 187–235.
Hamilton, David E. "The Causes of the Banking Panic of 1930: Another View."
    Journal of Southern History, 51:4 (November 1985), pp. 581–608.
Hubbard, Joseph B. "Hoarding and the Expansion of Currency in Circulation." *The
    Review of Economic Statistics*, 14:1 (Feb. 1932), p. 31–34.
Huertas, Thomas F., and Joan L. Silverman. "Charles E. Mitchell: Scapegoat of the
    Crash?" *Business History Review*, 60 (1), 1986, pp. 81–103.
McClure, Richard A. "The Toledo Guaranty Corporation." Unpublished manu-
    script, 1977, Local History Department, Toledo–Lucas County Public Library.
McMurray, David A. "The Willys-Overland Strike, 1919." *Northwest Ohio
    Quarterly*, 36:4 (Autumn 1964), pp. 171–181 and 37:1 (Winter 1964–65), pp. 33–43.
Nancarrow, William J. "The Voters Speak: The Ohio Judicial Election of 1910 and
    Progressive Era Jurisprudence." *Proceedings of the Ohio Academy of History*
    (2001), pp. 35–46.
Postlewaite, Andrew, and Xavier Vives. "Bank Runs as an Equilibrium
    Phenomenon." *The Journal of Political Economy*, 95:3 (June 1987), pp. 485–491.
"Pulling Thru the Crisis: How Toledo Leadership Met the Emergency of 1932 and

1933." Pamphlet, Center for Archival Collections, Bowling Green State University.

Robb, T. Bruce. "Safeguarding the Depositor." *American Academy of Political and Social Science*, 171 (Jan. 1934), pp. 54–62.

Rodkey, Robert G. "State Bank Failures in Michigan." *Michigan Business Studies*, vol. 7, No. 2 (Ann Arbor, 1935), pp. 1–169.

Skiles, John A. "Individual Personal Liability of Bank Directors for Negligent and Excess Loans." *Notre Dame Lawyer*, Vol. 7 (January 1932), pp. 185–208.

Spahr, Walter E. "Bank Failures in the United States." *The American Economic Review* 22:1 (March 1932), pp. 208–238.

Temzelides, Theodosios. "Beliefs, Competition and Bank Runs." Working Paper No. 95-26 (Federal Reserve Bank of Philadelphia, October 1995).

Theodorides, A. "Construction in the United States and Toledo Through Booms and Depressions: A Study of the Industry Covering the Period 1899–1939." Bureau of Business Research, University of Toledo, Bulletin 13, May 25, 1939.

Trefftzs, Kenneth Lewis. "The Regulation of Loans to Executive Officers of Commercial Banks." *The Journal of Political Economy* 50:3 (June, 1942), pp. 377–396.

Trescott, Paul B. "Bank Failures, Interest Rates, and the Great Currency Outflow in the United States, 1929–1933." *Research in Economic History* Vol. 11 (1988), pp. 49–80.

"Wage and Salary Payments and Average Wages in Lucas County, Ohio, 1925–1934." *Employment Studies of Lucas County*, Part 2, Bureau of Business Research, University of Toledo, Bulletin 3 (Dec. 16, 1936).

Weidenhammer, Robert. "Better Bank Management: An Analysis of Fifty Bank Failures." *The Annals of the American Academy of Political and Social Science* 171 (Jan. 1934), pp. 47–53.

White, Eugene Nelson. "The Merger Movement in Banking, 1919–1933." *Journal of Economic History*, 45:2 (1985), pp. 285–291.

"The Welles-Bowen Company, 1908–1968." Unpublished manuscript, n.a., n.d., Toledo–Lucas County Public Library.

Wernette, John Philip. "Branch Banking in California and Bank Failures." *The Quarterly Journal of Economics* 46:2 (Feb., 1932), pp. 362–375.

Theses and Dissertations

Ballert, Allan H. "The Primary Functions of Toledo, Ohio." Ph.D. dissertation, University of Chicago, 1947.

Ballinger, Allan H. "Methods of Relief and the Present Unemployment Emergency in the City of Toledo." Master's thesis, University of Toledo, 1933.

Bindley, Joe Hoover. "An Analysis of Voting Behavior in Ohio." Ph.D. dissertation, University of Pittsburgh, 1959.

Dorn, Richard D. "A New Deal for the Glass City: Local Initiatives for Federal Aid During the Great Depression in Toledo, Ohio." Master's thesis, University of Toledo, 1992.

Karolak, Eric J. "'Fighting Autocracy at Home': The Willys-Overland Strike of 1919." Senior honors thesis, University of Toledo, Dept. of History, 1986 (copy housed at the Carlson Library).

Miller, Gregory M. "A Short History of Automobile Workers in Toledo, 1907–1935." Master's thesis, University of Toledo, 2000.

Rinehard, John S. "The Negro in a Congested Toledo Area." Master's thesis, University of Toledo, 1940.

Schroeder, Charles H. "Some Aspects of the Toledo Bank Failures of 1931." Master's thesis, University of Toledo, 1939.

Sobczak, John N. "The Inadequacies of Localism: The Collapse of Relief in Toledo, 1929–1939." Master's thesis, Bowling Green State University, 1975.

Zieren, Gregory R. "The Propertied Worker: Working Class Formation in Toledo, Ohio, 1870–1900." Ph.D. dissertation, University of Delaware, 1982.

Books

Bell, Spurgeon, et al. *Industrial and Commercial Ohio Yearbook, 1930.* Columbus: Bureau of Business Research, Ohio State University, 1930

Bird, Caroline. *The Invisible Scar.* New York: David McKay Co., 1966.

Bogart, Ernest L., and Donald L. Kemmerer. *Economic History of the American People.* New York: Longmans, Green and Co., 1942.

Bremer, C. D. *American Bank Failures.* New York: Columbia University Press, 1935.

Calomiris, Charles. *U.S. Bank Deregulation in Historical Perspective.* Cambridge: Cambridge University Press, 2000.

Downes, Randolph C. *Industrial Beginnings: Lucas County Historical Series No. 4.* Toledo: Historical Society of Northwestern Ohio, 1954.

Downes, Randolph. *The Rise of Warren Gamaliel Harding, 1865–1920.* Columbus: Ohio State University Press, 1970.

Fairfield, William E. *Fire and Sand: The History of the Libbey-Owens Sheet Glass Company.* Cleveland: Lezius-Hiles Co., 1960.

Friedman, Milton, and Anna J. Schwartz. *A Monetary History of the United States, 1867–1960.* Princeton, N.J. : Princeton University Press, 1963.

Friedman, Milton, and Anna J. Schwartz. *The Great Contraction, 1929–1933.* Princeton, N. J.: Princeton University Press, 1967.

Goodbar, Joseph E. *Managing the People's Money.* New Haven: Yale University Press, 1935.

Hickerson, Frank R. *The Tower Builders: The Centennial Story of the University of Toledo.* University of Toledo Press, 1972.

Hinshaw, Seth. *Ohio Elects the President: Our State's Role in Presidential Elections, 1804–1996.* Mansfield, Ohio: Book Masters Inc., 2000.

Hoffman, Susan. *Politics and Banking: Ideas, Public Policy, and the Creation of Financial Institutions.* Baltimore: Johns Hopkins University Press, 2001.

Johnson, Wendell F. *Toledo's Non-Partisan Movement.* Toledo: H.J. Chittendon Co., 1922.

Jones, Marnie. *Holy Toledo.* Lexington: University Press of Kentucky, 1998.

Kennedy, Susan Estabrook. *The Banking Crisis of 1933.* Lexington: University Press of Kentucky, 1973.

Killits, John M. *Toledo and Lucas County, Ohio, 1623–1923.* 3 vols. Chicago and Toledo: S.J. Clarke Publishing Co., 1923.

Korth, Philip A. *I Remember Like Today: The Auto-Lite Strike of 1934.* East Lansing: Michigan State University Press, 1988.

Krooss, Herman E., ed. *Documentary History of Banking and Currency in the United States*. 4 vols. New York: McGraw Hill, 1969.

Markham, Jerry W. *A Financial History of the United States*, vol. 2. Armonk, New York: M. E. Sharpe, 2002.

McFerrin, J. B. *Caldwell and Company*. Nashville: Vanderbilt University Press, 1969; originally University of North Carolina Press, 1939.

McLaughlin, Glenn. *Growth of American Manufacturing Areas: A Comparative Analysis with Special Emphasis on Trends in the Pittsburgh District*. Westport, Connecticut: Greenwood Press, 1970, originally published 1938.

National Industrial Conference Board, Inc. *The Banking Situation in the United States*. New York, 1932.

O'Connor, J. F. T. *The Banking Crisis and Recovery under the Roosevelt Administration*. Chicago: Callaghan & Co., 1938.

O'Connor, William, ed. *History of the Toledo Fire Division, 1837–1977*, vol. 1. Marceline, Missouri: Wadsworth Publishing, 1977.

Olson, James Stuart. *Herbert Hoover and the Reconstruction Finance Corporation, 1931–1933*. Ames: The Iowa State University Press, 1977.

Park, Sangkyun. *Contagion of Bank Failures: The Relation to Deposit Insurance and Information*. New York: Garland Publishing, 1992.

Paterson, Joyce Shaw. *American Automobile Workers, 1900–1933*. Albany: State University of New York Press, 1987.

Pecora, Ferdinand. *Wall Street Under Oath: The Story of Our Modern Money Changers*. New York: Simon and Schuster, 1939.

Phelps, Ralph E. *Profiles of Toledo Mayors*. Toledo: Blade Publishing Co., 1957.

Phillips, Ronnie J. *The Chicago Plan & New Deal Banking Reform*. Armonk, N.Y.: M.E. Sharpe, 1995.

Porter, Tana Mosier. *Toledo Profile: A Sesquicentennial History*. Toledo: Toledo Sesquicentennial Commission, 1987.

Pratt, Lester A. *Bank Frauds: Their Detection and Prevention*. New York: The Ronald Press Co., 1947.

Rajner, Richard A. *The Comprehensive History of Plumbers and Steam Fitters U.A. Local No. 50*. Toledo: Plumbers and Steamfitters No. 50, 1998.

Robb, T. Bruce. *State Bank Failures in Nebraska*. Nebraska Studies in Business, No. 35. Lincoln: University of Nebraska Press, 1934.

Sheppard, Virgil. *William T. Jackson, Mayor, City of Toledo, 1928–1931*. Unpublished manuscript, Canaday Center, University of Toledo.

Sullivan, Lawrence. *Prelude to Panic: The Story of the Bank Holiday*. Washington, D.C.: Statesman Press, 1936.

Temin, Peter. *Did Monetary Forces Cause the Great Depression?* New York: W.W. Norton, 1976.

Temin, Peter. *Lessons from the Great Depression*. Cambridge, Mass.: M.I.T. Press, 1989.

Upham, Cyril B., and Edwin Lamke. *Closed and Distressed Banks: A Study in Public Administration*. Washington, D.C.: Brookings Institution, 1934.

Vickers, Raymond B. *Panic in Paradise: Florida's Banking Crash of 1926*. Tuscaloosa: The University of Alabama Press, 1994.

Walton, Gary M., and Hugh Rockoff. *History of the American Economy*. New York: Harcourt Brace Jovanovich, 1990.

Whitsett, J. M. *Banking Operations in Ohio, 1920–1940*. Columbus: The Ohio State University Press, 1941.

Wicker, Elmus. *The Banking Panics of the Great Depression*. Cambridge: Cambridge University Press, 1996.

Wolfe, Don. *Frazier Reams: His Life and Times*. S.l.:S.n. Local History Collection, Toledo–Lucas County Public Library. 1978.

Index